About this Book

George W. Bush has fundamentally changed America's place in the world. And for the worse, argue Roger Burbach and Jim Tarbell. Using September 11 not as tragedy but as a political opportunity, Bush has given us the war on terror, the blitzkrieg in Afghanistan, the Patriot Act, the doctrine of pre-emptive war, the invasion and occupation of Iraq, and an immense war bill that saps the economy and vital domestic programmes.

The clique surrounding Bush has altered US foreign policy more dramatically than at any time since the onset of the Cold War. In some neo-conservative circles the word 'empire' is back in fashion. Ironically, a great republic that broke away from the British empire is now supposed to be proud of its new imperial role. This book explains how the neo-cons, the Christian right and the petro-military complex have hijacked US foreign policy. It asks some very important questions. What is the price Americans will have to pay for this new era of endless projections of American military might – a price measured in terms of a never ending fear of terrorism; mushrooming spending on security, defence, and overseas military adventures; the erosion of civil liberties inside the United States; and most importantly the deaths abroad of tens of thousands of innocent civilian and military combatants on both sides?

At the heart of this disturbing and timely book is the ultimate question. Previous empires have foundered on the rock of imperial overstretch – the costs of trying to run and protect empires eventually outstripping the capacity and willingness of the citizenry to pay them. Is the US in danger of going down that road? Who around George W. Bush is pushing him along that path? Can Americans change direction and restore America's reputation in the world into the shining 'city on the hill'?

Roger Burbach is Director of Research and Publication at the Center for the Study of the Americas (CENSA) in Berkeley, California. A historian by training, he was for a number of years a staff member and writer with NACLA, the North American Congress on Latin America. During the 1990s he was Visiting Scholar in Peace and Conflict Studies, and subsequently at the Institute of International Studies, University of California, Berkeley. He is the author of numerous books, including most recently *The Pinochet Affair: State Terrorism and Global Justice* (London and New York, Zed Books, 2003), *Globalization and Postmodern Politics: Zapatistas versus High Tech Robber Barons* (London, Pluto Press, 2001) and *Globalize This! The Battle against the World Trade Organization* (Monroe, ME, Common Courage Press, 2000) (edited with Kevin Danaher). He coauthored with Orlando Núñez *Fire in the Americas* (London, Verso Books, 1987).

Jim Tarbell is a writer and broadcaster based in Northern California. Following spells as a staffer for Congressman Wendell Wyatt (1968–72) and Peace Corps volunteer (1973–75), he founded his own publishing house, Ridge Times Press, in 1981. Amongst many other activities, he is now the editor of the Alliance for Democracy quarterly journal *Alliance Alerts*, and co-hosts a radio programme on KZYX called Corporations and Democracy. He is the author of a previous book, *I Came Not Alone* (1994), which tells of ordinary people's experiences of globalization in Latin America, and is currently working on a new book, *Democracy versus Empire*.

ROGER BURBACH | JIM TARBELL

Imperial overstretch

George W. Bush and the hubris
of empire

Fernwood
NOVA SCOTIA

Books for Change
BANGALORE

World Book Publishing
BEIRUT

SIRD
KUALA LUMPUR

Spearhead
CAPE TOWN

Zed Books
LONDON | NEW YORK

Imperial overstretch: George W. Bush and the hubris of empire was first published in 2004, by

in Canada: Fernwood Publishing Ltd, 8422 St Margaret's Bay Road (Hwy 3) Site 2A, Box 5, Black Point, Nova Scotia, BOJ 1BO

in India: Books for Change, 139 Richmond Road, Bangalore 560 025

in Lebanon, Bahrain, Egypt, Jordan, Kuwait, Qatar, Saudi Arabia and United Arab Emirates: World Book Publishing, 282 Emile Eddeh Street, Ben Salem bldg, PO Box 3176, Beirut, Lebanon
www.wbpbooks.com

in Malaysia: Strategic Information Research Department (SIRD), No. 11/4E Petaling Jaya, 46200 Selangor

in South Africa: Spearhead, a division of New Africa Books, PO Box 23408, Claremont 7735

in the rest of the world: Zed Books Ltd, 7 Cynthia Street, London N1 9JF, UK and Room 400, 175 Fifth Avenue, New York, NY 10010, USA
www.zedbooks.co.uk

Cover designed by Andrew Corbett
Set in FF Arnhem and Futura Bold by Ewan Smith, London
Printed and bound in the EU by Cox and Wyman, Reading

Distributed in the USA exclusively by Palgrave Macmillan, a division of St Martin's Press, LLC, 175 Fifth Avenue, New York, NY 10010.

A catalogue record for this book is available from the British Library.
US CIP data are available from the Library of Congress.
Canadian CIP data are available from the National Library of Canada.

ISBN 1 55266 140 7 pb: Canada
ISBN 81 8291 000 5 pb: India
ISBN 9953 14 051 0 pb: Lebanon
ISBN 983 2535 29 8 pb: Malaysia
ISBN 0 86486 659 3 pb: South Africa
ISBN 1 84277 496 4 hb: rest of the world
ISBN 1 84277 497 2 pb

Contents

Acknowledgements

The research and writing of *Imperial Overstretch* required an over-stretch on the part of the authors as well as all those who helped us produce the manuscript in just over four months. Without the foresight and guidance of Robert Molteno at Zed Books, this project would not have come to fruition. Special thanks to Russell and Sylvia Bartley, who gave us sound advice on an early version, and to Spike Peterson, who gave us cogent direction at a pivotal moment. Before we started writing, Robert Armstrong provided assistance in conceptualizing the project. We give special thanks to Judy Tarbell for her editorial comments on several chapters and overall enthusiasm for making this a successful undertaking.

Ensuring that the book reflected the current state of the empire required leaving our northern California harbours to travel to Washington, DC, on two occasions. We thank our hosts on those trips, Cathy Schneider, Laurie Marshall, Gail Morrell, Scott Redford and Scott Cooper, for their generosity and interest in this project. We also thank the people who took time out of their busy lives to share their thoughts with us on these trips, including: Charlie Cray, Max Sawicky, Bill Goodfellow, Fareed Mohamedi, Cornell Metternich, Jeff Krehely, Meagan House, Emily Kernan, Steve Weiss, Chris Toensing, Congressman Mike Thompson, and especially Phyllis Bennis.

We also wish to thank Michael Lind and Dana Priest, as well as Michael Klare and Marc Herold, for their incisive thoughts and ideas. Pat and Gary Leiser, Aron Scalabrini, Cecile Earle, Glenn and Marilyn Borchardt, David Parkhurst, Mary Hayssen, Paul Cantor, Eric Leenson and Pat Flynn provided encouragement as well as logistical assistance. Maria Elena Martinez and Peter Rosset of the Center for the Study of the Americas and Ben Clarke of Freedom Voices were also very supportive. Finally thanks to Ewan Smith and Ian Paten for a fine job copyediting and laying out this book. Mostly, though, we thank our family members, Judy, Beca, Shamli, Crescent, Matt and Allie, for their patience and understanding in allowing us to concentrate on finishing this project in a timely manner.

To the victims of the empire.
May this age of belligerency soon pass.

Prologue: the toll of empire

In modern war there is nothing sweet nor fitting in your dying. You will die like a dog for no good reason. *Ernest Hemingway, Notes on the Next War*

There is much common ground between low- and high-tech terrorism, between the terrorism of religious fanatics and that of market fanatics, that of the hopeless and that of the powerful, that of the psychopath on the loose and that of the cold-blooded uniformed professional. They all share the disrespect for human life. Eduardo Galeano, *The Theater of Good and Evil*

It is 6 a.m. in a small, impoverished town in the desert. Seventy-five US National Guard soldiers march through the streets chanting: 'Kill! Kill! Kill! Swing your guns from left to right, we can kill those guys all night.' An hour later they stop in front of the house of the local cleric opposed to the US occupation of Iraq, and at the urging of their commander, the soldiers shout again: 'Kill, kill, kill.'

This scene did not take place in Iraq, but in a town in north-eastern New Mexico in November 2003 where a National Guard unit was preparing to go to Iraq. When the soldiers stopped in front of the house of an anti-war priest, John Dear, he put on his winter coat and went out of the front door into the middle of the street. The soldiers stopped shouting and heard him implore: 'In the name of God, I order all of you to stop this nonsense, and not to go to Iraq. I want all of you to quit the military, disobey your orders to kill, and not to kill anyone ... God does not want you to kill so Bush and Cheney can get more oil. God does not support war' (Dear 2003).

This scene reveals just one of the costs of war, how it divides and exploits communities, even on the home front far from the slaughter taking place abroad. The state of New Mexico, with the highest rate of poverty in the nation, is number one in military spending and first in nuclear weapons. It is the state most in need of disarmament and non-violence. It is the first place the Pentagon goes to recruit poor youth for the empire's army.

For these American soldiers, once they arrive in Iraq the enemy is everywhere. Specialist Corporal Michael Richardson, twenty-two, a combat veteran in Iraq, says: 'There was no dilemma when it came to shooting people who were not in uniform, I just pulled the trigger. It was up close and personal the whole time, there wasn't a big distance. If they were there, they were enemy.' Specialist Anthony Castillo adds: 'When there were civilians there we did the mission that had to be done. When they were there, they were at the wrong spot, so they were considered enemy.' The grim reality of the death they inflict is described by Sergeant First Class John Meadows: 'It's like snapshot photos of maggots on tongues, babies with their heads on the ground, men with their heads halfway off and their eyes wide open and mouths wide open ... The smells and the torsos burning ... nothing but burned bodies' (Graham 2003).

John Farrel, a theology student from Chicago who spent three weeks travelling around Iraq in the autumn of 2003 with Voices in the Wilderness (a non-profit organization that campaigns to 'end economic and military warfare against the Iraqi people'), states: 'You don't see US soldiers in Baghdad except an occasional well-guarded convoy of Humvees' (Farrel 2003). The Americans are lodged in Saddam's former palaces and barricaded inside a fortified enclave in central Baghdad. Outside these fortresses there is no American presence, except for well-armed patrols and counter-insurgency operations. John adds: 'There is sixty per cent unemployment, and the whole place has been made into a free trade zone. They've hired and fired the police three times and it's so dangerous they can't get anybody to do it' (ibid.).

It is an apt allegory for the American empire in the early twenty-first century. As the United States builds a Star Wars system to ensconce itself inside a fantasy missile shield, it turns the rest of the world into a free trade and free fire zone where the race to the bottom impoverishes the world's population and destroys the environment of the planet. 'It's all part of the corporate globalization,' says Eric Edgin, who also spent time in Baghdad with Voices in the Wilderness. 'We have to see and understand that Iraq is part of a bigger process' (Edgin 2003).

The Bush administration does not care how many civilians die in Iraq; in fact it connives with the established media to keep the US public ignorant of the true human toll of the war. In Baghdad, the Pentagon refuses to count the number of civilian dead. General Tommy Franks, the commander in chief of the US Central Command during the Iraq war, a man referred to as the 'proconsul' of a region extending from East Africa to Afghanistan, said, 'We don't do body counts.'

For the innocent, the toll of imperial warfare is staggering. The London-based Iraq Bodycount project has drawn on investigative and journalistic reports from Iraq to calculate that between eight and ten thousand civilians died in Iraq between March and December 2003 as a result of the conflict. According to the project: 'There is evidence that these deaths, often from indiscriminate use of firepower, increasingly fail to be reported or remain unacknowledged by occupation forces' (Iraq Bodycount 2003). This toll is roughly three times the number of people who died at the World Trade Center on 11 September 2001. And it is inflicted on a country with less than one-tenth the population.

Jonathan Steele (2003) reported in the *Guardian* after the end of the official war: 'As far as Iraqis are concerned all the dead are "martyrs", whether they fell defending their country or were struck when missiles or cluster bombs hit their homes.' There are those who live and remember. It is a memory that grows exponentially

3

and creates a determination among the popular classes that the empire must not be allowed to continue.

This scenario is not limited to Iraq. Afghanistan, the Philippines and Colombia, among other countries, have suffered thousands of deaths as George W. Bush uses his 'war against terrorism' as a cover for extending the tentacles of the empire into the far corners of the globe. The cost is not only in terms of the loss of human life. According to the Iraq Bodycount project: 'People may suffer deep psychological trauma, miscarriage, bereavement, dislocation, and loss of home and property. Destruction of civil infrastructure can have effects which last for generations.'

In Afghanistan and Iraq, death and hardship will continue for years after the Americans depart. The thousands of cluster bombs dropped contain shrapnel-filled packages that often lie unexploded, waiting for a curious hand to detonate a deadly explosion. Depleted uranium from American munitions now pollutes the landscape of these countries, poisoning the people and the environment for generations to come.

In the United States the economic costs of America's imperial adventurism are becoming increasingly unbearable. The proposed military budget for 2004 is almost $400 billion. That does not include the $87.5 billion specially allocated for operations in Iraq and Afghanistan. In the next six years the USA plans to spend $2.7 trillion on the military. This is at a time when federal budget deficits are expected to approach $500 billion a year. Economist Max Sawicky, who works at the Economic Policy Institute in Washington, DC, says that the American economy 'is headed for a train wreck'.

Moreover, war contributes directly to the increasing polarization of income between the rich and poor in the United States. Bush's wars act as a form of double taxation, redistributing wealth upwards. First the taxpayers turn their money over to the Pentagon and the military contractors to carry out the destruction caused by the war itself. Then they are taxed again as favoured companies such as Halliburton and Bechtel receive billions to rebuild the infrastructure that was destroyed by the war (Chomsky 2003).

All across America publicly funded programmes are being decimated by Bush's 'infinite war'. In Oregon, where the public education system has suffered severe cutbacks, school playgrounds are being sold for housing tracts to pay teachers' salaries. According to the National Priorities Project (2003), if the $87.5 billion dollars earmarked for occupying Iraq and Afghanistan were 'spent on other priorities in the United States, it could pay for: 105,319 new affordable housing units, creating 257,820 new jobs; 418,060 new firefighters, health care coverage for 5,723,077; $15.0 billion for school construction, resulting in 356,475 new jobs; and $15.0 billion for local and state roads and bridges, creating 423,131 new jobs'.

While Americans suffer from the outrageous costs, it is not even clear that unilateral, pre-emptive preventive war is good for business. Throughout the international community, outrage against American policies has elicited dozens of boycotts against American products. One German bicycle manufacturer stopped buying $300,000 of American supplies because of the Iraq war. 'Americans only pay attention when money is on the line,' the director of the company told Reuters (Kirschbaum 2003). The most vulnerable American products are the brands targeted by multiple boycotts around the globe. Coca-Cola, Budweiser, Marlboro, American whiskey and even American Express cards were taken off the menus in Europe after Washington politicians denigrated French products (ibid.).

On a broader economic plane *Business Week* ran an editorial the week the Iraq war officially began which stated,

As a foreign policy, [the Bush doctrine] is both arrogant – certain to generate opposition by even the most friendly of countries

5

– and corrosive, certain to undermine multilateral institutions and agreements, including those in the economic sphere ... Chief executives are beginning to worry that globalization may not be compatible with a foreign policy of unilateral preemption. Can capital, trade, and labor flow smoothly when the world's only superpower maintains such a confusing and threatening stance? US corporations may soon find it more difficult to function in a multilateral economic arena when their overseas business partners and governments perceive America to be acting outside the bounds of international law and institutions ... A world divided between multilateral economic and unilateral security policies is an uncertain and risky place. It is not likely to encourage economic growth or prosperity. The Administration risks turning what was once trumpeted as the American Century into the Anti-American Century. (Nussbaum 2003)

What seems particularly perverse is that Bush's war policy has a contingent domestic policy that targets immigrants with arbitrary arrests and unregulated detention in solitary holding cells that resemble animal cages. This barbaric treatment is imposed on people living in a nation that draws much of its strength from its diversity and its continual waves of immigrants. This onerous policy undermines the basis of our democratic experience and is a frontal assault on both our constitution and the ideals on which the country was founded. Suddenly Americans are living in a police state milieu where the government monitors everyday activities and crushes political dissent. This became particularly evident in Miami in November 2003 at the meetings for the Free Trade Area of the Americas. To 'provide security' for the hemispheric elites that attended the gatherings, the local police force received $8.5 million out of the special $87.5 billion war authorization bill. In fact the funds were used for repression. On the outskirts of the city the police stopped scores of buses carrying demonstrators who wanted to participate in a protest with official permits. Then the police used tear gas, pepper spray and fired rubber bullets at random to disperse the 20,000 citizens who managed to participate in the protests.

The allure and immediacy of this war divert political attention from more pressing needs. They divert attention from a healthcare system with skyrocketing costs that leaves many Americans without adequate medical treatment. They obscure the need to create sustainable production systems that will ensure the long-term existence of an environmentally sound planet. Finally they rob the creativity necessary to build an enlightened, forward-thinking America where the residents are intellectually alive and politically engaged.

For the planet as a whole, the biggest cost is the spread of the laissez-faire empire where money is power, people are landless commodities and the environment is ignored. In the following pages we look at the history of this empire, the money-based political drive that placed the Bush administration in power, the hubris of figures like George W., Dick Cheney and Donald Rumsfeld, and the costs and overstretch of their imperial policy, which is epitomized by their actions in Iraq. Finally we look at the hope embodied within a popular world democratic movement that is rising up against the American empire.

ONE
George W. Bush and the reality of empire

> The history of the rise and fall of Empires teaches us that it is when their own citizens finally lose faith in the virtue of infinite war and permanent occupations that the system enters into retreat. *Tariq Ali*

On 15 February 2003, one month before George W. Bush ordered the 'shock and awe' bombing of Iraq, his effigy, holding buckets of blood and oil, bobbed above the determined crowds in New York City on a frosty winter day. In Manhattan, the city borough that suffered the terrorist attacks of 11 September 2001, 400,000 people besieged the United Nations, calling for no war. Nobel Peace Prize winner Archbishop Desmond Tutu told the crowd, 'We are members of one family ... the human family ... President Bush, listen to the voice of the people ... "Give peace a chance."'

The demonstrators in New York joined citizens from around the world to call on Bush not to pursue his imperial wars in their name. The largest global demonstrations in the history of humanity took place that day. In London alone 1.5 million people turned out, in Spain over a million mobilized, in Berlin the *Frankfurter Allgemeine Zeitung* estimated that demonstrators numbered half a million. Protests in the United States took place from coast to coast in over a hundred cities (Pitt 2003).

In the nations of the South anti-war demonstrations were also widespread. In Jakarta, Indonesia, 100,000 marched on the US embassy, in São Paulo, Brazil, 30,000 turned out, and in Istanbul, Turkey, at least 5,000 demonstrated while thousands more mobilized in other Turkish cities, demanding that the United States not be allowed to station troops in their country to strike against Iraq. In the capitals of Egypt and Tunisia thousands protested against the impending US war, only to be beaten by local security forces. Even in Antarctica, fifty-one demonstrators formed a peace sign in the snow. All told, it is estimated that at least eleven million people demonstrated in seventy-five countries on that historic day. (See, for example, Internet F and Internet I.)

The crowds in New York came to the United Nations to address diplomats questioning the American rush to war. Within the walls of this global contemplative body coalitions were forming to with-hold the world's approval of pre-emptive war in Iraq. America's sanctimonious, unilateral aggression had sparked the creation of the largest countervailing alliance since the United States rose to global dominance with the end of the Second World War.

On this sullen Saturday in Washington, DC, the President, who excelled in salesmanship rather than statesmanship, kept to himself. He had only fear to sell. In his weekly radio address he announced, 'Last week the national terrorist threat level was raised to "high" ... inform[ing] the general public to be more alert to their surroundings and prepared for possible emergencies in the event of an attack ... Our enemies are still determined to attack America, and there is no such thing as perfect security against a hidden network of killers' (Bush 2003a). A month later on 16 March, Bush announced the 'moment of truth' for the world on Iraq. The next day he gave Saddam forty-eight hours to clear out. Then the bombs began the horrifying destruction.

After the fall of Baghdad, on 1 May 2003, George W. Bush landed on the USS *Abraham Lincoln* aircraft carrier and with great fanfare proclaimed the end of 'Operation Iraqi Freedom'. Dressed in a military flight suit, he projected the image of a mod-ern warrior king as he got out of the cockpit of a Navy Viking jet. Then, standing in front of a huge banner proclaiming 'Mission Accomplished', Bush, who had dodged the draft as a youth, made a triumphal speech, declaring 'major combat operations in Iraq have ended'.

This carefully orchestrated scene required the USS *Abraham Lincoln* and its crew to remain at sea off the coast of California for an extra day after months of duty in the Persian Gulf. It seemingly marked the successful conclusion of a long campaign to project US power around the world. Under the guise of a 'war on terrorism, that began with the events of September 11, 2001, the United States had established fourteen new military bases extending from eastern Europe through Iraq, the Persian Gulf, Pakistan, Afghanistan and the Central Asian republics of Uzbekistan and Kyrgyzstan' (Siddiqui 2003). The United States had also stepped up its military involvement in other key areas of the world, such as the Philippines and Colombia.

But the United States was in trouble. In the coming days and months after 1 May the emergence of the Iraqi resistance, along with a number of international challenges, indicated that the United States had over-extended itself abroad. By the summer of 2003, twenty-one of the army's thirty-three active-duty combat brigades were deployed in conflictive or potentially explosive areas of the world: sixteen in Iraq, two in Afghanistan, two in South Korea and one in the Balkans. And of the thirty-three active-duty brigades only three were actually free for new duties. Of a total of 491,000 troops, about 370,000 were deployed overseas (*New York Times*, 21 July 2003). In July 2003 the Pentagon began debating the need to increase the size of the US armed forces and the possible reinstatement of the military draft to meet the need for US troops abroad.

Bush and Imperial Overstretch

A momentous consequence of the belligerent policies pursued by George W. Bush around the globe is imperial overstretch. Bush's adventurism is wreaking havoc on the United States, adversely affecting its standing in the world. Most Americans do not think of the United States as an empire, but the turmoil brought on by Bush's foreign adventures is compelling many to reconsider the US role in the world.

The phrase imperial overstretch first gained prominence in 1987 when Paul Kennedy, a historian at Yale University, published *The Rise and Fall of Great Powers*. In this book he argued that empires in their waning years engage in overstretch, 'like Imperial Spain around 1600 or the British empire around 1900' (Kennedy 1987). Kennedy did not shy away from comparing these earlier empires to the United States in the 1980s, asserting that because of 'a vast array of strategical commitments' made over the years, the United States 'runs the risk, so familiar to historians of the rise and fall of previous Great Powers, of what might roughly be called "imperial overstretch"' (ibid.).

At the time Kennedy wrote his book the Reagan administration was engaged in a massive military build-up. It sponsored a series of counter-revolutionary wars in Africa, Central America and Asia, attempting to counteract the earlier US setbacks in Vietnam and other parts of the world. Simultaneously, US economic pre-eminence appeared to be threatened by the more dynamic economies of Japan and western Europe.

Interestingly, when Kennedy wrote his tome in the 1980s his first argument in relation to US imperial overstretch focused on 'American obligations in the Middle East. Here is a region, from Morocco in the west to Afghanistan in the east, where the United States faces a number of conflicts and problems whose mere listing (as one observer put it) "leaves one breathless".' In what would be words of premonition for the second Bush administration, Kennedy went on to point out that petroleum 'makes the region very important to the United States, but at the same time bewilderingly resistant to any simple policy option. It is, in addition, the region in the world which, at least in some parts of it, seems most frequently to resort to war' (ibid.: 515–16).

In the short term Kennedy's thesis of imperial overstretch for the United States appeared to be wrong. Like virtually all historians and political observers, Kennedy failed to anticipate the fall of the Berlin Wall and the collapse of the Soviet Union. The success of Bush Senior in the first Gulf war and Clinton's interventions in Bosnia and Kosovo along with a resurgent US economy in the 1990s also nurtured the belief that 'Pax Americana' was once again in fine shape. At the turn of the millennium, Kennedy's argument of imperial overstretch was largely forgotten and appeared to be irrelevant.

The rise of the administration of George W. Bush and its turn to a unilateral, pre-emptive imperial modus operandi re-established the concept of overstretch as the likely outcome of US foreign policy. Placed in power by the vagaries of the US electoral system and the Supreme Court, the Bush administration constructed an aggressive imperial plan driven by neo-conservative hawks touting the righteousness of the American democratic model. Their rhetoric promoted the virtues of spreading liberal democracy across the planet. But the reality of their actions revealed that they were fundamentally intent on advancing the narrow interests of an imperial plutocracy that plunders the planet's resources regardless of the political consequences.

Mythology and the American Empire

This US empire conflicts with the ideals that every American schoolchild is raised upon. Children are taught that, in contrast to brutal human conquests and empires of the past, the United States emerged as the world's first truly democratic society with equal opportunity for all. To this day many in school memorize passages from the Declaration of Independence such as: 'We hold these truths to be self-evident, that all men are created equal, that they are endowed ... with certain unalienable Rights, that among these are Life, Liberty and the pursuit of Happiness.'

Then in 1876, on the centennial of the Declaration of Independence, France seemingly recognized this unique role when it gave the United States the Statue of Liberty. The statue inspired Emma Lazarus, a fourth-generation Jewish immigrant in New York, to pen the words on the statue that distinguished the new American colossus from past imperial powers. Her words, impregnated in the conscience of American history, state:

> Not like the brazen giant of Greek fame,
> With conquering limbs astride from land to land;
> Here at our sea-washed, sunset gates shall stand
> A mighty woman with a torch, whose flame
> Is the imprisoned lightning, and her name Mother of Exiles.
> From her beacon-hand
> Glows world-wide welcome; her mild eyes command
> The air-bridged harbor that twin cities frame.
> 'Keep ancient lands, your storied pomp!' cries she
> With silent lips.
> 'Give me your tired, your poor,
> Your huddled masses yearning to breathe free,
> The wretched refuse of your teeming shore.
> Send these, the homeless, tempest-tost to me,
> I lift my lamp beside the golden door!'

Even when the United States colonized the Philippines and occupied Cuba in the aftermath of the war with Spain in 1898, many in the United States and the rest of the world continued to hope and believe that America would serve as a 'shining city on the hill' for other nations. The period from 1900 to 1930 did witness repeated military interventions in the Caribbean and Latin America. But when Franklin Roosevelt became President in 1933 and proclaimed the 'Good Neighbor Policy', it appeared that the United States had rectified its wanton ways.

After the Second World War, the United States became the

dominant world power, and the new era was dubbed 'the American Century'. Now the United States clearly acted as an imperial nation, flagrantly imposing its will on others, as the violent CIA coups in Iran and Guatemala in the early 1950s confirmed. But here again the US government was able to mask the existence of an empire of 'conquering limbs' behind the rhetoric and fear of the Cold War, asserting that it was a struggle between 'the free world and communism'. Only with the Vietnam war in the late 1960s and early 1970s did the American people question and rise up against the military and the imperial adventures of its leaders.

The Empire of Deceit

Finally, with George W. Bush, under the banner of 'compassionate conservatism', the Christian right and a band of neo-conservatives and militarists seized full control of the government. With the earth-shaking events of 11 September they were able to run wild in promoting the interests of a reactionary, corporate elite on a global scale while cloaking these interests in the rhetoric of the American myths. The back-slapping Texas oilman in the White House was able to foist his views on ordinary Americans because he not only had God on his side but also the Supreme Court, the House of Representatives and Senate, and the most powerful military force in the history of the world.

Bush's pomp on the USS *Abraham Lincoln* on 1 May reflected what he had learned to do best during the early years of his presidency: project the aura of a true believer bent on a righteous mission of ridding the world of 'evil-doers'. But his speech on the aircraft carrier also revealed the fatal flaw that runs through his presidency – a self-delusional capacity to distort and bend reality to fit his narrow world view.

On the *Lincoln* Bush asserted that by winning the war against Saddam Hussein, 'we've removed an ally of al-Qaeda'. This statement was a fabrication, perhaps even more of a distortion than the oft-repeated claim that the United States went to war to rid Iraq of weapons of mass destruction. No links ever existed between al-Qaeda and Saddam. But by banging the drums of war with false statements for well over a year before the invasion of Iraq, Bush managed to mobilize and manipulate US public sentiment to back the Iraqi adventure. When the war began over half of Americans mistakenly believed that the Iraqi regime had been involved in the destruction of the World Trade Center on 11 September 2001.

Aboard the USS *Abraham Lincoln* Bush declared he would continue his global campaign, stating 'the battle of Iraq is one victory in the war on terror', adding: 'our mission continues: al-Qaeda is wounded, but not destroyed'. The image of al-Qaeda would be manipulated ad infinitum in an effort to frighten the American people into supporting continued US adventures abroad. What makes these interventions even more problematic is that they are intertwined with Bush's belief that he is on a divine mission. As Bush told Palestinian Prime Minister Mahmoud Abbas in June 2003, 'God told me to strike at al-Qaeda and I struck them, and then he instructed me to strike at Saddam, which I did, and now I am determined to solve the problem in the Middle East' (cited in Kamen 2003). Bush's moral mission is global in scope, extending well beyond al-Qaeda, the Middle East and the Gulf. The war against terrorism is simply the most visible feature, and at times even a subterfuge, for the efforts of Bush and a loyal band of hard-core conservatives to project US power around the world.

Moreover, the Bush administration reflects the core interests of a petro-military complex, a very narrow group of largely national-based economic interests that are not as interlocked with global capital as other business sectors in the United States. It is astounding, but the diverse entity called the United States of America has placed in political power one of the narrowest ruling cliques in recent history. Many of the executive orders and policies, before and after 11 September, have served the narrow interests of this economic group. The US abandonment of the Kyoto treaty to control global warming, the attempts to drill in the Arctic Circle, and calls for the disavowal of nuclear arms treaties in order to pursue a multibillion-dollar Star Wars programme – these and other policies cater directly to the interests of the petro-military complex. And it is this complex which is benefiting the most from the occupation of Iraq and the war without end against terrorism. Small wonder that Germany, France and Russia broke with the United States over the Iraq intervention, recognizing that their interests would be largely excluded once the United States was in control of the Gulf region.

Militarization of the Empire

With the war on terror, the militarization of US foreign policy accelerated dramatically. Early 2002 found 660 soldiers in the Philippines searching for members of Abu Sayyaf, allegedly linked to al-Qaeda. In Kenya, where the United States has used bases since 1980, 3,000 US troops took part in exercises as the Bush administration sought to build a permanent facility there. Thousands more troops were pouring into oil-rich central Asia. Over 4,000 were in Afghanistan and 2,000 in Uzbekistan. The United States also began building a base in Kyrgyzstan to house 3,000 troops, and Tajikistan was considering a long-term base on its soil. On a more symbolic level, it is notable that the established corporate media give extraordinary attention to the press conferences of Secretary of Defense Donald Rumsfeld while minimizing the importance of Secretary of State Colin Powell (himself a former head of the Joint Chiefs of Staff), unless his views clash with those of the Defense Department.

It is not widely recognized, but prior to 11 September 2001 the United States already constituted a global power heavily reliant on its military to control a world it perceived as unruly and increasingly unwilling to accept US domination. As Dana Priest points out in *The Mission*, 'long before September 11, the US government had grown increasingly dependent on its military to carry out its foreign affairs' (Priest 2003: 14). During the Clinton administration, the Pentagon, through its five regional commands, each with its own commander-in-chief called CinC, had become more active in advancing US interests in key areas of the world, ranging from eastern Europe and the Gulf to south-east Asia and Latin America. The CinCs constituted the 'proconsuls to the empire', exerting enormous power in their regions, often bypassing diplomats and civilian figures in their influence on US policy (ibid.: 61, 72). The CinCs also commanded the potent special forces in each region.

Relations with surrogates in other countries have become increasingly militarized in recent years. The United States pays Kyrgyzstan $7,000 every time a US aircraft lands there. In the aftermath of 9/11, the United States arranged for the transfer of billions of dollars in loans and grants to the notoriously corrupt Pakistani regime in exchange for its agreement to break off its alliance with the Taliban and to allow the country to be used as a staging base for the war against Afghanistan (see Burbach and Clarke 2002). The CinCs, with State Department funds, train over eight thousand foreign military officers each year, while another 18,700 military students are trained by US officers with funds from their own countries (Priest 2003: 75). Since 9/11 these programmes have accelerated, with a particular emphasis on the Central Command CinC, which includes central Asia, the Gulf and north-eastern Africa.

The less fortunate social classes, on the other hand, often react in horror to the US military penetration of their countries. In the Basilian region of the Philippines, where troops ravaged the land in their search for Abu Sayyaf, one local pointed out that, 'The solution ... is not a military one. The problem is poverty, and the government should listen to the cry of the people here. We need livelihood for our people, we don't need war.' In the Amazon basin, where American corporations are spraying the jungle as part of Plan Colombia, the peasant women grieve over the deaths of their children and the destruction of their crops due to the use of these poisonous sprays. Meanwhile Kenyans are outraged at the thought of a permanent base in Kenya, where journalist Philip Ochieng (2003) exclaims, 'No matter how much the dollar offers, nothing can be more perilous than to allow a US military base in Kenya.'

US military bases also cause extensive social problems in local communities. Historically, prostitution and violence have been endemic in communities that host US military bases. As Chalmers Johnson notes in *The Sorrows of Empire*, conditions at the US military installations in Okinawa, Japan, the 'expropriation of the island's most valuable land for bases, extraterritorial status for American troops who committed crimes against local civilians, bars and brothels crowding around the main gates of bases, endless accidents, noise, sexual violence, drunk-driving crashes, drug use, and environmental pollution – are replicated anywhere there are American garrisons' (Johnson 2004). Attendees at a conference entitled 'Women and Children, Militarism and Human Rights in Okinawa' reported that they 'see militarism as a system of structural violence which turns its members into war machines and creates victims among women and children in our local communities' (IWW 1997). They also held a 'clear conviction that the US military presence is a threat to our security, not a protection'. A sixteen-year-old Kyrgyz student says, 'I don't think American soldiers will protect us if someone attacks us from outside. They will first leave our country if there is something dangerous. And they will never protect us, because they think that their lives are much more expensive than others' (Koerkamp 2002).

Multi-polar Resistance to Empire

These US military trends conform to Paul Kennedy's description of how earlier imperial powers haemorrhaged in their final stages. As he notes: 'The Triumph of any one Great Power ... or the collapse of another, has usually been the consequence of lengthy fighting by its armed forces; but it has also been the consequence of the ... utilization of the state's productive economic resources in war time, and further in the background, of the way in which that state's economy had been rising or falling, "relative" to the other leading nations' (Kennedy 1987: xv).

As the quote above indicates, Kennedy also defined the concept of overstretch in relation to the relative pecking order of the other Great Powers. Georgetown University professor Charles Kupchan picks up on this theme in his book *The End of the American Era*, published in 2002. He argues that 'Pax Americana' will come to an end because of the 'rise of alternative centers of power and a declining and unilateralist US internationalism'. Even before France and Germany headed up Western opposition to the US war in Iraq, Kupchan asserted that the European Union would be in the forefront of an emergent 'multipolar world' that will eclipse US ascendancy in the early part of the twenty-first century.

Relations with the other major powers did not augur well for the United States in the aftermath of the 2003 Iraqi invasion. Dealings with 'old Europe' led by France and Germany remained frigid, with many signs pointing to a widening breach between the United States and members of the NATO alliance. The lack of European support in Iraq also made it virtually impossible for the United States to get the United Nations and other multilateral institutions more deeply involved in its efforts to rebuild an occupied Iraq. For the past sixty years the United Nations has been used to back many US policies around the world, ranging from the Korean war to the first Gulf war. The disregard the United States has shown for the United Nations in its drive to go to war in Iraq is undermining the very existence of that institution, which is essential for the world if we are ever to achieve long-term stability. Writing in *The Hindu*, Boutros Boutros-Ghali, former UN Secretary-General, observed, 'unilateralism may destroy the United Nations'. He then went on to contemplate that it was hard for the UN to chastise the United States, its main income source, for its actions. 'The real problem', he wrote, 'is that the UN is not able to speak up. How can it defend itself by saying that a given dispute is due to member-state A, when member-state A is its boss?' (Boutros-Ghali 2003).

In a globalized and media-oriented age, the US imperium's loss of both international and domestic public legitimacy is another clear sign of imperial overstretch. The demise of the democratic myth and the hard reality of empire now conjure up abroad the image of the arrogant and incompetent 'ugly American'. On the second anniversary of the 9/11 attacks, a *New York Times* article entitled 'Foreign Views of US Darken since Sept. 11' included what it called a commonly expressed view that 'A lot of people had sympathy for Americans around the time of 9/11, but that's changed, [now Americans] act like the big guy riding roughshod over everyone else.' The article went on to say that people blame the change on Bush, whom they see 'at best, as an ineffective spokesman for American interests and, at worst, as a gunslinging cowboy knocking over international treaties and bent on controlling the world's oil, if not the entire world'. Another common view was that 'the United States is a classically imperialist power bent on controlling global oil supplies and on military domination'. It then pointed out that the glib US President has become the laughing stock of the world. One British subject observed, 'President Bush is a very poor salesman for the United States ... Whether it's Al Qaeda or Afghanistan, people have just felt that he's a silly man, and therefore they are not obliged to think any harder about his position' (Bernstein 2003).

21

A majority of Europeans no longer want America to 'have a strong global presence'. Even in Poland, one of the strongest members of the 'Coalition of the Willing', 60 per cent of the people did not want Polish troops to go to Iraq. And in the Third World resentment is even stronger. In Indonesia favourable views of Americans fell by 75 per cent to the point where only 15 per cent of the population had a favourable view of the USA (ibid.).

In Latin America, the historic back yard of the United States, problems are also emerging. Brazil, Venezuela, Ecuador and Argentina have all elected governments that question US neo-liberal and free trade policies. Bush proclaimed in April 2001 in Quebec City that the Free Trade Area of the Americas was one of the highest priorities of his administration, but the November 2003 FTAA meetings in Miami, Florida, made it clear that the leading nations of South America were not interested in hemispheric economic integration. And Vicente Fox of Mexico, the first foreign leader invited to Bush's Crawford ranch in 2001, was increasingly disgruntled and disillusioned with the policy of benign neglect Bush adopted towards Mexico in the aftermath of 11 September. At the World Trade Organization meetings in Cancún in September 2003, a collective of Third World nations shut down the talks. Emboldened by demonstrations on the outside, delegates on the inside stood up to the United States and walked out when their concerns were disregarded. Suddenly the world has realized that America is not the mythological paradise it has always been portrayed as. The mask has fallen and the despotic and grasping imperial ruler has been revealed.

The Empire Confronts the Republic

Americans have also turned against the war policies of the Bush regime. In the autumn of 2003, a Pew poll discovered that 59 per cent of Americans did not like the expense of keeping troops in Iraq and 70 per cent favoured involving the United Nations more in creating the future of that country. In another poll 62 per cent of Americans felt that the United States was acting too frequently as the policeman of the world and only 12 per cent felt that it should 'continue to be the preeminent world leader in solving international problems' (Feffer 2003).

Two years after 9/11, 26 per cent of Americans felt more insecure than they did immediately after the Twin Towers were attacked, while 53 per cent said they felt only as secure as they did then, which was not very secure. One oft-repeated reason for this failure in the war on terrorism is the reality that undirected, wanton American violence in the Middle East creates a breeding ground for future generations of terrorists. As one Vietnam war veteran pointed out, 'Overcoming evil with more evil will not result in a good end. We only create more terrorists' (ibid.).

As with the republics of antiquity, Greece and Rome, the American republic and its liberties are menaced by the rush to empire. The Bush administration's cancellation of many civil liberties as part of the war on terrorism raised alarm cries across the country. Suddenly Americans were held incommunicado for an indefinite period. Prisoners were tried outside the public criminal justice system. Invasion of privacy was rampant as the government sought access to a plethora of private information including Internet searches, e-mails and phone records. Standard search warrants were becoming passé. And if you were arrested, your lawyer could be monitored by the government.

Bush's Democratic presidential opponent in 2000, Al Gore, speaking in the Hall of the Daughters of the American Revolution in Washington, DC, observed: 'It makes no more sense to launch an assault on our civil liberties as the best way to get at terrorists than it did to launch an invasion of Iraq as the best way to get at Osama Bin Laden' (Gore 2003). He went on to point out that while the government is seeking private information on citizens it is also withholding information from the public. Not only is it limiting use of the Freedom of Information Act, but it has also refused to submit critical information to the panel studying 9/11.

Most amazingly, in the land where the Statue of Liberty implores the world to 'give me your tired, your poor, your huddled masses yearning to breathe free', immigrants are the most often attacked. Addressing this reality, Al Gore pointed out that

> the disgraceful treatment suffered by ... vulnerable immigrants at the hands of the administration has created deep resentments and hurt the cooperation desperately needed from immigrant communities in the US and from the Security Services of other countries ... these gross violations of their rights have seriously damaged US moral authority and goodwill around the world ... our moral authority is, after all, our greatest source of enduring strength in the world.

The repression of the demonstrations against the FTAA in Miami in November 2003 revealed that the war for empire had come home. Symbolically, funding for the police repression came from the special war appropriations bill for Iraq and Afghanistan. And some of the antics employed by the police took a page right out of US military operations in Iraq. Reporters from the established media, such as the *Miami Herald*, were 'embedded' among the police. Spies and infiltrators were placed among the protest organizers. Rubber bullets were fired at the demonstrators at random, and pepper gas pellets inflicted severe pain and suffering on many protesters. And while the police rioted in Miami, recently retired General Tommy Franks, who had commanded the invasion of Iraq, said it might be necessary to suspend the constitution of the United States in the event of another terrorist attack (Solnit 2003).

24

Rise of the 'Second Superpower'

Walden Bello, a leading critic of US militarism, declared in a speech to an assembly of alternative and anti-war organizations in Berlin in June 2003 that the world has

> entered a historical maelstrom marked by prolonged economic crisis, the spread of global resistance, the reappearance of the balance of power among centre states, and the re-emergence of acute inter-imperialist contradictions. We must have a healthy respect for US power, but neither must we overestimate it. The signs are there that the United States is seriously overextended and what appear to be manifestations of strength might in fact signal weakness strategically. (Bello 2003)

In his speech, Bello also discussed 'the forging of a powerful global civil society movement against US unilateralism'. This is a critical development. In the world of the twenty-first century, the challenges faced by US rulers go beyond the traditional economic and military challenges presented by other nation-states.

George W. Bush scoffed at the eleven million people who protested against the American war on 15 February 2003, calling them 'a focus group'. Continuing opposition to his policies at home and abroad reveals that his words could not have been farther off the mark. One of the concepts presented in these pages is that a 'second superpower' is emerging. This power is rooted in the mobilization of popular forces on a global scale. It includes the anti-war and anti-globalization movements, the gatherings of the Porto Alegre Forum and a multitude of human rights and global justice organizations, many of which are non-governmental organizations, or NGOs. If there is one slogan that unites these groups and organizations, it is that 'another world is possible'. This vast and diverse movement is at once autonomous and interacts with governments and international institutions to pose a challenge not only to the United States war machine but also to the world system of Great Powers that has been predominant for half a millennium.

To understand the enormous tasks faced by this global movement, we need to reflect on the origins of the American empire. Inadvertently, George W. Bush, by engaging in a policy of reckless imperial overstretch, is compelling the American people to look at their history and seriously to consider whether or not they want to endure the world's last remaining empire.

TWO

Empire as the American way of life

Mine eyes have seen the orgy of the lancing of the Sword;
He is searching out the hoardings where the stranger's wealth
   is stored;
He hath loosed his fateful lightnings, and with woe and death
   has scored;
His lust is marching on.

*Mark Twain, Battle Hymn of the Republic (Brought Down to
Date), written for the Anti-Imperialist League in February 1901
to denounce the US war of occupation in the Philippines*

In 1997 Irving Kristol wrote in the *Wall Street Journal*: 'One of
these days, the American people are going to awaken to the fact
that we have become an imperial nation, even though the public
and all our institutions are hostile to the idea' (Kristol 1997).
Kristol, paraphrasing an old saw that the British empire emerged
in a 'fit of absent-mindedness', argued 'there does seem to be
an awful lot of absent-mindedness about the way an American
imperium ... has come (and is coming) into existence'.

A leading ideologue of the neo-conservatives since the early
Reagan years, Kristol may have distorted the role of imperial
absent-mindedness, but he did capture the widespread belief
that the American people are hostile to the idea of empire. Even
during the Vietnam war, when many protesters and opponents
of the war used the term 'imperialism' to describe US actions in
south-east Asia, the American public by and large rejected the idea
of the United States as an imperial nation.

However, the militaristic policies of the Bush administration
have ignited a renewed discussion about the United States as an
empire. Before the Iraqi invasion, the *New York Times Magazine*

27

ran a feature article by Michael Ignatieff, a mainstream scholar at Harvard University, who asked rhetorically, 'what word but empire describes the awesome thing that America is becoming?' The United States, he pointed out, 'is the only nation that polices the world through five global military commands; maintains more than a million men and women at arms on four continents; deploys carrier battle groups on watch in every ocean; guarantees the survival of countries from Israel to South Korea; drives the wheels of global trade and commerce; and fills the hearts and minds of an entire planet with its dreams and desires' (Ignatieff 2003).

The Bush administration, of course, officially eschews the use of the term empire. George W. himself proclaimed before a group of veterans assembled at the White House in November 2002 that the United States has 'no territorial ambitions. We don't seek an empire.' And Secretary of Defense Donald Rumsfeld, when asked by a reporter in April 2003 whether the United States was building a global empire, responded in typical Rumsfeld fashion: 'We don't seek empires. We're not imperialistic. We never have been. I can't imagine why you'd even ask the question' (Boot 2003b).

But there is little doubt that the concepts of empire and global domination are in the forefront of the minds of the foreign policy strategists of the Bush administration. Richard Haass, who became the Director of Policy Planning in the State Department under Colin Powell, presented a paper entitled 'Imperial America' in Atlanta just days after the presidential election of 2000. He asserted that for the United States to achieve global pre-eminence, Americans would need to 're-conceive their role from a traditional nation-state to an imperial power'. Max Boot, a neo-conservative who writes for the *Wall Street Journal* and who supports the interventionist policies of the Bush administration, also believes that 'America's destiny is to police the world'. In a talk at the University of California, Berkeley, he declared that the United

States is engaged in 'liberal imperialism' and that the discussion of 'American empire has become respectable' (Boot 2003a).

Of course, when these officials and apologists for the Bush administration use the words imperial or empire, they claim to be employing them in a benign manner. Haass, for example, rejected the more aggressive term 'imperialist', proclaiming it meant 'territorial control' and 'exploitation, normally for commercial ends' (Haass 2000). Boot, in his book *The Savage Wars of Peace*, argues that the United States has continually intervened on the side of peace and righteousness since its founding, and that as the world's only superpower its destiny is to shape the world of the twenty-first century.

In October 2003, however, a broad coalition of prominent foreign-policy scholars and analysts whose political views ranged from right to centre-left announced their opposition to the imperial policies advocated by neo-conservatives like Max Boot. Forming the Coalition for a Realistic Foreign Policy, they charged that the Bush administration was moving 'in a dangerous direction toward empire', an idea that had never been embraced by the US public. Among the more prominent conservative members were Doug Bandow, a special assistant to former President Ronald Reagan and a senior officer at the Cato Institute, and Scott McConnell, chief editor of *The American Conservative* magazine (Lobe 2003).

Defining Empire, the American Way

The concept of empire has bedevilled American history. Perhaps it is a step forward that some of the current advocates of US dominance in the world are at least acknowledging the concept of an American empire. But in order to understand US intervention in countries such as Iraq we need to grapple with the history of the US imperium, to sort out its origins and relation to other empires. If we are not willing to recognize our history as an aggressive empire, then we are destined to repeat the mistakes and errors of our past, to inflict great pain and suffering on the rest of the world while corrupting our democratic institutions at home.

A major reason why the term empire is so alien to many Americans is that it is associated with the 'old' empires of Europe. The British colonial empire of the nineteenth century on which the 'sun never set' is probably the most well known. Great Britain exercised territorial control over colonies in Africa, Asia, Australia and the Caribbean and Latin America. And aside from the British, the Belgians, the Germans, the Dutch, the French and the Portuguese all possessed formal empires well into the twentieth century, exerting direct military and political control over distant lands.

Because the United States of America became the first modern nation in the world to declare its independence from an empire, the American people by and large believe that the United States is inherently anti-colonial and anti-imperialist. However, the truth of the matter is that the United States throughout its history has always been on the 'cutting edge of empire', looking with disdain on the old empires of Europe, while employing new rhetoric and concepts to forge its own empire. Early on, Thomas Jefferson captured this tendency to cast US expansionism in the best light when he proclaimed that the United States was an 'empire of freedom'.

A related fact that helps us understand why the concepts of empire and imperialism are largely absent in the discussion of US history is that the leading theorists of imperialism emerged in Europe in the late nineteenth and early twentieth centuries. John A. Hobson of Great Britain, Rudolf Hilferding of Germany and Lenin of Russia all produced major studies on the origins and dynamics of imperialism. Lenin, who wrote what is probably the most well-known treatise on imperialism in 1916, argued that imperialism is the product of a particular stage of capitalism, which he called monopoly capitalism.

These 'scientific' analyses of imperialism had only a limited impact on American politics and culture. A few early critics of imperialism in the United States, such as Scott Nearing, did produce insightful studies (see, for example, Nearing 1921), but unfortunately they did not ignite broad public debates. The reality is that Marxist analyses, along with communist political parties, did not sink deep roots in American culture or politics, and thus discussions of imperialism and empire were limited to a relatively small group of leftist intellectuals and members of radical political formations.

In the United States a more systematic discussion of empire and imperialism did begin to take hold in the years after the Second World War when the United States emerged as the world's dominant capitalist power. In the 1950s William Appleman Williams, more than any other scholar of the post-war era, managed to break out of the European mould of analysis and to develop a 'native' school of study that opened up a wide-ranging discussion in scholarly circles on the US empire. The key to his success in developing such a new school of thought at the University of Wisconsin lay in his ability to capture the uniqueness of US international expansion, especially in comparison to European empires. His ground-breaking work, *The Tragedy of American Diplomacy*, first published in 1959, traces the origins of the current US imperium back to the late nineteenth century when the United States first espoused an 'open door' policy and forged an 'informal empire'.

Williams used the work of a historian of the late nineteenth century, Frederick Jackson Turner, to argue that the closing of the western frontier compelled the United States to expand abroad. While Turner never employed the terminology of empire or imperialism to describe the US role in the world, his analysis of the 1890 census data led him to proclaim that the frontier was closed and that in order for the United States to avoid the social upheavals and political strife that were so pronounced in Europe it would have to expand beyond its continental limits. 'For nearly three centuries the dominant fact of American life has been expansion,' Turner proclaimed. He was confident that this expansion would persist in a new form, noting that 'the demands for a vigorous foreign policy, for an inter-oceanic canal, for a revival of our power upon the seas, and for the extension of American influence to outlying islands and adjoining countries, are indications that the movement will continue' (cited in Williams 1992: 32). Williams, borrowing from Turner, made the closing of the frontier the linchpin of his study of the US empire in the twentieth century, asserting that the closure compelled US leaders to search aggressively for new international markets and to intervene in other countries to ensure that their economies would be 'open' to US penetration.

The Foundation of the American Empire

In a subsequent work, *The Contours of American History*, Williams went back to the foundations of the republic in the late eighteenth century to demonstrate that the United States had always been intent on forging an empire, although the early leaders gave it a different content and meaning from the empire that emerged around the turn of the twentieth century. This early empire had a distinct '*Weltanschauung*', a term Williams uses to describe the imperial world views the United States would develop over two centuries.

The signers of the Declaration of Independence and the founders of the republic were more frank than their twentieth-century political descendants in discussing the importance of empire in relation to the new republic. John Adams of Massachusetts, who would become the second President of the United States after George Washington, called on the Second Continental Congress in 1775 to get on with the business of writing 'a constitution to form for a great empire'. Representing South Carolina at the same congress, William Henry Drayton proclaimed, 'The Almighty ... has made choice of the present generation to erect the American Empire ... ' (Williams 1973: 116).

Popular books of the time also revelled in the idea of a new American empire. The first spelling book, written in 1783 when the former colonies were grouped together under the Articles of Confederation, spoke pointedly of how it provided the intellectual tools needed by 'this infant Empire'. Its author, Noah Webster, boasted that the book was dedicated to 'encourage genius in this country, [so that] the EMPIRE OF AMERICA will no longer be indebted to a foreign kingdom for books' (ibid.: 143).

Then, at the end of the eighteenth century after the ratification of the US constitution, Jedidiah Morse, in the authoritative and widely used *American Geography*, asserted that the United States had 'risen into Empire'. And he captured at this early date the fascination of the new nation with the territories on its western frontier as the basis of a new imperium. Morse stated: 'It is well known that empire has been travelling from east to west,' and he predicted that the new nation would soon be 'the largest empire that ever existed' (ibid.: 179).

Some of the founding fathers did worry about whether a nation of republican origins was compatible with the establishment of a large empire. The eighteenth-century French political philosopher Baron de Montesquieu, who exerted a strong influence on the drafters of the US constitution, believed that a republic could be preserved only in a small territory. With the early expansion into the Ohio river valley and the addition of new states to the Union, however, the first US leaders soon became confident that the two were compatible. In 1801 Thomas Jefferson wrote that American expansion 'furnishes a new proof of the falsehood of Montesquieu's doctrine, that a republic can be preserved only in a small territory. The reverse is the truth' (ibid.: 179). Eight years later, as his presidency came to its end, Jefferson declared: 'I am persuaded no constitution was never before as well calculated as ours for extensive empire and self-government' (Williams 1980: vii).

Williams sees US leaders in the nineteenth century as adopting two main economic philosophies to guide the new empire: mercantilism in the early years, and then laissez-faire for much of the nineteenth century. The mercantilists, such as Adams, Jefferson, Madison and Monroe, advocated a strong role for the state to bind the new republic together. The national government would look after the common good, control competing factions and use tariffs and public works to foment the development of the new nation as a whole. In this early period, the federal government became the single largest economic enterprise in the country.

This economic approach predominated from the founding of the republic until 1829 when Andrew Jackson became President. Having built his fame as an army officer and Indian-fighter, Jackson accelerated the westward drive that relied on a strong individualist bent as well as genocidal warfare against the Indians. A laissez-faire economy took hold among the settlers, the businessmen and the national leaders who asserted that the government had no role to play, other than providing land grants and an army to fight the Indians. 'Manifest Destiny' soon became the rallying cry for these nineteenth-century expansionists. From 1845 to 1849, under President James Polk, the United States annexed Texas, went to war with Mexico, seizing the entire south-west of the present United States, and finally took over the north-west territories that were in dispute with Great Britain.

Williams does not discuss the relationship of the nineteenth-century US imperium to earlier empires, but US leaders of that period were well versed in the empires of antiquity, especially those of Rome and Athens. One only has to see the architecture of the prominent government buildings in Washington, DC, dating from the turn of the nineteenth century, to realize the presence of these ancient empires in the minds of those who built the new republic. While few of the founding fathers verbally expressed their desire to forge an empire like those of the ancient world, there are striking similarities with the early expansion of the Roman republic dating from the third century BC onwards. These were the years when the Romans marched eastwards to conquer Greece, then Carthage, most of the Mediterranean basin, and westwards into Gaul and Britain where they fought the 'barbarians'. Rome's early institutions were republican, drawing on the traditions of the Greek city-states, with Roman citizenship granted to many of the residents of the conquered territories. Edward Gibbon, the famous eighteenth-century historian and author of *The Decline and Fall of the Roman Empire*, claims that 'if man were called to fix the period in the history of the world during which the condition of the human race was most happy and prosperous, he would, without hesitation' look to Roman history before the beginning of its decline in the late second century AD (cited in Doyle 1986: 82).

Contemporary author Michael Doyle, in his outstanding work *Empires*, describes the dynamics of the early Roman empire in terms that sound amazingly similar to what took place in the United States in the nineteenth century. In the following passage from Doyle, the words 'the United States' could easily be substituted for Rome: 'Rome's constitution was fit for empire. It rested upon liberty (for nonslaves, of course) and thus freed the energies and ambitions of the people who could safely be armed to guard the state' (ibid.: 88). Doyle also notes that in early Rome, 'a growing population demanded more land'. To the west of Rome, as in the US west, the thirst for land meant the conquest of 'tribal societies'. At another point Doyle, in a phrase that eerily captures traits that could be used to describe Americans up to today, states that in republican Rome 'liberty, ambition and patriotism are conjoined' (ibid.: 85).

There were, of course, differences regarding the foes that Rome and the United States faced in taking on the 'civilized states', both of which lay to the geographic east. Rome conquered many of the ancient states in the Persian and Middle East regions and subsumed them into its empire. The United States in its early years recognized the overwhelming power of its 'civilized' rivals to the east, the European states, opting to steer clear of 'entangling alliances' with them. But in the nineteenth century the United States did seize control of territories that Europe possessed on the American continent, and early on challenged the European powers to get out of the western hemisphere with the proclamation of the Monroe Doctrine in 1823.

The new Weltanschauung   With the conquest and settling of the continent by the end of the nineteenth century the building of the US empire entered a new stage, a new *Weltanschauung* that went beyond that of the founders of the US republic. The war that broke out in 1898 with Spain, the 'splendid little war' as it was called, marked a turning point in the consolidation of a new US empire based not on territorial conquest but on the conquest of foreign markets so as to guarantee the prosperity and growth of US agriculture and its burgeoning manufacturing sector. As the Department of State declared on the eve of the war of 1898: 'Every year we shall be confronted with an increasing surplus of manufactured goods for sale in foreign markets if American operatives and artisans are to be kept employed the year around. The enlargement of foreign consumption of the products of our mills and workshops has, therefore, become a serious problem of statesmanship as well as of commerce' (Williams 1992: 28).

The classic view is that in the aftermath of the war of 1898 the United States was divided between the imperialist and anti-imperialist camps over whether to take the Philippines and Puerto Rico and exert direct control over Cuba. Williams argues that there was a third camp that emerged triumphant and that would to a large extent subsume the other two positions. This camp viewed access to foreign markets as the key to US expansionism, not the conquest of foreign territories. Secretary of State John Hay articulated this position in several diplomatic dispatches between 1899 and 1900, referred to as the 'Open Door Notes'. They did not deal with the 'spoils' of the war of 1898, but with the demands of the United States for access to the markets of China as the European powers set about carving up the country, securing territorial control over key ports and territories. In the first note Hay stated that US entrepreneurs in China 'shall enjoy perfect equality of treatment for their commerce and navigation', even within the spheres of interest controlled by foreign powers (cited in ibid.: 51). In his third and final note, Hay went on to set the tone for US intervention in the Caribbean and Central America for the next two decades when he proclaimed that 'it is axiomatic that trade follows the loan'. The collection of loans, along with the protection of US investments and trade, became the basis for expansion and repeated US interventions in other countries.

Williams asserts that the Open Door Notes set the foundations for the US empire down to the years of the cold war in the mid-twentieth century. The United States forged an 'informal empire', one based on the quest for foreign markets and the search for investment outlets for US capital, not on the direct control of colonies or territories. He argues that while the United States did take control of the Philippines and Puerto Rico, these were viewed mainly as outposts or bases for commercial entry into the larger markets of Asia, the Caribbean and Latin America. Borrowing in part from Lenin's *Imperialism*, Williams notes that this new empire coincided with the rise of large corporations which became increasingly influential in shaping US foreign policy as they sought raw materials, foreign markets and manufacturing subsidiaries abroad.

This new empire grew out of the consolidation of wealth and power created during the American industrial revolution of the late 1800s. In the years before the 1898 Spanish–American War, a robust populist movement emerged to challenge the robber barons who dominated this gilded age. To defeat this movement of farmers and workers, Mark Hanna, a cohort of Ohio-based oil monopolist John D. Rockefeller, headed up a corporate fund-raising drive in the 1896 presidential election to back the candidacy of Ohio governor William McKinley. The drive set new standards for electoral fund-raising. McKinley's subsequent defeat of William Jennings Bryan completed the corporate takeover of government that had been enhanced a year earlier when J. P. Morgan and the English bank of the Rothschilds underwrote half the gold supply of the US Treasury at a time when panic threatened to destroy the American economy.

Run by the rules of Wall Street, this empire took on a singular narrow market ethos. The laissez-faire market reigned supreme as costs were determined only by narrow market costs. The costs of human lives, the costs of environmental degradation, the costs of human alienation were not considered. As far as the commercial empire was concerned, these costs did not exist. The financial and industrial corporations looked to and expected the US government to support and protect their international commerce and holdings. Their expansive interests were embodied in the Open Door Notes. This approach, Williams argues, characterized US policy from the years of Theodore Roosevelt and William Howard Taft down to the administrations of John F. Kennedy and Lyndon Johnson. The post-Second World War years in particular are portrayed by Williams as the heyday of 'corporate liberalism', the period when corporate interests went hand in hand with the influence of the eastern liberal establishment in setting the course of US foreign policy.

But Williams, by lumping this long period of history into

one grand *Weltanschauung*, does not tease out the importance of the distinct conceptions and strategies of expansionism that emerged with the rise of the new empire. Some administrations were more assertive in sending US troops abroad to occupy countries and fight in local wars, while others were more patient, preferring to rely more on diplomacy and commercial pressures and sanctions to secure US interests abroad. Also, different policies elicited different popular reactions among the US body politic, sometimes leading to non-interventionist and even anti-imperialist movements that placed constraints on US policies of blatant aggression. These deliberations over the direction of US foreign policy include the early debate over whether or not to take possession of the Philippines, the opposition to the US war against Sandino's guerrilla army in Nicaragua in the 1920s, the domestic strife over the Vietnam war, and finally, today, the debate over the waging of pre-emptive wars by the Bush administration.

Of these great discourses concerning the proper US role in the world, only the first, the taking of the spoils of the war with Spain, was explicitly framed in terms of imperialism and empire. A number of prominent Americans – including ex-Presidents Benjamin Harrison and Grover Cleveland, corporate tycoons such as Andrew Carnegie, radical reformers such as Jane Addams, and prominent thinkers and writers like Thorstein Veblen, William James and Mark Twain – staked out clear anti-imperialist positions. Robert Beisner, who wrote about twelve of the key figures who led this movement, notes that between 1898 and 1900: 'Hundreds of prominent politicians and private citizens denounced American imperialism in newspapers, magazines and pamphlets, made countless speeches on the subject, fought the acquisition of Puerto Rico, Hawaii, and the Philippines in Congress, organized anti-imperialist leagues and associations ... ' (Beisner 1968: x). The movement failed to stop the US Senate from ratifying the Treaty of Paris, which annexed the Philippines and Puerto Rico in 1899. Hawaii was annexed in 1898 and made a US territory in 1900. Then, with the defeat of William Jennings Bryan, who ran on an anti-imperialist platform in the presidential elections of 1900, the opposition movement collapsed.

New imperial leadership   For the next quarter-century it is actually difficult to distinguish the US policy of empire, particularly in the Caribbean and Central America, from the actions of the major European powers. Teddy Roosevelt, who became President in 1901, orchestrated a plot to seize control of the Colombian province of Panama to build an inter-oceanic canal. He subsequently boasted: 'I took the isthmus [and] started the canal' (Internet K). His administration became known for its gunboat diplomacy, as the United States sent the marines into Cuba, the Dominican Republic, Haiti and Nicaragua. Roosevelt's successor, William Howard Taft, seemingly tried to put a different spin on this policy of direct intervention by calling for 'dollar diplomacy'. But he also wound up deploying US troops in the Caribbean basin to secure the interests of the almighty dollar.

Woodrow Wilson, who criticized both gunboat and dollar diplomacy in the presidential elections in 1912, declared in a university lecture in 1907: 'Since trade ignores national boundaries and the manufacturer insists on having the world as a market, the flag of his nation must follow him and the doors of the nation which are closed must be battered down ... Colonies must be obtained or planted, in order that no useful corner of the world may be overlooked or left unused' (Williams 1992: 72). As President, Wilson was as aggressive as his predecessors, seizing control of the Mexican port of Vera Cruz, sending General Pershing to pursue Pancho Villa's rebels in northern Mexico, and ordering US troops into Haiti, the Dominican Republic, Nicaragua, Cuba, Honduras and Panama.

The genocidal approach to warfare that had become ingrained

in the American psyche during the conquest of the North American Indians was carried over into the new empire. In the Philippines, the US military conquest left a deep scar on both the local residents and the American occupiers. Filipinos resisted the American occupation for a decade after the Spanish–American War. As in the Iraqi war a century later, no count was kept of the local populace that died as a result of the war. It was not a cost that the US empire concerned itself with. Two years after the counter-insurgency campaign began an American general told the *New York Times* that 600,000 Filipino lives had been lost owing to the war. Philippine researcher Luzviminda Francisco makes a guesstimate that by the end of the war perhaps a million people had died (Francisco 1985).

The barbaric incivility of the American conquest tore at the roots of the mythological American democratic culture. Only by denying reality and characterizing Filipinos as 'niggers, babarians and savages' could the Americans rationalize the horror of the Philippines (ibid.). It internationalized the racism of American culture, dealing a heavy blow to the dream of equality. The denial by the American populace of the link between racism and the new imperial expansionism that took hold in the Philippine war has continued for more than a century. In that time this denial has allowed the government to sell wars – in Asia, Latin America, and now in the Gulf – that are implicitly based on a racist world view that the cultures and peoples of these lands are inferior and do not meet our 'civilized' standards.

For the Filipinos, as for the subsequent victims of the American empire, the costs are incalculable. The victims of the American empire were forced to accept the money-powered, market values of the American financier class. The will of a strong and independent people was crushed, humans beings commodified, the landscape razed and turned into sugar plantations and anything that would turn a profit for the emergent multinational corporations. But the memory and grief never die. The resentment that becomes ingrained in the heart of a conquered people is always there, always an impediment to the future of the empire.

Smedley Butler, who rose in the ranks of the Marine Corps to major-general during the first three decades of the twentieth century, saw action on three continents. At the end of that experience he said,

> I spent most of my time being a high class muscle-man for Big Business, for Wall Street and for the Bankers. In short, I was a racketeer, a gangster for capitalism ... I helped make Mexico, especially Tampico, safe for American oil interests in 1914. I helped make Haiti and Cuba a decent place for the National City Bank boys to collect revenues in. I helped in the raping of half a dozen Central American republics for the benefits of Wall Street. The record of racketeering is long. I helped purify Nicaragua for the international banking house of Brown Brothers in 1909–1912. I brought light to the Dominican Republic for American sugar interests in 1916. In China I helped to see to it that Standard Oil went its way unmolested. (Internet D)

In the early twentieth century the United States clearly possessed both an informal and a formal empire. Aside from the colonies it controlled after the war with Spain, the United States acted as a sovereign power in the Caribbean and much of Latin America, intervening with troops thirty-one times in the region between 1901 and 1925 (see Collier 1993). And US foreign investments during the first quarter of the twentieth century expanded in tandem with the advance of the US flag, just as Wilson had advocated. In 1900 investments abroad stood at $500 million, in 1909 at $2 billion, in 1913 $2.5 billion, and by 1924 they had reached about $8 billion. The heart of these holdings was in the Americas with $4 billion of the 1924 investments located in Latin America and another $2.4 billion in Canada (Nearing and Freeman 1925/1970:

12, 16). As Nearing stated in the 1925 study of *Dollar Diplomacy* that he co-authored with Joseph Freeman, 'this is the economic structure of American imperialism' (ibid.: 17).

The rapid expansion of US entrepreneurs and business investments aroused the wrath of divergent social classes throughout Latin America in the 1910s and 1920s. Peasants, trade unions, the emergent middle classes and even sectors of the local elites came to resent US intrusion and the takeover of their most productive lands and the dynamic mining and manufacturing enterprises (see O'Brien 1999: 73–81). The cry of 'Yanqui imperialism' became a common refrain in Latin America. Moreover, the repeated interventions to protect US interests did not create stability, as US forces intervened repeatedly in countries such as Cuba, Haiti, Nicaragua and the Dominican Republic, only deepening local hostility.

Fighting Communism

Under Calvin Coolidge, who succeeded to the presidency when Warren Harding died in office, the United States embarked on its first anti-communist campaign in an effort to keep the republics to the south in line. The radical policies of the Mexican Revolution in particular aroused the ire of Washington. US oil companies lobbied hard against Article 27 of the 1917 Mexican constitution, which granted the national government control of all subsoil rights. Under Coolidge a representative of the oil companies declared that Mexican laws threatened their 'basic right to produce oil and make money'. When the liberal government of Juan B. Sacasa took power in Nicaragua in 1926 and received limited support from the Mexican government, the US ambassador to Nicaragua proclaimed that 'a semi-Bolshevik regime' like Mexico's was being established. A rump government was set up by the United States in Nicaragua, but when it encountered local opposition the United States sent in 5,000 troops. At about the same time Secretary of State Kellogg released a State Department paper entitled 'Bolshevik Arms and Policies in Mexico and Central America'.

The new US invasionary force found no Bolsheviks, but it soon inspired opposition from a ragtag, peasant army led by Augusto Cesar Sandino. This marked the first guerrilla warfare waged against the US occupation of a Latin American country. For several years Sandino's fighters fought hit-and-run battles against US marines. Responding as it would in latter-twentieth-century wars, the United States used aircraft to bomb guerrilla positions. And just as in subsequent years, sustained native resistance precipitated the formation of a non-intervention movement in the United States. An interview with Sandino in *The Nation* magazine fomented awareness in the United States of Sandino's cause and led to popular protests. Soon other US magazines and newspapers, along with a student movement and congressional opponents in Washington, came out against the war, calling for the immediate withdrawal of US troops from Nicaragua. In 1928 Congress came within one vote of denying funding for the war.

In 1929, Henry Stimson, Herbert Hoover's Secretary of State, began to negotiate an end to the Nicaraguan conflict and the gradual withdrawal of US troops. In the rest of Latin America, US policy-makers, and even US businessmen, began to realize that the heavy-handed policy of US intervention was provoking ever deepening hostility towards the United States. As a result Hoover and Stimson began to pull out most of the US forces stationed in the Caribbean basin.

Relaunching the informal empire The tilt away from direct intervention and control of Latin American countries marked a decided shift back towards the original intent of US expansion abroad, that of creating an informal empire. The reversion to informal rule in the Caribbean and Central America was driven by both the resistance of the peripheral societies to US domination and the belief of US rulers that it was difficult or impossible to manage and produce stability in those countries subject to US intervention in the Caribbean basin. As Thomas Lamont of the J. P. Morgan bank declared: 'The theory of collecting debts by gunboats is unrighteous, unworkable and obsolete. While I have, of course, no mantle to speak for my colleagues of the investment banking community, I think I may safely say that they share this view ... ' (Gardner 1964: 51).

To understand these twists and turns of US expansionism in the twentieth century it is important to grasp the dynamics that have shaped and reshape the US empire. Doyle, in his book *Empires*, goes beyond the classic analysts of late nineteenth and early twentieth-century European imperialism to argue that it is not simply the internal dynamics of the imperial nations, such as monopoly capitalism, which determine whether or not a given country becomes an empire. Doyle believes that in addition to the 'capacities and interests' of the imperial power, the characteristics of the peripheral societies, along with the 'transnational system' and the 'international context', explain the rise (and decline) of an imperial nation. In other words the nature of the peripheral societies and the characteristics of the international system of power relations are critical to understanding the role of a given imperial nation at a particular moment in history.

For the United States in the late 1920s and the early 1930s it was the growing resistance and diversification of the class structures of the Caribbean countries which made it increasingly difficult for the United States to continue the dispatch of US troops to control their internal affairs. Franklin Roosevelt's Secretary of State, Cordell Hull, realized that in order to maintain and expand existent US economic interests in Latin America, the United States would have to abandon its formal interventions. Almost immediately after he took office, however, Hull faced a challenge on the US doorstep as the Cuban dictatorship of General Gerardo Machado was overthrown by a group of revolutionary officers and civilians led by Ramon Grau San Martin.

Distrustful of the new government, the United States sent gunboats to patrol the waters around Cuba, and dispatched an envoy to Havana, who soon requested that US troops be sent ashore to depose the new government. After a prolonged debate within the Roosevelt administration, intervention was ruled out. As Cordell Hull stated: 'I am telling people who have property there to let it be injured a little, while the Cubans are establishing a government themselves, because should the Cubans themselves establish a government, the outbreaks will gradually cease, business will return to normalcy and the Americans will recover their losses' (ibid.: 48). This approach was also adopted in Haiti and the Dominican Republic. There the United States replaced its collection of debts via occupation of the main ports with a system in which the customs receipts were deposited directly in New York banks for payment to US debtors. As one State Department official acknowledged in the case of the Dominican Republic, this preserved 'the fiction of Dominican sovereignty over the customs service' (Rabe 1988: 9).

To reinforce its political control without direct intervention, the US government began to train local leaders and dictators to take the place of US occupation forces. In Nicaragua, the United States established the Nicaraguan National Guard, recruiting a Nicaraguan car salesman living in Philadelphia, Anastasio Somoza, as its commander-in-chief. Somoza subsequently assassinated Sandino and installed a family dictatorship that ruled the country for almost half a century. As Roosevelt declared, 'Somoza may be a son of a bitch, but he's our son of a bitch.' In Cuba the United States cultivated a similar relationship with Falencio Batista, one of the young military officers who originally sided with Grau San Martin. In 1934 he toppled San Martin with the acquiescence of the United States, becoming the country's de facto strongman.

US control now came to depend on the forging of political and commercial alliances with the ruling classes of Latin America. Under the Spanish colonial system, a caste of Spaniards and Spanish descendants controlled the lands and local commerce of the New World. Then, with the declaration of independence in the early 1800s, the new Latin American rulers broadened their international ties to include Europeans, particularly the British, and then the Americans. These ties were strengthened, sometimes through marriage, but even more importantly through cultural and economic bonds as children of the elite were sent abroad to study and absorb the values of the metropolitan countries. The ruling strata looked with distain on the mixed-race populations of their societies, preferring to hobnob with the foreigners as they facilitated the extraction and sale of their countries' resources and wealth, often in exchange for a portion of the profits that accrued to the international interests.

The forging of strong relations with subservient internal political elites enabled the United States to consolidate an informal empire that allowed US economic expansion to continue apace in Latin America. By 1934, US direct investments in Latin America stood at $5 billion. And in the midst of the Great Depression, Latin America became a critical trading partner of the United States. As of 1935, Latin America absorbed 54 per cent of US cotton manufactured exports, 55 per cent of steel mill exports, roughly one-third of its leather, rubber, silk, paper, electrical and industrial exports, and 22 per cent of auto exports. One Commerce Department official exclaimed: 'we are entrepreneurs in Latin America, but are mere creditors in Europe' (Gardner 1964: 52). The Roosevelt administration even began to speak of a 'Common wealth of the Americas', borrowing a concept from the British, who had established their own Commonwealth to hold together the disparate countries of the British empire.

By the mid- and late 1930s another of Doyle's defining tenets of major empires, the competing interests of other great powers, began to impact on the US role in Latin America. Germany contested US interests in the region, particularly in Argentina, Brazil and Chile in South America, and Guatemala in Central America. In these countries German capital along with German immigrants exerted significant influence on the countries' economies and politics. To help contain these German advances in the region, in 1940 the US Congress broadened the mandate of the Export-Import Bank (established in 1934) so it could finance development projects, as well as provide loans to countries to purchase US exports.

In the case of Brazil, where Germany along with Japan was particularly active in trying to gain access to the country's iron ore reserves, the Eximbank extended its largest loan to the Volta Redonda steel mill project. It marked the first time that the United States financed a major industrial project that did not directly involve US investors and which potentially competed with US steel interests. However, as in the case of all Eximbank loans, the funds had to be used to import machinery and equipment from the United States, thereby creating a new form of dependency. Simultaneously the US government began underwriting the expansion of Pan American Airways as the semi-official airline of the United States in Latin America. To keep out German air competitors, PanAm received US mail concessions and federal funds to build air bases in South America (ibid.: 69, 129–30).

With the outbreak of the Second World War, Latin America became vitally important to the United States as trade with Europe and other parts of the world was curtailed because of the war. Latin America became the 'commodity arsenal' for the United States as it went to war in Europe and the Far East. Trade between the United States and Latin America almost doubled, focusing in particular on key strategic wartime commodities such as copper, manganese, quartz crystals, tin, tungsten, zinc and oil. This expansion in trade occurred largely under the domination of US corporations as the number of American firms operating in the region increased dramatically: in Mexico the total jumped from 200 in 1939 to 359 in 1943, in Brazil from 112 to 265, and in all of Latin America from around 1,000 to 2,000 (ibid.: 205). As a result of the war the United States exerted a virtual stranglehold on the Latin American economies. A White House aide in the Roosevelt administration declared: 'The petroleum resources of Mexico, Colombia, Venezuela and other Caribbean countries must be considered to be the reserves of the United States.'

The United States also continued to intervene overtly in the political and economic affairs of Latin America. In 1943 the Roosevelt administration pointedly told Chile that it would not receive post-war economic assistance if it did not declare war on Germany and Japan. And in 1943–44 in Bolivia, the United States refused to recognize the government of Gualberto Villarroel because of its alleged Nazi sympathies. To counter Nazi proclivities and propaganda throughout the hemisphere, the State Department's Office of the Coordinator of Inter-American Affairs, headed by the young, ambitious politician Nelson Rockefeller, funded a pro-US propaganda campaign that penetrated Latin American newspapers, radios and cinemas. The State Department later declared that this was 'the greatest outpouring of propagandistic material by a state ever' (Rabe 1988: 10). US military influence in South America also expanded during the war as US military advisers replaced Europeans in much of the continent. With the approaching end of the Second World War, the United States was set to usher in a new imperial age, one that would rely on ideology and propaganda as well as unprecedented economic and military power.

The United States had become a global empire. Americans may have been in denial but the rest of the world knew the truth. While Latin American and Filipino peasants and workers chafed at the American bit, their elite patrons merrily colluded with the

49

American imperium. The costs of the empire were buried in betrayal and denial.

Rise of the Bushes

Throughout the early part of the twentieth century, men who worked in the legal firms and brokerage houses of Wall Street helped forge and run the new American empire. An eastern establishment grew up around the Council on Foreign Relations in New York City. It provided pivotal policy figures for Republican and Democratic administrations. Wall Street lawyers such as Elihu Root, Henry Stimson and John Foster Dulles served in every cabinet from the presidency of Teddy Roosevelt to that of Dwight Eisenhower. Averell Harriman, the son of the wealthiest railroad magnet in America in the late nineteenth century, is perhaps the leading diplomat of this group, serving at least five presidents.

It was within this group that the Bush family first moved into Wall Street and the political world. George W. Bush's maternal great-grandfather, Herbert Walker, masterminded the creation of the W. A. Harriman & Co. investment house in 1919. In 1931 it merged with the British-American Brown Brothers Bank and formed Brown Brothers Harriman. This bank became the 'largest and politically the most important private banking house in America', as well as a core supporter of the American Open Door policy (Tarpley and Chaitkin 1992).

Prescott Bush, George W.'s grandfather, went to work for his father-in-law, Herbert Walker, in 1926, and became a partner in the firm along with Percy Rockefeller, Averell Harriman and his brother 'Bunny'. They invested in Nazi Germany until 1942 when under the Trading with the Enemy Act they were forced to end their financing of major corporations in the Third Reich. It was one of the few times when the US government moved to close the worldwide trade door it had pried open at the beginning of the century.

With the emergence of 'the American Century' at the end of the Second World War, Prescott Bush became a US senator from Connecticut and a fully fledged member of the eastern establishment. His son, George H. W. Bush, transplanted his family to the 'new south', thereby putting one foot in the emergent camp of Republican conservatives who began to take control of foreign policy from the eastern establishment. And his son, George W., would prove to be the ultimate opportunist, serving the interests of a petro-military complex based largely in the south, while courting the old scions of the eastern establishment through massive tax cuts and the hubris of empire.

THREE

The 'American century'

In the postwar world, petroleum's 'center of gravity' – not only
for the oil companies, but also for the nations of the West – was
indeed shifting to the Middle East. The consequences would be
momentous for all concerned. *Daniel Yergin, The Prize (Yergin
1992: 422)*

The Whites and the rich people make fun of us indigenous women
for our clothing, for our speech, for our language, for our color,
which is the color of the earth that we work ... When the rights and
the culture of the indigenous peoples are recognized ... the law will
begin to ensure that their hour will come. *Comandante Esther of the
Zapatista National Liberation Movement*

The powerful financial world of Wall Street that the Bush and
Walker families became enmeshed in during the early part of
the twentieth century made its bid for global domination as
soon as the United States became confident it would win the
Second World War. America's ascension to the leading role in an
expanding global commercial empire took place in the summer
of 1944 on the spacious verandas and within the elegant meeting
rooms of the Mount Washington Hotel in Bretton Woods, New
Hampshire. As the success of the allied D-Day invasion of Nazi-
occupied Europe appeared imminent, Franklin Delano Roosevelt
realized that the United States would emerge from the war as the
world's leading power. To ensure that the global economy after
the war would promote 'the opportunity for investment, under
proper safeguards, of capital from many lands' (UN 1944), the
United States convened the United Nations Monetary and Financial Conference at the sprawling Mount Washington Hotel. This
venue, which had been a retreat for presidents and princes since

America's first appearance on the global scene at the beginning of the twentieth century, served as an apt location for the establishment of its imperial dominion.

Almost half of the forty-five nations that attended what became known as the Bretton Woods Conference came from the western hemisphere and were closely allied to US interests. For three weeks, 700 representatives of governments and private financial interests laboured to create the International Monetary Fund (IMF) and the International Bank for Reconstruction and Development (World Bank). The conference established the US dollar as the basic world currency and promised the US government overwhelming influence in the policies of the IMF and the World Bank. It truly catapulted the United States into the role of an economic superpower.

This power was enhanced on a grey February day in Washington, DC, almost three years after Bretton Woods. President Truman's Secretary of State, George Marshall, had left for the weekend. Under-Secretary Dean Acheson oversaw the workings of the State Department as it prepared to move into its new quarters, fit for a world power, in Foggy Bottom. He received a message that Lord Inverchapel, British ambassador to Washington, had an important message for State. An hour later it was delivered by H. M. Sichell, first secretary of the British embassy. Britain was broke. The British empire could no longer afford to support the efforts of the Greek government to fend off an insurgency movement. Britain was pulling out in a month. Acheson knew he had to act quickly. Calling his staff together, he told them to 'Work like hell.' He had to prepare for American assumption of the responsibilities of the British empire (Isaacson and Thomas 1986: 387–9).

Henry Luce Booth, owner of *Time* and *Life* magazines, dubbed this age 'the American Century'. US troops occupied Japan and Germany, while Great Britain and France, owing to the devastating costs of two world wars, were compelled to acknowledge the ascendancy of the United States and reconcile themselves to substantially reduced roles as imperial powers. The Soviet Union, which suffered more war casualties than any of the other Allied powers, initially looked to the United States for assistance to reconstruct its country. Washington made it clear, however, that aid would be contingent upon the Soviet Union's acceptance of the 'open door policy'.

Setting the Ground Rules for Empire

The American empire became the latest in a series of imperial nations that set the rules for the domination of global trade and finance. This process had begun half a millennium earlier with the age of discovery and exploration when the Genoese bankers, allied with the Spanish monarchy, dictated the terms of Western trade and finance. They were displaced by the Dutch in the 1600s. After that came the British in the nineteenth century, followed by the United States in our day and age. These hegemonists have all served as dominant financial centres, exercising informal and/or formal control over other territories and countries. Usually military power backed up these global economic interests, especially with the latter-day hegemonists (Arrighi 1994: 36–75).

In 1945, in terms reminiscent of the John Hay notes after the Spanish–American War, President Harry Truman proclaimed that in eastern Europe the United States would not accept 'spheres of influence of any one power' (Williams 1992: 252). The United States was intent on expanding its commercial and corporate interests to all corners of the globe, including eastern Europe and the Soviet Union. As the *New York Times* noted at the time, 'France, Britain, and the United States in seeking to absorb eastern Europe into a unified continental system, are aiming to weaken the Eastern bloc, and at the same time they are being forced with varying degrees of reluctance into the formation of that very Western bloc that Russia dreads' (ibid.: 258).

Truman: Scaring the Hell Out of Americans

In March 1947, a month after the British had turned over their empire to the Americans, Harry Truman began the job of selling the American people on the empire they want to deny they have. Senator Arthur Vandenberg, an avowed believer in America's international mission, convinced Truman that he had to 'scare hell out of the American people', to make them accept the responsibilities of an empire. In an appeal to both chambers of the US Congress to get extensive funding to fend off popular movements in Greece and Turkey, he outlined the Truman Doctrine, which declared that the United States would support 'free peoples who are resisting attempted subjugation by armed minorities or by outside pressure'. He then went on to talk about the 'terrorist activities of several thousand armed men, led by communists', and that resistance was 'essential to the preservation of order in the Middle East'. In tones similar to those of George W. Bush he proclaimed that 'totalitarian regimes imposed on free peoples, by direct or indirect aggression, undermine the foundations of international peace and hence the security of the United States', and that the alternative to the American way 'relies upon terror and oppression, a controlled press and radio, fixed elections and the suppression of personal freedoms'. He assured his listeners that if they did not accede to his programme, 'Confusion and disorder might well spread throughout the entire Middle East' (Truman 1947).

In two speeches prior to this declaration, Truman outlined the true intent of his doctrine, the need to 'act and act decisively' to maintain the open door policy. He went on to argue, 'the pattern of international trade which is most conducive to freedom of enterprise ... is one in which major decisions are made not by governments but by private buyers and sellers'. Asserting that the United States was 'the giant of the economic world', Truman also asserted 'the choice is ours' to sustain and expand private enterprise (Williams 1992: 269). The Marshall Plan, announced as a counterpart to the Truman Doctrine, provided massive assistance to the countries of Europe, but only if they would accept the rules of the free market and recognize the economic pre-eminence of the United States.

George Kennan, chief architect of the Truman Doctrine and US policies at the commencement of the cold war, outlined the problem in 1948. He pointed out that 'we have about 50% of the world's wealth, but only 6.3% of its population ... In this situation, we cannot fail to be the object of envy and resentment. Our real task in the coming period is to devise a pattern of relationships which will permit us to maintain this position of disparity' (Chomsky 1993).

This was the golden age of the US empire. At the time it had sole possession of the ultimate weapon of mass destruction, the atomic bomb. It had achieved this position while decisively breaking with the formal empires of Britain, France, Portugal and Belgium. Indeed, this was a major sideshow of the early post-war period; the United States, while focusing on the Soviet Union as its principal adversary, hammered away at the old European empires, demanding that they abandon their colonial 'spheres of influence' which limited US commercial access to their markets.

With the proclamation of the Truman Doctrine the importance of US economic and imperial interests abroad was obfuscated by the rhetoric of the cold war. Any frank discussions of the ascendancy and advance of the US corporate and commercial classes were set aside in favour of the simplistic view that this was a struggle of 'the free world versus communism'. In 1950 the use of this narrative was codified with National Security Doctrine 68, which became the central canon guiding US policy throughout the cold war. In its opening paragraphs, the doctrine proclaims that as a result of two wars the world has witnessed 'the collapse of five empires – the Ottoman, the Austro-Hungarian, German, Italian, and Japanese – and the drastic decline of two major imperial systems, the British and the French. During the span of one generation, the international distribution of power has been fundamentally altered.' It went on to proclaim that power had now gravitated to two centres: the Soviet Union and the United States. In terms later employed in the 'evil-doers' rhetoric of George W. Bush, NSC 68 asserted: 'the Soviet Union, unlike previous aspirants to hegemony, is animated by a new fanatic faith, antithetical to our own, and seeks to impose its absolute authority over the rest of the world' (Internet H).

The Soviet Union certainly did not turn out to be an ideal model for the world's population as it intervened repeatedly in eastern Europe. But the United States in its quest to maintain its position as the world's dominant imperial power employed violence and force on an unprecedented scale, negating the democratic principles that supposedly distinguished it from the Soviet Union. In Italy, with the start of the cold war, the United States intervened covertly and overtly to prevent the Italian Communist Party from winning power via the ballot box. During the crucial elections of 1948 the United States used a variety of techniques, including the restoration of the Fascist police, the busting of unions and the withholding of food assistance, to stop the Italian communists. The first National Security Memorandum, NSC 1, specified a number of actions if the Italian communists won the elections, including armed intervention via military assistance for underground operations in Italy. Some US diplomats, like George Kennan, advocated military action in Italy even before the elections (Chomsky 1993).

With the advent of the Truman Doctrine and its concerns about the Middle East, US policy after the Second World War became increasingly intent on securing control over what became known as 'the Prize', the immense oil reserves of the Persian Gulf. Here it was not only a question of pushing out the Soviets, who had control of northern Iran, but of gaining the upper hand in competition with the British interests throughout the region. In 1944, even before the war ended, the United States, in preparation for negotiations with the British over the divvying up of the global petroleum market in the region, drew up a government report entitled 'Foreign Petroleum Policy of the United States'. It declared that US policy should assure 'a substantial and geographically diversified holding of foreign petroleum resources in the hands of United States nationals'. The paper went on to add that this would mean the 'insistence upon the Open Door principle of equal opportunity for United States companies in new areas' (Painter 1986: 59).

In the Middle East the Truman administration aligned itself with the efforts to establish an Israeli state. While this antagonized the Arab peoples of the region, Truman believed that the United States could compel the other Middle Eastern and Gulf countries to accept a Jewish state as a fait accompli. Truman, who in his private conversations made derogatory remarks about blacks and Jews, favoured the establishment of Israel in part because it meant that the migration of Jewish refugees from the European Holocaust to the United States could be kept in check. The United States also believed that a European-populated Jewish state in Palestine would be a dependable ally to support US interests in the region. Accordingly, when the armed Zionists in Palestine partitioned the region and established the Israeli state in 1948, the United States became the first country to extend full diplomatic relations and quickly became Israel's primary financial backer (Bennis 2003: 29–34).

The Subjection of Latin America

With US interests increasingly focusing on Europe, the Middle East and the Gulf, the Latin Americans began to feel abused by their post-war role in the US imperium. No Marshall Plan appeared in Washington to assist the development of the countries south of the border, even though they had served as a vital commercial arsenal for the United States in the Second World War and desperately needed assistance to develop their economies. During the war the United States had fixed the prices it paid for raw materials from the region, meaning that Latin America in effect gave the United States a $3 billion subsidy for the war effort. With the end of the war the United States insisted that the 'free market' should once again prevail. But the free market now meant that while the prices of raw materials rose, the demand for, and cost of, manufactured and capital goods from the United States skyrocketed (Rabe 1988: 16). The 'terms of trade' for Latin America, as well as for most of what would become known as the Third World, were adverse, meaning that these countries experienced ever growing balance of trade deficits. Locked into an inferior economic position, the undeveloped countries became dependent on appeals for international financial assistance to stay afloat.

The Economic Commission for Latin America (ECLA), an agency of the United Nations, demonstrated in academic-like reports that the prices of raw materials and food exports were declining relative to the price of manufactured goods. How American advisers did not realize the costs this incurred in long-term resentment and poverty is hard to understand. But the US State Department, instead of recognizing the inequality of these basic economic trends, argued that the messenger and not the message should be dealt with as it lobbied (unsuccessfully) for the abolition of ECLA (ibid.: 19).

While the informal empire of the United States expanded beyond the Caribbean basin and Latin America, the region remained critical to US interests. In the immediate post-war years Latin America accounted for 30 per cent of US international trade and nearly 40 per cent of US direct investments (ibid.: 18). But instead of economic cooperation, the United States focused on strengthening its ties with the Latin American militaries. In 1947, two years before the founding of the North Atlantic Treaty

Organization (NATO), the United States foisted the Rio Treaty on the Latin Americans. While this proclaimed that collective armed force (meaning primarily US forces) could only be used to repel an internal or external threat to the region with a two-thirds vote of its members, the United States used the accord throughout the cold war when it believed it could garner the votes it needed, and ignored the treaty when it felt it could not get the necessary support. As the Truman administration declared in 1950, 'US security is the objective of our world-wide foreign policy today', and 'US security is synonymous with hemisphere security'. After the Korean war broke out, the United States, in an effort to bolster its hold on its 'backyard', finally extended assistance to Latin America. But it was not economic aid. The United States sent $38 million in military equipment and assistance to Latin America in 1951 and another $51 million in 1952 (ibid.: 23).

Seizing the Prize

Relegating Latin America to a subservient position, the United States moved aggressively to secure its hold in the Persian Gulf and the Middle East. It initially recognized the ascendancy of the British in Iran, where the Anglo-Iranian Oil Company exercised a monopoly over Iranian petroleum production. In Kuwait and Iraq, the USA divided up the petroleum market with the British, while the country with the largest reserves in the Gulf, Saudi Arabia, fell under exclusive US influence. The United States became top dog in this country owing in part to the astute diplomacy during the Second World War of Franklin Roosevelt, who cultivated a close personal relationship with Ibn Saud, the charismatic Bedouin leader who founded the modern Saudi kingdom and established its dynastic monarchy.

The personable style of Roosevelt helped bring the Saudis within the American sphere. After the historic Yalta Conference in January 1945, Roosevelt met with Ibn Saud aboard a ship in the Suez Canal. Knowing that the ruler's Islamic religion forbade drinking or smoking, Roosevelt, a chain-smoker, puffed away on two cigarettes in the ship's elevator on the way up to the banquet room in his wheelchair. At dinner the king commented on Roosevelt's wheelchair and noted that he too had a serious disability due to combat injuries to his legs. In an act of generosity, Roosevelt gave Ibn Saud the spare wheelchair he had on the ship.

Infuriated by Roosevelt's meeting with Ibn Saud and other potentates from the Gulf region, Winston Churchill rushed to the Middle East three days later, where he met with the Saudi king at a hotel in the Egyptian desert. A notorious drinker and cigar smoker, Churchill refused to abide by the religious scruples of the head of the Saudi kingdom, later proclaiming: 'I was the host and I said ... my religion prescribed as an absolute sacred rite smoking cigars and drinking alcohol before, after, and if need be during, all meals' (Yergin 1992: 404–5). His insensitive Anglocentrism offended the king and drove the Saudis towards the Americans.

Two US petroleum companies, Texaco and Socal, initially formed Aramco, a subsidiary that dominated Saudi oil production. Aramco became a mechanism for the enrichment of the ruling family (Ibn Saud had fifty-six sons) as roughly half the oil revenue went to the Saudis. The relationship with the Saudis became in many ways a strange alliance of Bedouin Arabs and Texas oilmen, a traditional Islamic autocracy and autocratic American capitalists (ibid.: 428). This alliance endured and flourished for decades in a variety of forms. It provided the opportunity for George W. Bush to stake out his first business endeavour in the petroleum industry by working with Saudi business partners in the 1970s to found Arbusto Oil. Only the dramatic events of 11 September 2001 – fifteen of the nineteen hijackers came from Saudi Arabia – would finally begin to disrupt the close relationship between the two countries.

Along with the Middle East and Latin America, Asia constituted the other critical region for the US imperium in the Third World. Because the United States had ousted Japan as the occupying power in Asia, Americans were generally looked on with favour in this region in the immediate aftermath of the Second World War. The United States even made noises against France's reclamation of its empire in Indochina. The granting of independence to the Philippines in 1946 also contributed to the view of the United States as a benevolent power in the region.

On Revolutions and CIA Coups

However, the Chinese revolution under the leadership of Mao Zedong in 1949 profoundly transformed Asia and the US role on the continent. China had been the object of the original open door policy and 'the millions of Chinese consumers' had always been seen as the solution to US agricultural and manufacturing overproduction. Suddenly that was no longer possible as the communist revolution in China shook the US ruling elite and made it determined to draw the line against further advances by communist nationalists, which cut American companies out of many of the economic opportunities in Asia. In Korea this overriding concern led the United States into its first sustained conflict of the post-war era with the outbreak of hostilities in 1950. Instead of trying to work out an arrangement with the northern communists, who had resisted the Japanese occupation of the country, the United States backed the corrupt regime of Syngman Rhee. The war ultimately ended in a stalemate in 1953 with over 37,000 US combat casualties.

In the US presidential elections of 1952, the conflict in Korea was a decisive factor in ousting the Democrats after twenty years in power. Dwight 'Ike' Eisenhower became President, promising to bring the troops home, a political promise that subsequent presidential aspirants would make to get elected when US foreign adventures went awry. Under Ike, two brothers from the

Wall Street corporate world, Allen and John Foster Dulles, took centre stage in shaping US policy, the first as head of the CIA and the second as Eisenhower's Secretary of State. John Foster Dulles had particularly strong anti-communist views which shaped the US role in the world in the 1950s.

As a result of the Truman Doctrine and the inception of the cold war the US government constructed what became known as the 'national security' apparatus. Designed to advance US interests abroad, the Central Intelligence Agency (CIA) sat at the centre of this bureaucracy. Growing out of the Second World War Office of Strategic Services, the CIA worked at 'providing strategic warning and conducting clandestine activities' on behalf of US foreign policy, while using 'confidential fiscal and administrative procedures' (History of the CIA 2003).

The Dulles brothers' ideological bent in favour of private property and against the communality of property under communism, combined with the direct concern of controlling Middle Eastern oil, led the United States to undertake the first CIA-sponsored coup, in Iran. The Anglo-Iranian Petroleum Company, partially owned by the British government, earned £250 million in profits between 1945 and 1950, while Iran received only £90 million in royalties (Yergin 1992: 451). At least somewhat cognizant of the political costs of such a policy, the Roosevelt and Truman administrations had been highly critical of the British for their oil profiteering. Iranian nationalists detested British domination of their country, and the Truman administration, fearful of growing Soviet influence in Iran, pushed the British to increase the royalties accruing to the Iranian government. The British reacted adversely, leading US Secretary of State Dean Acheson to decry 'the unusual and persistent stupidity of the company and the British Government' (ibid.: 453).

In 1951 the conflict between the British and the Iranians reached a boiling point when the Iranian parliament selected an ardent nationalist, Mohammed Mossadegh, to become the country's prime minister. Within days he nationalized the Anglo-Iranian Company. The United States tried to mediate between the two foes. A young congressman from Massachusetts, John F. Kennedy, showed up in Tehran at this historic moment, declaring, 'it would be a good thing for American concerns to step into the breach' (ibid.: 459). However, no accord was forthcoming, and the British mounted an economic embargo against Iran, threatening legal action against any oil tankers that picked up 'stolen oil'. British diplomats in Tehran were subsequently expelled from the country.

In early 1953, with the Dulles brothers now exercising the levers of power under Eisenhower, the USA decided to throw in its lot with the British, organizing 'Operation Ajax' to carry out 'regime change' in Iran. The battle with the communists in Korea helped shape the administration's fears that if it didn't act in Iran the communists might be able to take advantage of Iranian instability to expand into the Gulf. Teddy Roosevelt's grandson, Kermit Roosevelt, coordinated CIA operations with British Intelligence (SIS). The British operation failed, however, and Shah Mohammad Reza of the Pahlavi dynasty, the titular head of the country, fled Iran because of his involvement in the failed coup. But Kermit Roosevelt, on his own initiative and with virtually no help from the SIS, staged another coup attempt a few days later which succeeded in ousting Mossadegh and installing the Shah as the new absolute ruler of the country.

This coup reshaped the tactics, if not the strategies, of the cold war. Ike was ecstatic with the result, saying, it 'read more like a dime store novel than a historical fact' (ibid.: 470). In succeeding years the United States increasingly turned to the CIA to conduct clandestine operations, toppling governments and, more often than not, replacing them with brutal, repressive regimes always friendly to American commercial needs.

However, as Stephen Kinzer notes in *All the Shah's Men: An American Coup and the Roots of Middle Eastern Terror*, the Iran adventure did spawn substantial human costs. He points out that it 'set off a sequence of events in that country that led to civil war and hundreds of thousands of violent deaths. Later, the CIA set out to kill or depose foreign leaders from Cuba and Chile to the Congo and Vietnam. Each of these operations had profound effects that reverberate to this day. Some produced immense misery and suffering and turned whole regions of the world bitterly against the United States.'

This intervention in the affairs of other countries ushered in a new era in the dynamics of the US empire. The constant use of covert interventions combined with the periodic deployment of military forces in effect transformed and transcended the meaning of 'informal' and 'formal' empires. The United States did not occupy any new territories or countries on a permanent basis, but as the self-proclaimed leader of the 'free world' it acted as an arrogant and self-serving imperial power determined to impose its will on the world. In 1970, Henry Kissinger summed up the hubris and deceit of this post-war empire when he proclaimed on the eve of socialist Salvador Allende's victory in the Chilean presidential elections: 'I don't see why we need to stand idly by and watch a country go communist due to the irresponsibility of its own peoples' (Burbach 2003: 10).

This became a central tenet of US foreign policy from the 1950s to the fall of the Berlin Wall in 1989. The United States appropriated to itself the right to decide which governments it found acceptable and those it deemed 'unfit' to rule their countries. This approach was similar to the imperial rule the United States exerted in the Caribbean basin in the early decades of the twentieth century, only now the United States operated on a global scale. Its determination to extend its rule around the globe now drew it into ever deeper conflicts with militant nationalist movements that presented more profound challenges than Sandino's guerrillas had in Nicaragua a quarter of a century earlier.

The cold war apologists for this empire assert, of course, that the United States was resisting the 'evil empire' of the Soviet Union. But William Appleman Williams and other critics of US policy got it right when they pointed out that the United States was predominantly interested in securing and expanding its economic interests. This was blatantly apparent in Guatemala in 1954, when the CIA, fresh from its adventure in Iran, overthrew Jacobo Arbenz, who had been elected president in 1952. The Guatemalan Communist Party supported his government, but it was not the dominant force in his governing coalition. The main threat to US interests came from the decision of the Arbenz government to modernize the country by undertaking an agrarian reform programme that expropriated idle lands, including vast uncultivated expanses owned by the principal banana exporter in Guatemala, the United Fruit Company. The takeover of its idle 'reserve' lands goaded in particular Allen and John Foster Dulles, who had close connections to the United Fruit Company, to orchestrate the overthrow of Jacobo Arbenz.

Under Ike and the Dulles brothers, the United States remained determined to keep its imperial adversaries in western Europe in check in order to advance its own interests. When the British and the French along with the Israelis invaded Egypt after Gamal Nasser nationalized the Suez Canal in 1956, the Eisenhower administration made it clear that it was opposed to this effort to assert traditional European control in the region. As a result the invasion forces withdrew. Thenceforth the British aligned themselves tightly with the US imperium, particularly in the Gulf and the Middle East, an alliance that came to serve them badly when Prime Minister Tony Blair fell into line with George W. Bush's policy of 'pre-emptive war' in Iraq.

The American débâcle in Indo-China began with a debate

among US rulers over how to deal with the French and their colonies. During the war the Roosevelt administration had generally regarded Ho Chi Minh as a Vietnamese nationalist, a 'George Washington' who resisted the Japanese occupation forces. With the onset of the Korean war, however, the United States began to extend military assistance to the French in their war against the Viet Minh, assistance that actually surpassed the economic aid given to France under the Marshall Plan. Before the onset of the decisive battle of Dien Bien Phu in 1954, the French pleaded with the United States to intervene on its side, and discussions even took place within the Eisenhower administration about conducting US air strikes to stave off a French defeat. In the end, however, the United States decided to allow the French forces to fall to the Vietnamese (Gardner 1976: 222–4).

In south-east Asia, as in the Persian Gulf, once the United States had replaced the European powers, it assumed the imperial mantle and steadfastly insisted on maintaining what in effect became its own 'sphere of influence'. The Geneva peace treaty of 1954 had called for elections in 1956 in all of Vietnam to determine who would lead a reunified country. Owing to the popularity of Ho Chi Minh, the United States opposed popular democracy and never implemented this part of the peace accord. Instead, in 1954, it installed Ngo Dinh Diem, who had been residing at the Maryknoll Catholic Seminary in Ossining, New York. As a model for future American interventions in which expat mercenaries would be called 'freedom fighters', the government referred to Deim as the 'George Washington of South Vietnam'. Never mind that a Catholic would lead a country that was overwhelmingly Buddhist. Even the French questioned the installation of this inappropriate leader. But the United States would hear none of it, backing Deim's inept regime until 1963, arguing that he constituted a 'one man democracy' (ibid.: 226). As history would once again demonstrate with the occupation of Iraq in 2003, the United

States had a knack for ignoring the costs of opposing nationalists and deposing governments. It was particularly clueless about
establishing new regimes with national, let alone democratic,
credentials.

Counter-revolutionary Warfare

As the United States discovered during the height of the cold
war, the destiny of an empire is shaped not only by the interests
and ideology that emanate from the imperial centre, but also
by the class structure and the beliefs and particular interests
of the societies that it attempts to subsume into its imperium.
While Washington sided with some of the Third World countries
that broke with the old imperial powers, the United States continually underestimated the strident nationalism that erupted
in Asia, Africa, the Middle East and Latin America. In all these
continents, national liberation movements emerged in opposition to US-backed regimes that were appropriately portrayed as
'neo-colonialist'.

It was no historic accident that the first successful revolution
in the western hemisphere occurred in Cuba, the country with the
most extensive US corporate investments and where probably the
American imperialists were most blind to the human costs of their
empire. Prostitution, illiteracy and slave-wage underemployment
on giant sugar plantations characterized Cuban society under the
US puppet Batista government. Finally the Cuban people rose in
revolt in 1959. Ernesto Che Guevara, who rode his motorcycle
through Central America in 1954 and had learned well the lessons of the CIA coup that toppled Jacabo Arbenz in Guatemala,
helped lead the charge.

Any country that wished to pursue its authentic national interests and carry out deep-seated social and economic reforms would
face the wrath of the United States. Rather than accede to the
advance of national revolutionary movements, in the 1960s and

1970s the USA engaged in counter-revolutionary warfare and military interventions around the globe, particularly in Latin America and Asia. As we saw, the United States lost the war in south-east Asia. But in Latin America it succeeded in containing the revolutionary challenges by sending special counter-insurgency units into countries like Venezuela, Peru and Bolivia, by invading the Dominican Republic and by overthrowing the socialist government of Salvador Allende. By the mid-1970s three-quarters of the peoples of Latin America lived under military dictatorial regimes backed by the United States.

But a new revolutionary tide emerged in the latter part of the 1970s in countries as diverse as Angola, Iran, Grenada and Nicaragua. In the early and mid-1980s it was not at all clear that the United States could turn back these movements. In the US back yard it looked as if revolutionary movements in El Salvador and Guatemala, along with the Sandinista government of Nicaragua, might succeed in freeing the region from its historic subservience to the United States. Ultimately two factors enabled the USA to triumph in Central America: 1) the overwhelming violence it unleashed on a region of just over 20 million people which decimated and demoralized broad swathes of the populace (leading in particular to the defeat of the Sandinistas in the 1990 Nicaraguan elections); and 2) the fall of the Berlin Wall in 1989, which sapped the will and capacity of the Soviet Union to provide material support for the Central Americans as well as other liberation movements.

In hindsight we can see that the Soviet Union was actually not an empire in the modern sense of the term. It held sway in eastern Europe through the use of force but it wrested few economic benefits from its control of the region. As Williams and the revisionist historians argue, Russia viewed its control over eastern Europe as providing a security buffer to protect it from invasion from the west. In fact an argument can be made that the Soviet Union, after appropriating some resources from the eastern countries as post-war reparations to rebuild its own country, actually pumped more material aid into the eastern socialist bloc countries than it took out. This was definitely true of the Third World countries that aligned themselves with the Soviet Union, such as Vietnam, Angola and Mozambique. In the case of Cuba, it became abundantly clear with the break-up of the Soviet system that the Cuban economy relied on Soviet assistance to provide an adequate standard of living for the Cuban people. The United States, on the other hand, even after the setback it experienced in the Indo-China war, continued to flourish as a commercial and economic power because of the resources and profits its multinational corporations extracted on a global scale via the 'free market'.

Moreover, the triumph of the United States was due also to its capacity to transfigure the nature of its empire. Up until the end of the Second World War, capital and even multinational enterprises were almost exclusively nation based. As Lenin points out in his treatise on imperialism, German national cartels competed intensively with the trading and financial houses of Great Britain as well as the capitalist classes of other countries. To advance their interests the national bourgeoisies relied on their nation-states to protect and advance their interests. This competition led to over thirty years of war, conflict and protectionism, extending from 1914 to 1945.

Globalizing the Empire

Today, in the age of globalization, the dominant centres of finance capital and the multinational corporations are opposed to war among their respective nation-states. The reason is quite simple. The world's largest enterprises are highly integrated, with diverse stockholders from around the world and, even more importantly, with subsidiaries in virtually every corner of the globe. National wars and conflicts are antithetical to their interests, particularly if they were to occur among the dominant powers. Any such war would throw into crisis the entire capitalist system, rupturing international commerce and the free flow of goods that is critical to their prosperity. We need look no further than the European Economic Community – which emerged out of the ashes of two world wars originating in Europe – to demonstrate the fact that the bourgeoisies of today are overwhelmingly opposed to national wars (Burbach 2001: 49–50).

In the late 1970s and 1980s these new transnationalized sectors of capital set out to create and strengthen multilateral institutions to advance their global interests. The Thatcher and Reagan governments in the early 1980s pushed for neo-liberal trade and financial policies through institutions such as the International Monetary Fund (IMF) and the World Bank. International capital transformed these institutions to promote capitalist expansion throughout the world and impose a financial discipline on the rest of the world that favoured transnational capital. In 1995, the World Trade Organization (WTO), which grew out of the principles established at the Bretton Woods conference, became a central institution for mediating trade disputes and advancing the interests of multinational corporate and banking interests.

US Presidents from Reagan to Clinton actively used these institutions to advance global economic integration and to make the political systems of other countries more responsive to corporate interests. By the mid-1980s the United States even began to realize that many of the dictatorships established during the cold war were no longer viable in the context of neo-liberalism and the emergent process of globalization. Dictatorial regimes, of the right as well as the left, tended to exercise forms of authority over their societies and economies that were increasingly anathema to international capital. The expansion of Western interests required not only open international markets, but also pliable political institutions.

Accordingly, during the second Reagan administration the

United States shifted to a strategy of supporting what some call 'low intensity', or controlled democracies. As William Robinson argues in *Promoting Polyarchy*, in order to integrate the Third World into a global, neo-liberal economy, the United States turned against many of the dictators it once nurtured and adopted a policy of supporting, and even imposing, controlled democracies (see Robinson 1996). This explains why under Ronald Reagan the United States moved against Ferdinand Marcos in the Philippines and 'Baby Doc' Duvalier in Haiti, as well as Augusto Pinochet in Chile. It then replaced them with conservative or moderate governments that would accept the regime of international capital while containing social and political movements that advocated radical or nationalist policies.

Reagan created the National Endowment for Democracy (NED) in 1983 to manage this new foreign policy that sought to resolve the contradictions between capitalism and democracy, and to move from coercive to consensual mechanisms of control. It promoted a concept called polyarchy, which had been advanced in the 1970s by academics and the Trilateral Commission. Robinson writes that polyarchy

> refers to a system in which a small group actually rules and mass participation in decision-making is confined to leadership choice in elections carefully managed by competing elites...The state is the domain of the dominant classes, while the popular classes are incorporated into civil society under the hegemony of the elite ... which is the formula for the exercise of consensual domination.

He adds: 'Equality of conditions for electoral participation is not relevant to whether elections are "free and fair". These conditions are decidedly unequal under capitalism owing to the unequal distribution of material and cultural resources among classes and groups and to the use of economic power to determine political outcomes' (ibid.: 58).

He then goes on to quote Samuel Huntington (1989), a supporter of the polyarchic vision of democracy, as saying: 'Defining democracy in terms of goals such as economic well being, social justice and overall socio-economic equity is not ... very useful.' In fact polyarchy uses civil society institutions to legitimize initiatives supporting the political elite and delegitimizing the demands of popular democracy that challenge the economic order.

NED complemented the role played by the CIA in manipulating elections around the world. The CIA continued its covert operations while NED worked on an overt level. A supposedly private organization, NED is fully funded by the US government through the US Agency for International Development and the United States Information Agency. NED came out of a project conceptualized by three former National Security Advisors, the US Chamber of Commerce and the Democratic and Republican parties, as well as members of the business, labour and intelligence communities. It is a bipartisan effort of liberals and conservatives, Democrats and Republicans. As noted in a Project Democracy report, 'One byproduct [of this new "democracy initiative"] may well be the restoration of bipartisanship to its central place in the American foreign-policy-making process' (Robinson 1996: 98).

The New World Order

George H. W. Bush and Bill Clinton advanced the policies and activities of NED. Bush Senior, even more than his predecessor, was a president at ease with other international leaders, particularly those of the Western world. With the first Gulf war, his administration headed up a broad international coalition designed to protect the dominant global interests against Saddam Hussein, an upstart ruler who wanted to rearrange the map of the Gulf and the Middle East. This is why western Europe and Japan underwrote most of the costs of the conflict while the United States concentrated on providing the troops and the firepower.

There was an early perception that Clinton would be a 'domestic president', that he was less interested in handling foreign policy issues. But his deeds demonstrated that he was committed to international policies aimed at merging the interests of the US empire with those of international capital. In a major policy address to the United Nations in September 1993, Clinton proclaimed that his administration would pursue an activist foreign policy designed to foment the continued expansion of what he called 'free market democracies', meaning controlled democracies that would recognize the prerogatives of international capital.

Along with his Secretary of the Treasury, Robert Rubin, from Wall Street, Clinton acted repeatedly to advance the interests of the emergent globalized order. From the intervention in Mexico's economic crisis in 1994 to the US military involvement in Bosnia, Serbia and Kosovo, the Clinton administration demonstrated a determination to stabilize the world in cooperation with the world's dominant economic interests. The IMF, the World Bank and the World Trade Organization served as key global financial institutions to promote a new 'open door' that would serve the interests of global capital. As might be expected, the more explicitly political institutions designed to promote globalization trailed behind in their development. But the annual meetings of the G8, along with the Organization for Economic Cooperation and Development and the Organization for Security and Cooperation in Europe, as well as the United Nations and NATO, came to play increasingly important roles in the march towards an integrated global order.

Of course, the threat of military force is an integral part of the globalization project. As Thomas Freidman notes in his sympathetic tome on globalization (1999): 'The hidden hand of the market will never work without a hidden fist. McDonald's cannot flourish without McDonnell Douglas, the designer of the US Air Force F-15. And the hidden fist that keeps the world safe for Silicon Valley's technologies to flourish is called the US Army, Air Force,

Navy, and Marine Corps ... ' In addition to the US-sponsored wars in the Balkans, the Clinton administration also laid the groundwork for expansion in south central Eurasia by establishing military ties with Kazakhstan, Uzbekistan, Georgia and Azerbaijan, while carrying out periodic bombing forays in Iraq (Klare 2003a: 55).

However, by the end of the 1990s neo-liberalism and corporate-driven globalization were facing major challenges. The economic crisis that struck Indonesia, Malaysia, South Korea and other countries in south-east Asia in 1997 revealed that the free movement of international finance capital could throw economies into disarray and depression virtually overnight. Popular movements in countries ranging from Brazil and Mexico to the Philippines and Russia also protested against the cuts in basic social services and expenditures that were orchestrated by the IMF and the World Bank in order to open up national economies to international capital. Then in late 1999 tens of thousands of demonstrators gathered in Seattle to denounce the meeting of the World Trade Organization. In the 'Battle of Seattle', environmentalists, trade unionists, farmers, human rights activists and many others tried to shut down the meetings, marching under banners denouncing the 'tyranny of the WTO', and calling for 'Fair Trade not Free Trade'.

When George W. Bush assumed power, the globalization project was in serious trouble. Beyond the popular protests, the collapse of the high-tech boom and the lethargy of the global economy precipitated increasing tensions among the leading capitalist nations. This was a potent mix that would challenge even the most astute of global leaders. The new Bush administration could have tried to maintain the process of globalization, perhaps making some modifications and changes in the model in an effort to deal with its more egregious effects on the world. But the cohort of leaders around Bush had a different agenda, one that harked back to the more strident years of the early twentieth century when the United States had acted unilaterally to maintain and expand its imperium.

FOUR

The rise of the Bush people

> It is the international system of currencies which determines the
> totality of life on this planet. That is the natural order of things today.
> That is the atomic and subatomic and galactic structure of things
> today. And you have meddled with the primal forces of nature. And
> you will atone. *From the 1976 movie Network*

> The love of money is the root of all evil. *New Testament,*
> *I Timothy, vi, 10*

Money put William McKinley in office in 1896. The same can be
said for George W. Bush in 2000. Both were reactionary movements
against popular democracy movements. In the 1890s American
populists, anarchists and union members organized against the
concentrated wealth that manipulated the national democratic
process. In the 1990s people across the planet rose up against a
worldwide commercial empire intent on enacting planetary rules
written in the boardrooms of multinational corporations.

The think-tank neo-conservatives, cold war militarists and
Christian conservatives who provide the reactionary base for the
Bush administration are part of a conservative institutional infrastructure that was developed in the 1970s in response to popular
movements of the 1960s. In those years the civil rights movement,
the women's movement, the environmental movement and the
anti-war movement coalesced around a social vision that began to
assess the hidden costs of the American imperial system.

The Movement that Upended the Establishment

Broadly known as 'The Movement', the insurgents of the
1960s managed to reshape the political dialogue in the country to

address the social costs of an imperial corporate-driven order. By mobilizing those oppressed and disenfranchised by the system, the movement was able to challenge racism, sexism, imperialism and environmental degradation. The civil rights movement ended blatant segregation and empowered a black political movement to challenge the forces that kept broad sections of the Afro-American community in a dependent status as low-paid workers. The women's movement questioned the market-based value system that made them sex objects in the media and undervalued their domestic role in the household. The environmental movement concentrated on rectifying the costs to the people and the planet of pollution, costs that did not show up in the financial formulas of the corporations. The anti-war movement critiqued the human and cultural costs of an American empire cloaked in the rhetoric of the cold war. It sought to disarm America's militarist foreign policy which depended on the direct intervention of American troops.

Major initiatives rattled the established order throughout the early seventies. By 1973 a couple of long-haired reporters for the *Washington Post* doggedly pursued the Watergate story, which would drive the American President from office. That spring an empowered and righteous movement of women pushed the legalization of abortion through the courts. The first Earth Day in 1970 educated Americans about the unacknowledged poisoning of the planet due to industrialism and consumerism. On the international front, the major oil-producing countries led by Saudi Arabia and Iraq formed the Organization of Petroleum Exporting Countries (OPEC) to control world oil production. They cut off the free flow of oil to the industrialized world. Both within the United States and around the world, from south-east Asia to Latin America, people stood up to the American empire.

In 1973 the empire began to retreat. That spring the Nixon administration began withdrawing US military forces from Vietnam. Never before had US troops withdrawn in defeat. More importantly, the biggest American foundations, institutions endowed by the wealth of the creators of America's monopoly empire, started funding radical economic solutions that dealt with the root causes of poverty in America (Dowie 2001).

Corporate Right

As the forces of empire fell back, a corporate right began coalescing to reverse the advances of the social/cultural revolution taking place on the streets of America. Lewis F. Powell, a highly successful corporate lawyer and president of the American Bar Association, a man who later surprised everybody by becoming a moderate swing vote in the US Supreme Court, gave voice to the initiative in a letter to the US Chamber of Commerce. His letter complained that 'One of the bewildering paradoxes of our time is the extent to which the enterprise system tolerates, if not participates in, its own destruction. The campuses from which much of the criticism emanates are supported by (i) tax funds generated largely from American business, and (ii) contributions from capital funds controlled or generated by American business.'

Then he emphasized that 'the time has come – indeed, it is long overdue – for the wisdom, ingenuity and resources of American business to be marshaled against those who would destroy it'. He then went on to urge the Chamber to create a broad-based campaign to counteract the popular social movements by subverting and regaining control of academics, scholarly journals, the media, the courts and politicians (Powell 1973).

After circulating Powell's letter around a core group, the Chamber declined to take on this campaign. But others stepped into the breach. That same year, after reading Powell's plea, Joseph Coors provided $250,000 to Ed Feulner and Paul Weyrich, who quit their jobs as congressional aides to start the Heritage Foundation. Their mission was to 'formulate and promote conservative public policies based on the principles of free enterprise, limited government, individual freedom, traditional American values, and a strong national defense'.

Other conservative veterans of the Washington scene joined the drive to build a corporate-right counter-movement in America. William E. Simon, Nixon and Ford's Treasury Secretary, wrote, 'Funds generated by business must rush by the multimillions ... to scholars, social scientists, writers, and journalists who understand the relationship between political and economic liberty.' He wanted business leaders to 'cease the mindless subsidizing of colleges and universities whose departments of economy, government, politics, and history are hostile to capitalism', and to stop funding 'the media which serve as megaphones for anti-capitalist opinion' and support 'pro-business' media (cited in Callahan 1999a).

When Simon became the head of the John M. Olin Foundation in 1977 he formed a relationship with the Lynde and Harry Bradley Foundation, the Scaife Family Foundations, and the Smith Richardson Foundation, which became known as the 'four sisters' (Dowie 2001). Richard Behan adds another eight foundations to these four sisters and asserts that they established a stable of conservative think tanks and legal foundations across the country to promote the thinking of the corporate right (Behan 2003).

They used the think tanks to manipulate capitalist tenets into more democracy-friendly terms. In place of greed they promoted entrepreneurialism. Instead of environmental regulation they promoted market mechanisms or voluntary initiatives to alleviate the costs of pollution. The control of politics and the economy by monopolistic economic institutions was renamed the 'free market', which negated the reality that in any market situation money is power. They reached back into the 1800s, when 'liberalism' meant the right of wealthy international entrepreneurs to have rights of access to markets and resources anywhere on the planet.

Thus they became known as the neo-liberals and free traders. They had a mission to re-establish the dominance of the money-powered market system and the attendant patriarchal hierarchy that controlled women's lives and kept people of colour in a permanent underclass of low-paid workers. To back up this mission, they called for a strong military that would operate overtly or covertly anywhere on the planet to achieve purely American goals.

Rise of the Neo-cons

A new study by the National Committee for Responsive Philanthropy (NCRP) shows that conservative foundation funding of this political movement is still strong. Between 1999 and 2001, as the reactionary corporate-right movement elevated George W. Bush to the White House, eighty-two conservative foundations gave $253 million in conservative public policy grants (Krehely et al. 2003a). As the NCRP study states, 'Regardless of presidential approval ratings and the outcomes of the 2004 elections, it is undeniable that conservative public policy institutions and their philanthropic supporters have had a tremendous impact on Congress's and the Administration's penchant for waging war, curtailing civil liberties, and slashing taxes and social spending' (Krehely et al. 2003b).

Almost all observers of this thirty-year trend wherein conservative foundations have funded like-minded think tanks agree that their persistency has led to success. Whereas the large foundations like Ford and Rockefeller give to specific projects, the strategy to build a conservative political movement in the United States has succeeded because their foundation supporters provided general operating funds to build entire institutions. As the NCRP study says, 'This type of unrestricted grant gives their grantees the flexibility they need to build strong institutions, do innovative work without having to worry about attracting new donors, and respond in a timely fashion to policy issues without having to wait for a project-specific grant' (ibid.).

Much like the support Bush received at the polls, the bulk of the assets for the eighty-two foundations resides in thirteen rural, conservative states, with Arkansas, Oklahoma and Colorado serving as a home for 37.25 per cent of the conservative foundations' assets. 'Five foundations[1] make up just over 50 percent of total conservative public policy grantmaking for [1999–2001] ... [and] organizations within the policy arena received ... 46 percent of total funding, or $115,994,347.00 ... The national think tanks received $77,746,388 ... Included in this category are the large think tanks such as the Heritage Foundation, American Enterprise Institute, and the Cato Institute' (ibid.).

Besides this,

many conservative foundations are laying the groundwork for conservative ideals in universities by either giving to traditionally conservative schools, such as the George Mason University in Virginia or Hillsdale College in Michigan, which promote self-government and conservative law and economics programs, or specifically to professors or departments for their continued work and research to promote conservative ideals. Total conservative giving to universities equaled $23,140,307 ... Media organizations have also been well funded by the conservative movement. They received $6,775,169 to shape the public's opinion on the issues, to further develop conservative media organizations, and to bring the right's point of view to the public ... There has also been significant targeting of college media outlets to shape college dialogue on a variety of issues, train future journalists, and provide internships at national media outlets with a conservative perspective.

In addition, over the three-year period 1999–2001 $5,842,131 went to the Philanthropy Roundtable and State Policy Network, two organizations that provide services for conservative foundations at national and state level (ibid.).

Although there is no official coordination of conservative grantmaking to create 'a vast right wing conspiracy', the study does note that

> people associated with the foundation (a board member, founder, family member, CEO, etc.) would engage in some type of direct lobbying, organizing peer foundation leaders, or supporting political campaigns strictly as individuals, not as representatives of the foundations. The founders of several of the foundations interviewed were prominent individuals within the Republican Party, and/or very successful and visible business leaders. Their connection to politics, therefore, was rather natural, a legacy that often persists long after their deaths ... In many cases, the foundation money ... is coming from the same original source that the individual is using to push the agenda in a more overtly political manner. So while it's accurate for the interviewees to state that foundations have not engaged in coordination, it's also accurate to say that the leaders and founders of these institutions have had a very heavy – and well financed – hand in directly and personally pushing the agenda forward (ibid.).

The study also notes:

> There is a great deal of overlap between the boards and staffs of conservative foundations and the boards and staffs of their non-profit grantees. Twenty-three of the individuals in our database are leaders of three or more foundations and/or nonprofits, with nineteen of them serving on the board or staff of at least one foundation and of at least one nonprofit. Notably, the leading family members who direct foundations also serve on the boards of various nonprofits, to which their foundations often provide grants. For example, Richard M. Scaife serves as chairman of the Sarah Scaife Foundation and also sits on the board of the Heritage Foundation.

Basically these foundations have perpetrated their conservative ideas on America and the world by building institutions such as the Heritage Foundation, the American Enterprise Institute, the Committee on the Present Danger, and the Center for Strategic and International Studies. They not only funded their think tanks but also funded the media to promote the think tanks and programmes within the think tanks to provide free literature to journalists from all sectors of the media. As Stuart Butler, Vice-President of Domestic and Economic Policy at the Heritage Foundation writes, 'The unique thing we have done is combine the serious, high-quality research of a "traditional think tank" ... with the intense marketing and "issue management" capabilities of an activist organization' (Commonwealth Institute 2004).

Instead of relying solely on traditional conservative thinkers, these corporate-right think tanks emulated the CIA's post-war funding of former communists and leftists to counter the western European communist parties (see Bartley 2001). In the United States this meant concentrating on using a group of disaffected New York intellectuals who had initially been Trotskyists in the forties but slowly evolved into Democrats during the fifties and sixties. Alarmed by the changes instituted by the early seventies, however, these intellectuals wanted to create a vision that would promote what they called American exceptionalism. They viewed American society as the ideal habitat for the human race, even though it had a corporate-funded democracy and increasing concentration of wealth. They rallied around Francis Fukayama's *The End of History and the Last Man*, which posits that the American government and society are the final stage of human development with few flaws. While embracing all the neo-liberal and free-trader philosophies of money and market power, they overlaid them with a patina of Americana that promoted a strong military to spread the 'Exceptional American' culture across the planet. They became known as the neo-conservatives or neo-cons.

As the money flowed into the think tanks of the seventies, the ranks of the neo-cons swelled. Ronald Reagan, financed by the corporate right and drawing electoral strength from a burgeoning Christian right, provided the neo-conservatives with power and legitimacy by turning to their think tanks to fill many of the posts in his administration after his 1980 election. Immediately the new administration set about reversing the policies of the popular democratic movements throughout the hemisphere.

The neo-cons in the Reagan administration, joined by cold war militarists, pushed for an enormous increase in military spending. This led to a new arms race, which almost bankrupted the United States government as it experienced unprecedented fiscal and trade deficits. Under George H. W. Bush, the neo-cons maintained most of their positions of power, but Bush Senior began to deal with the enormous deficits and called for a New World Order that would involve the other global powers.

Irving Kristol, the man they call the godfather of the neo-conservatives and the John M. Olin Distinguished Fellow at the American Enterprise Institute, as well as the author of *Neo-Conservatism, Autobiography of an Idea*, has written that

> Neoconservatism is ... a 'persuasion' ... [with] the historical task and political purpose ... to convert the Republican Party, and American conservatism ... into a new kind of conservative politics suitable to governing a modern democracy ... In earlier times, democracy meant an inherently turbulent political regime, with the 'have-nots' and the 'haves' engaged in a perpetual and utterly destructive class struggle. It was only the prospect of economic growth in which everyone prospered, if not equally or simultaneously, that gave modern democracies their legitimacy and durability ... It is a basic assumption of neoconservatism that, as a consequence of the spread of affluence among all classes, a property-owning and tax-paying population will, in time, become less vulnerable to egalitarian illusions and demagogic appeals and more sensible about the fundamentals of economic reckon-

ing ... The steady decline in our democratic culture, sinking to new levels of vulgarity, does unite neocons with traditional conservatives ... The upshot is a[n] ... alliance between neocons, who include a fair proportion of secular intellectuals, and religious traditionalists ... [In] foreign policy ... patriotism is a natural and healthy sentiment ... world government is a terrible idea since it can lead to world tyranny ... statesmen should, above all, have the ability to distinguish friends from enemies ... Behind all this is ... the incredible military superiority of the United States ... planned by no one ... And it is a fact that if you have the kind of power we now have, either you will find opportunities to use it, or the world will discover them for you. (Kristol 2003)

The neo-cons are in denial about the costs and tragedies perpetrated by the American empire. By calling for the end of class conflict, they implicitly leave their wealthy patrons in control. They refer to egalitarian illusions as if the ideals of equality that America is built upon are unattainable. By leaving the decision to go to war in the hands of the political elite, they forsake the government of 'we the people' and institute a regime that pursues policies that cater only to the needs of the imperial establishment. By insisting that world government will lead to tyranny, they show no faith in humanity. By implying that the growth of American military power was a fluke, they ignore the century-long drive by corporate America to construct a military used to open doors to resources around the world. Finally, by promoting the pre-emptive use of military power, they promote a wanton military force that plays upon the fear-mongering that has been used to sell the use of military power for centuries.

The Next Generation

With the election of Bill Clinton to the US presidency in 1992, the neo-cons lost their official influence in Washington, although Clinton avidly followed the neo-liberal, free trade tenets that they espoused. Still the neo-cons watched in despair as the USA followed a foreign policy that focused on nation building and depended upon multilateral institutions such as the WTO to carry out global rule-making. By 1997 the neo-cons had watched helplessly for long enough. That year Irving Kristol's son, William, and Robert Kagan, a speechwriter for Reagan's Secretary of State, George Shultz, co-founded the Project for the New American Century (PNAC).

Kristol, editor of Rupert Murdoch's conservative publication the *Weekly Standard*, initially operated the PNAC out of the *Weekly Standard* offices. PNAC sought to 'rally support for American global leadership'. Their principles included a 'need to increase defense spending significantly ... to carry out our global responsibilities today and modernize our armed forces for the future' and promoted a 'need to accept responsibility for America's unique role in preserving and extending an international order friendly to our security, our prosperity, and our principles' (PNAC 1997).

They were joined in this project by a group we call the militarist cold warriors. With strong connections to corporate America, this group espoused the use of military force to achieve American imperial objectives. The two salient figures of this group were Dick Cheney and Donald Rumsfeld. Both had served as Secretary of Defense in Republican administrations. Both worked as CEOs of major corporations after their terms at the Pentagon. Rumsfeld headed the pharmaceutical company G. D. Searle, which produced the product aspartame or Nutra Sweet. They were in some trouble because they had apparently falsified the lab tests for the approval of the drug even though they knew that it produced a series of cancers in test animals. Rumsfeld helped smooth the political waters and promoted this product as CEO even though he must have suspected that it might cause cancer in consumers.

Dick Cheney began the process of privatizing the military while he was Secretary of Defense. At that time he hired the oil and military contractor Halliburton to 'produce a classified report detailing how private companies [such as itself] could provide logistical support for American troops in potential war zones around the world' (Christener 2003). Once out of the Pentagon, Cheney went to work as the CEO of Halliburton. In his years there Halliburton doubled its defence contracts and moved from seventy-third to eighteenth on the list of defence contractors. In 1997, as Halliburton CEO, Cheney appeared in an advertising campaign for Arthur Andersen, saying: 'I get good advice, if you will, from their people [Arthur Andersen], based upon how we are doing business and how we are operating, over and above the normal, by-the-books auditing arrangement' (cited in ibid.). Subsequently the Halliburton subsidiary KBR became the subject of an accounting fraud investigation by the Securities and Exchange Commission (ibid.), as did Arthur Andersen.

Twenty-five leading politicians, militarists and neo-cons signed the PNAC principles, including Dick Cheney, Rumsfeld, Paul Wolfowitz, Francis Fukuyama and Jeb Bush. Five years before George W. Bush went to war in Iraq, eighteen PNAC associates, now including Richard Perle and Robert Zoellick, sent a letter to President Clinton, encouraging a strategy of 'removing Saddam Hussein and his regime from power'. They emphasized that this policy 'now needs to become the aim of American foreign policy'. They went on to point out that 'In any case, American policy cannot continue to be crippled by a misguided insistence on unanimity in the UN Security Council' (PNAC 1998).

This letter drew on a document known as the Draft Defense Planning Guidance of 1992, produced under the aegis of Paul Wolfowitz, Under-Secretary for Policy in George Bush Senior's Defense Department. The report alarmed many observers with the declaration: 'Our first objective is to prevent the re-emergence of a new rival ... requir[ing] that we endeavor to prevent any hostile power from dominating a region whose resources would ... be sufficient to generate global power ... the world order is ultimately backed by the US [and] the United States should be postured to act independently when collective action cannot be orchestrated' (Frontline PBS 2003).

According to the *Washington Post* (11 March 1992, p. A1), all the military chiefs and secretaries received the 1992 draft document. Wolfowitz, subsequently a professor of international relations at Johns Hopkins University's School of Advanced International Studies, denies that he had reviewed the document. Its publication caused such an uproar that Wolfowitz admits they had to 'sand off a few corners' for its final publication, which no longer included the concept of the USA becoming the world's only superpower.

The draft document took on renewed importance, however, as PNAC issued its prescriptions for the future in September 2000. In the midst of the presidential race between Al Gore and George W. Bush, PNAC issued *Rebuilding America's Defenses: Strategy, Forces and Resources for a New Century*. This document cited Wolfowitz's Defense Policy Guidance of 1992 as the basis for its strategy, which it claimed 'provided a blueprint for maintaining US preeminence, precluding the rise of a great power rival, and shaping the international security order in line with American principles and interests'. The introduction featured the statement that 'At present the United States faces no global rival. America's grand strategy should aim to preserve and extend this advantageous position as far into the future as possible' (Donnelly et al. 2000).

Among the doctrines promoted in *Rebuilding America's Defenses* were:

- Increase defense spending gradually to a minimum level of 3.5 to 3.8 percent of gross domestic product, adding $15 billion to $20 billion to total defense spending annually.
- As a supplement to forces stationed abroad under long-term

basing arrangements, the United States should seek to establish a network of 'deployment bases' or 'forward operating bases' to increase the reach of current and future forces ... seen as a precursor to an expanded structure.

- Raising US military strength in East Asia is the key to coping with the rise of China to great-power status.
- Global missile defenses. A network against limited strikes, capable of protecting the United States, its allies and forward-deployed forces, must be constructed. This must be layers of land, sea, air and space-based components ... No system of missile defenses can be fully effective without placing sensors and weapons in space.
- creat[e] capabilities for operating in space, including ... launch vehicles, new satellites and transatmospheric vehicles ... Control the new 'international commons' of space and 'cyber-space,' and pave the way for the creation of a new military service – US Space Forces – with the mission of space control. (ibid.)

By the time that PNAC had published this strategy for extending the American empire throughout the universe, Dick Cheney had chosen himself as George W. Bush's vice-presidential running mate. He had served George Bush Senior as Secretary of Defense when Wolfowitz's staff had produced the Draft Planning Guidance 1992.

In December 2000, with George Bush the declared winner of the disputed autumn 2000 election, Cheney headed up the transition team and brought a host of PNAC associates into the administration. Eleven of the thirty-four people who signed either PNAC's statement of principles in 1997 or the letter to Clinton in 1998 urging a war on Iraq ended up as high-ranking officials in the George W. Bush administration.

Donald Rumsfeld became the Secretary of Defense, his second

stint in that position. Paul Wolfowitz, the overseer of the 1992 Defense Planning Guidance, became his second-in-command. Peter W. Rodman became Assistant Secretary of Defense for International Security Affairs. William Schneider Junior was appointed chairman of the Defense Science Board. Richard Perle became chairman of the Defense Policy Board and Randy Scheunemann served as a consultant to the Office of the Secretary of Defense. In addition, the neo-con Douglas J. Feith (an advocate of the Israeli Likud Party) became third-in-command at the Pentagon as Under-Secretary of Defense for Policy.

Over at the State Department the flood of adherents to the Project for the New American Century inundated the new administration. Richard L. Armitage became Deputy Secretary of State. Paula J. Dobriansky was confirmed as Under-Secretary of State for Global Affairs and John R. Bolton went to work as Under-Secretary of State for Arms Control and International Security. David Wurmser, Middle Eastern affairs specialist at the American Enterprise Institute and co-author with Perle and Feith of a 1996 study for the Israeli Likud Party, was appointed Special Assistant to John Bolton.

Lewis Libby, who helped Wolfowitz with the 1992 Defense Planning Guidance, became Dick Cheney's chief of staff and national security aide. Elliott Abrams was appointed to be Special Assistant to the President and Senior Director for Near East and North African Affairs. Bush named Robert Zoellick to a cabinet position as his principal trade policy adviser and chief trade negotiator in charge of dealing with the World Trade Organization and the Free Trade Area of the Americas. Finally, Zalmay Khalilzad, an Afghani native who had advised Unocal on their pipeline negotiations in Afghanistan, headed the Bush–Cheney transition team for the Department of Defense and served as an adviser to Secretary of Defense Donald Rumsfeld. He also served on the National Security Council, became Bush's special envoy to Afghanistan after the United States military removed the Taliban from power, and served as the administration's envoy to the Iraqi groups opposed to the government of Saddam Hussein.

American Enterprise Institute for Public Policy Research (AEI)

All of this had come out of the think tanks that the corporate right had begun funding in the seventies and which by 2000 had spent over a billion dollars to promote their agenda (Callahan 1999a). For the Bush administration, the American Enterprise Institute was showcased as the premier organization promoting the position of the corporate right. George W. Bush, speaking at the Annual American Enterprise Dinner in February 2003 as he was preparing to go to war in Iraq, told the crowd, 'At the American Enterprise Institute, some of the finest minds in our nation are at work on some of the greatest challenges to our nation. You do such good work that my administration has borrowed twenty such minds' (Bush 2003c).

Thanks to years of financial support by the corporate right, the facile manipulation of ideas by their associates and their aggressive lobbying efforts, AEI had become a corporate-right administration-in-waiting. Robert Bothwell, president of the National Committee for Responsive Philanthropy, observed that, 'It doesn't take a rocket scientist to figure out that the millions effectively spent by conservative think tanks have enabled them virtually to dictate the issues and terms of national political debates' (Callahan 1999a). The top twenty think tanks spent more on politically directed issues than the Republican Party collected in corporate soft money.

According to the National Committee for Responsive Philanthropy, 'these groups operate like "extra-party" organizations, adopting the tactics of a permanent political campaign' (ibid.). As Lawrence Korb, who has worked for both the Defense Department and Raytheon, says, 'All you have to do to move from AEI to the Administration is walk across the street ... You don't have to move your family to DC, because you're already there. You don't have to give up a good job you might not get back, because the think tank will always take you back' (Easterbrook 1986).

Unlike most of the post-1960s think tanks, the American Enterprise Institute has been around since the 1940s, when it was a blatantly corporate-funded attempt to match the influence of the Brookings Institution. The production of AEI became more serious in the 1950s when William Baroody took over, but he also made AEI into a more activist organization. Greg Easterbrook quotes Baroody as saying, 'I make no bones about marketing ... We pay as much attention to the dissemination of the product as we do to the content. We're probably the first major think tank to get into the electronic media. We hire ghost writers for scholars to produce op-ed articles that are sent to the one hundred and one cooperating newspapers, three pieces every two weeks' (ibid.). AEI also produced free tapes for radio and put on its own television show.

When the money began flowing in the 1970s, AEI increased its stable of scholars to 'achieve a critical mass' (ibid.) to meet up with enough politicians and journalists to make AEI's political opinions the dominant ideas of the day. In 1976 AEI had twelve thinkers. A decade later they had forty-five. In 2003 they had fifty-seven people they called Scholars and Fellows, including Lynne Cheney, Newt Gingrich, Jeane Kirkpatrick and Robert Bork.

In 2001 AEI brought in $23.6 million and spent $16.5 million. Fifty-eight per cent of its income came from corporations and foundations. Half of their board are CEOs of Fortune 500 companies. Half come from the next tier of American enterprises. Foundation donors included corporate foundations as well as the Four Sisters.

On 17 July 2003 AEI held a forum entitled 'The United States Is, and Should Be, an Empire'. Its announcement for the conference stated:

America is not just the most powerful nation on earth but, argu-
ably, the most powerful nation in history. To protect the global
trade routes of democratic capitalism and its own security interests, the United States can intervene anytime, anyplace. Although
America's domain is more sea-borne and space-based than territorial, some are beginning to refer to this Pax Americana as the
American empire. Is the United States an empire? Should we call
it that? (Internet B)

This is just one of many projects that this influential think
tank for the Bush administration has taken on in the cause of
promoting empire and protecting the interests of its corporate
sponsors. Their various projects are thinly veiled support efforts
for their sponsors. Their Liability Project attacks consumer law-
suits. Their Federalism Project attacks anti-trust policy. Their
Transition to Governing project is involved with attacking congressional ability to oversee the executive branch. Their Continuity
of Government Commission is promoting placing the Director of
Homeland Security in the presidential succession while taking
congressional leaders out of it and creating a mechanism for ap-
pointing a Congress in time of national emergency.

Finally, AEI has begun a new project it calls NGOWATCH.ORG,
which monitors the re-emergence of a civil society movement that
they think is aimed at disempowering the globalized empire of
the new millennium. It asks, 'Do NGOs influence international
organizations like the World Trade Organization? What are their
agendas? Who runs these groups? Who funds them? And to whom
are they accountable?'

Their major concern is that 'The extraordinary growth of advocacy NGOs in liberal democracies has the potential to undermine the sovereignty of constitutional democracies, as well as
the effectiveness of credible NGOs' (Internet A). The oddity of
this project is that neither the incredibly influential American

Enterprise Institute nor any of their other right-wing brethren is on their list of NGOs to keep a watch on.

Things Go Better with God

The October/November 2003 issue of AEI's magazine *American Enterprise* featured a cover displaying celestial heaven with the words 'Things Go Better with GOD' emblazoned across the front. Over the past thirty years the Republicans have discovered that their plans for expanding the American empire certainly go better with God. Reagan's election in 1980 was due largely to the fact that the Christian right registered millions of voters and got them to the polls.

As with the corporate drive against the liberation movements of the 1960s, the growth of fundamentalist Christianity can be seen as a reaction against the social changes implemented in that same time period. Whereas the environmental movement encouraged a holistic relationship with the planet and women demanded a bigger voice in world affairs, the fundamentalists depended on a strict biblical interpretation that declares a right for humanity to dominate nature and gives the male head of the household the duty to dominate the family. In addition the fundamentalist Christians view themselves as the chosen people and the United States as a chosen Christian nation. They blanched at the anti-Vietnam war movement which questioned America's imperial mission.

Several other social factors combined to help build this movement. The amoral market system that treated humans as commodities and utilized sex and violence to sell its products failed to fulfil the community and ethical needs of the American populace. Television evangelists took advantage of all these factors to build a huge following in the 1970s.

By 2000, the Christian Coalition of fundamentalist believers professed to be 'the largest and most active conservative grassroots political organization in America', claiming two million members. They distributed 70 million voter guides for the November 2002 election. They are reported to have 1,700 chapters throughout the United States. The religious right has an entire media industry generating over $2.5 billion per year with television, radio, magazine, newspaper and book outlets. If they don't agree with an issue they have the power to shut down the congressional switchboard (Diamond 1995). Their ability to mobilize voters has allowed the Christian fundamentalists to join the corporate right as the main pillars that support the Bush II administration.

The Christian right has inculcated the values of the corporate right into its theological fold. Christian groups give conferences based on 'the moral and ethical basis of free market economies'. They also 'work to instill a stronger appreciation of the morality of capitalism in the US and around the world' (cited in Borosage 2002).

In discussing the strategy of the right, Sally Covington, a researcher for the National Committee for Responsive Philanthropy, points out that the 'The National Federation of Independent Business, the National Rifle Association and the Christian Coalition are totally separate entities – strategically they move synchronously' (Covington 1998). Robert Borosage agrees, writing that 'spending consistently propagated by a wide range of conservative grantees has contributed to the movement's overall political coherence, helping unite religious right activists and the ... more secular fiscal conservatives' (Borosage 2002).

The godfather of the Christian evangelical movement, Billy Graham, played a pivotal role in George W. Bush's conversion to politics. Christian Coalition founder Pat Robertson signed on early to his campaign. The Christian right's efforts in South Carolina, at a point at which McCain was leading the race, helped swing that primary and eventually the Republican nomination in Bush's favour.

The ebullient Grover Norquist brings the Christian right and other conservative groups together at an invitation-only weekly Wednesday meeting in Washington, DC, where strategies and objectives are discussed and agreed upon. *USA Today* reports that the room where Grover convenes his gatherings 'is the incubator for Bush's political strategy ... a White House aide attends each week. Vice President Cheney sends his own representative. So do GOP congressional leaders, right-leaning think tanks, conservative advocacy groups and some like-minded K Street lobbyists.' Cheney calls the conclave 'a very positive influence' (Page 2001).

The degree to which the Bush administration has been influenced by the values of the Christian right was demonstrated in October 2003 when a controversy arose around Army Lieutenant General William G. 'Jerry' Boykin, Deputy Under-Secretary of Defense for Intelligence. Boykin created a stir because for a year and a half, while in uniform, he had been lecturing conservative Christian groups about George W. Bush and America's War on Terrorism. He said, for example, that George W. Bush was 'appointed by God' (American Humanist Association 2003) to be President and that he 'is in the White House because God put him there'. Most interestingly he described the American War on Terror as fighting a '"spiritual enemy" named Satan' (Bradley Graham 2003). The size and responses of his audiences indicate that he is not alone in these beliefs.

Republikud

In October 2002 the Christian Coalition sponsored a Christian Support for Israel Rally on the ellipse behind the White House to 'tell the world that Christians stand firmly behind the Jewish State and are unalterably opposed to trading land for a paper peace'. Roberta Coombs, president of the Christian Coalition (2002), commended Donald Rumsfeld's support for Israel by saying, 'the secretary is again showing leadership by supporting America's only real ally in the Middle East'. Richard Land, a reverend with the Southern Baptist Convention, says: 'We need to bless Israel more than America needs Israel's blessing, because Israel has a far greater ally than the United States of America, God Almighty' (Kaise 2003).

Christians believe in the cause of Israel because in Genesis 15: 18 God gives Israel to the Jews. They have become particularly supportive of the resurgence of the Jewish fundamentalist Likud government in Israel, though, because they feel that the Likud will establish the necessary circumstances for the Second Coming of Christ. In the past fifty years Israel has facilitated two of three pre-requisites critical to Christ's prophesied return. The modern con-vergence of Jews in Israel fulfilled the first requirement. The 1967 Middle East war in which the Israelis took over all of Jerusalem and particularly the Temple Mount fulfilled the second. Christians are particularly interested in the Temple Mount, because accord-ing to biblical teachings the Second Coming of Christ is dependent on the reconstruction of a Jewish temple there. That is the third requirement. Unfortunately there is an entire Muslim religious establishment on top of the Temple Mount and the mosque there is the third most holy site in the Islamic world. When the Israelis took over the Temple Mount in 1967 the secular defence minister Moshe Dayan gave jurisdiction of the Temple Mount back to the Muslims. Now the supporters of the Likud government in Israel are pushing to vanquish the Muslims and build a new temple on the Temple Mount, which is necessary in their belief for the coming of the Messiah.

Additional support for the policies of the Likud government in Israel is widespread throughout the Bush administration. Besides the Christian right, the neo-conservatives, many of whom come out of a Jewish tradition and see the corporate and militarist Israeli society as a natural ally of the American empire, have functioned as strong supporters of Ariel Sharon's Likud government. As far back as 1996, neo-cons Douglas Feith and Richard Perle co-wrote a paper advising the Likud government to drop 'land for Peace', increase its defences against Syria and Iraq, and build a stronger relationship with the United States.

James Zogby, president of the Arab American Institute in Washington, calls it a 'marriage ... between the religious right and the neoconservatives' (ibid.). Republican political strategists see this as an opportunity to add to their voter base. Ralph Reed, Georgia Republican and former head of the Christian Coalition, says, 'It could really make a difference' and predicts that the Jewish Republican vote could almost double in 2004.

With the appointment of Elliott Abrams as the Middle East specialist for the National Security Council, Thomas Neumann, executive director of the Jewish Institute for National Security Affairs (JINSA), says, 'The Likudniks are really in charge now.' He goes on to call Bush's team the 'best administration for Israel since Harry Truman' (ibid.).

In a study entitled *US Policy towards Iraq: Unraveling the Web*, Laurence A. Toenjes looks at the connections between the institutions that drove the decision to go to war in Iraq. He discovered that JINSA was at the heart of a group of five organizations instrumental in promoting the war. JINSA is a Washington, DC-based think tank 'committed to explaining the need for a prudent national security policy for the United States, addressing the security requirements of both the United States and the State of Israel, and strengthening the strategic cooperation relationship between these two'. Besides advising on US security and defence policy, JINSA runs a series of military tours to Israel for US military personnel. Retired General Jay Garner, the first post-war commander of US-occupied Iraq, is only one of the many former and future military officers who have been on these excursions. The trips include lectures on 'misconceptions about Israel, its past and recent history; its security requirements and the capabilities Israel brings to meeting its defense needs' (JINSA 2004).

Toenjes discovered that nine people, including Richard Perle, Douglas Feith and John Bolton, were affiliated with JINSA and the other central groups promoting the war. JINSA had seven people connected with the Project for the New American Century, six with the Committee to Liberate Iraq, six with the American Enterprise Institute, five with the Defense Policy Board and five with the Washington Institute for Near East Policy (WINEP) (Toenjes 2003).

WINEP is another DC think tank. It was started by Martin Indyk, a former research director of the American Israel Public Affairs Committee (AIPAC), and according to Stanford history professor Joel Beinin is the 'most influential think tank with effects on the United States government's Middle East policy. Fourteen members of WINEP are also associated with AIPAC, which calls itself "America's Pro-Israel Lobby"' (Beinin 2003). According to the *Washington Report on Middle Eastern Affairs*, between 1978 and 2000 AIPAC contributed over $34 million to US political candidates. One analyst points out that

> pro Israeli lobbying groups, most of whom are members or affiliates of the American Israeli Public Action Committee, have amounted to the largest single-interest PAC contributors to candidates for public office in the US for nearly a decade and a half and the fourth largest overall contributor to the Presidential races of 1992, 1996 and 2000. Additionally, pro-Israeli lobbying groups have established a virtual media monopoly on coverage of issues relating to Israel and the Middle East. (Crouse 2001)

Such influence has apparently been successful. As University of San Francisco Professor Stephen Zunes writes (2003),

> The Bush Administration's support for the Likud's right-wing stance ... has been quite clear since it first came to office ... Bush appointees ... have supported the expansion of Israeli settlements in the occupied territories and have opposed the

Israeli–Palestinian peace process from the beginning ... The Bush Administration has consistently supported Sharon's refusal to resume peace negotiations with the Palestinians until all Palestinian violence is halted.

Rumsfeld refers to the Israeli occupation of Palestine as 'so called'. House Majority Leader Tom DeLay says, 'I didn't see any occupied territory. I saw Israel.' Israeli commentator Gideon Samet noted that the USA is 'more Israeli than the Israelis' (ibid.).

Costs of Empire

For thirty years concentrated corporate wealth has followed a strategy of building a national institutional infrastructure that promotes the needs of capital and private property while reflecting the narrow values of self-serving business leaders. Entrepreneurs often work best when faced with a challenge. The rise of popular democracy movements both in the 1960s and the late 1990s threatened to take power away from a corporate-based plutocratic elite that has largely made decisions behind closed doors.

The ability of foundations, inspired by their conservative donors, to establish right-wing idea factories and fundamentally control US government policy is a new development in American politics. It once again proves that money is power. Scholars who enhance the position of business and private property are funded; those who do not go begging.

A strategic alliance between this new conservative-concepts apparatus and a traditionalist Christian movement has provided a grassroots political base to help make conservative political dreams legal realities. It is an odd-couple marriage of convenience between an amoral money-based system and a strict fundamentalist adherence to principles developed two thousand years ago. The money-changers whom Christ banished from the temple are embraced by the devotees who want to see the temple rebuilt

Foundation and religious money, which by virtue of its tax-free status is partially funded by the US taxpayer, represents quasi-public money serving completely private ends. The major problem with this formulation is that the narrow goals of the foundations and the Christian right do not serve the needs of the broader public. Their vision of creating a Christian world based on corporate-owned private property involves spreading American corporate and cultural values around the world. It does not take into account the financial costs, the human costs, the incredible loss to humanity of the destruction of cultural diversity, or the loss of creativity as an American corporate invasion, unimpeded by local laws, seeks to access all the resources of the planet.

Note

1 The Sarah Scaife Foundation, the Lynde and Harry Bradley Foundation, the John M. Olin Foundation, the Shelby Cullom Davis Foundation, and the Richard and Helen DeVos Foundation.

FIVE

The making of George W. Bush

In America anyone can become President. That is one of the chances you take. *Adlai Stevenson*

I'm living proof you can get a C average and still succeed. *George W. Bush*

In January 2001 the corporate right and the Christian right ushered in a new President of the United States who touched many of the diverse elements of traditional American culture. Baseball, Christianity and cowboys – George W. Bush could be connected with all three of these bastions of traditional Americana. As a descendant of the East Coast moneyed aristocracy he related to the traditional American power structure. In addition, many Americans can identify with his ordeal as a recovered alcoholic and even more with his experience as an average student.

On the other hand, as someone who was not involved in the social unrest of his baby-boomer generation he does not identify with the deeply felt social issues that rocked the country in the 1960s and 1970s. As an adherent of the male hierarchy preached in the Christian Church and ensconced in both Texan and his family's culture, he has a hard time identifying with the women's movement or any of the alternative lifestyles that have blossomed in America over the past forty years. As a man of wealth and social connections, he cannot identify with the plight of the dispossessed of the world. As a believer in the virtue of traditional American ways, he has no tools with which to assess the immense costs those ways have inflicted on America and the world.

George W. Bush grew up in Midland, Texas. Michael Lind, a Texan and an astute commentator on the Washington scene, writes that West Texas is 'perhaps the purest example of native, white, Anglo-Saxon Protestant culture in Texas ... with Baptists and Methodists dominant and the Disciples of Christ, the Church of Christ and various other evangelical sects prominent'. It is, he points out, 'a routinely segregationist society ... [where] the Ku Klux Klan found strong support ... [and] the most reactionary community in English-speaking North America' (cited in Lind 2003: 2).

Lind identifies the Protestant Scots-Irish frontiersman as the progenitor of Texas culture and states that the Protestant Scots had been 'conquering and expropriating other ethnic nations for centuries', from the Catholic Irish to the highly evolved Cherokee. These practices turned these Anglo-Saxons into 'a people as militaristic as the ancient Spartans' (ibid.: 30).

He goes on to point out that in East Texas 'oligarchs took their inspiration from the landlords of ... Alabama, Mississippi and Georgia'. The Ku Klux Klan arose as a defender of their culture and lynchings were rampant in the early part of the twentieth century. In this setting Texas became a 'master race democracy – a democracy in which the ethnic majority controls the government and uses it to repress ethnic, racial and religious minorities'. Ruling this democracy was 'a hereditary ruling class with a premodern mentality whose power rested in ownership of land and domination of politics and the military ... a grandee who was born on top and plans to stay there' (ibid.: 50).

So it is not surprising that George W. Bush has opted for the politics of traditional, privileged, white, male-dominated America. From claiming the right to pre-emptive war to his connection to Christian fundamentalism and his disregard for the fate of Middle Eastern residents, many of the roots of his policies can be found in the West Texas culture where he grew up in an American dream.

George H. W. Bush moved his wife and George W. to Texas after the Second World War to escape 'the parental gaze' of Prescott Bush, a member of the eastern Republican establishment (Barbara Bush, cited in Lardner and Romano 1999). George Senior says of those years in the 1950s, '[we] lived the dream' (George H. W. Bush, cited in ibid.), and his wife Barbara recalls that she spent a lot of time behind the backstop at Little League games where George W. dreamed of being a baseball star.

American privilege and success oozed from all sides of George W.'s family. His great-grandfather had been the money manager for E. H. Harriman, one of the railroad barons of the previous century. His grandfather had been a successful Wall Street lawyer and US Senator. His father was a war hero, college baseball star and successful oil magnate, a US Congressman, ambassador to the United Nations, head of the Republican National Committee, ambassador to China, head of the Central Intelligence Agency, Vice-President and then President of the United States. There were fabulous summer homes in the most exclusive enclaves. His mother grew up in the privileged surroundings of Westchester County, went to private schools, met George H. W. Bush at a dance when she was sixteen and married the first man she ever kissed.

George W. lived in Midland until junior high, when his parents moved to the Houston suburbs, but Texas culture stayed in his gut. His father and grandfather represented the values of the elite eastern establishment, while Bush Junior always remained closer to the provincial culture of conservative West Texas. He left Texas when his parents sent him off to Andover, Massachusetts, to high school. For the next decade George W. – known as Georgie in his family – tried to match up to his father – called Big George by the family – and consistently failed: first at private school, then at Yale and finally in his attempt to get into law school.

His father was head of the Republican Party. Family connections got him out of serving in Vietnam. He became a party boy until he went off to Harvard Business School in 1973. There he sat in the back of the class in old clothes and a bomber jacket emanating a cowboy persona, spitting chewing tobacco into an empty cup.

After getting his MBA at Harvard he retreated to Midland, Texas. Over the next dozen years he took refuge in the bottle. Rumours abound that cocaine usage plagued his life. He related to the roughneck world of the oil drillers and wildcatters who are at the heart of the corporate right. Although he excelled at raising money from friends and associates for risky oil ventures, he failed at producing results that paid dividends. Several ventures had to be bailed out by his family's contacts.

Atonement

Billy Graham, the preacher to presidents since Ike Eisenhower and a man called 'a fervent red hunter ... and an overall basher of the left' (Bloom 1999), came to George W. Bush with a mission in the summer of 1985. With his striking white mane ruffled by the breeze as they walked along the rocky shore of Walker Point, he counselled George W. Bush that 'To recommit your life to Jesus Christ, you have to give up one last demon before you can become a new man' (Hatfield 2000: 71). Bush's parents' summer estate rose behind them as waves crashed against the shore.

George must atone for his drunken and drug-filled ways. George W. calls Billy Graham's words 'a seed that grew' (Bush 1999: 136). He atoned, stopped drinking and found Jesus. Over the next dozen years he made money in the baseball business and got himself elected Governor of Texas.

Finding His Persona

The year he stopped drinking, George W. went to work for his dad's 1988 presidential bid. Changes in the Soviet Union made it appear that his father could oversee the demise of the Soviet Union and the ascension of the United States as the world's only superpower. He joined his father's campaign with a vengeance, undertaking the disparate jobs of cheering squad, loyalty enforcer and hatchet man. Bush's 1988 campaign political director commented: 'If the Vice President wasn't happy with any member of his campaign staff, George W. was the guy he sent in.' He disciplined the brash Lee Atwater and verbally attacked journalists who questioned his father or called him a wimp. He helped create an aggressive attack campaign that included pandering to racist fears by connecting Massachusetts Governor Dukakis to murderer and rapist Willy Horton. Finally he took control of squelching a late-campaign rumour that his dad had been involved in an extra-marital affair by barking at a *Newsweek* reporter, 'the answer to the "Big A" question is N-O'. By all accounts he loved the experience, even though the campaign had so disgusted Americans voters that turnout was low (Hatfield 2000: 78).

When he went back to Texas in 1988, fresh from the success of his father's campaign, he avoided the failures of his earlier years and tapped into an old family dream. When he had been a boy his great-uncle had been part-owner of the New York Mets, and when George returned to Texas he got the opportunity to become an owner of the Texas Rangers. Unfortunately his oil ventures had been such a bust he did not have enough money to buy the team. But he did know how to raise money for risky adventures, and in his baseball enterprise he utilized all the mean tricks that can be used in the money-powered economic system to come out on top.

It helped to have connections. He raised $75 million, half of it from eastern money he could tap through a clannish network that included people who had bailed him out of the oil business. His personal $606,302 investment in the venture was collateralized by the Harken oil stock he had received when he bailed out of the oil business. To put the deal together he became the managing partner of the Texas Rangers on a $200,000-a-year salary with a promise that he would get 10 per cent of the ownership when the partnership sold the franchise (ibid.: 89).

The Rangers were playing in an old minor-league stadium in Arlington, Texas, between Dallas and Fort Worth. In a drive to increase revenues, Bush threatened to move the team if the voters of Arlington did not provide $135 million to build a new stadium that Bush and his partners could buy back for $60 million. In the process of procuring a monopoly ownership of all the land around the new ballpark, Bush helped push the Texas legislature to create the Arlington Sports Facility Development Authority (ASFDA). This government agency then proceeded to use powers of eminent domain to try to acquire adjoining land at 60 per cent of its appraised value (ibid.: 115–17).

In their new stadium, the Rangers became a roaring financial success, with revenues climbing from $28 million to $116 million. George W. sold his Harken stock to pay off his loan. The value of the stock had increased two and a half times; one week after he sold it the company announced unprecedented losses and the stock value fell almost 50 per cent. The SEC investigated the now-President's son for insider trading but eventually terminated the investigation, although it admitted that this 'must in no way be construed as indicating that the party has been exonerated or that no action may ultimately result' (ibid.: 103).

Finally, in 1998, after George W. had used his public position as managing partner of the Rangers to boost himself into the Texas Governor's mansion and was ready to run for the presidency of the United States, he convinced his partners to sell the Rangers. His 10 per cent ownership clause kicked in; they sold the business for $250 million and Bush collected $15 to $17 million (Lardner and Romano 1999), a comfortable sum to rest on while running for the presidency.

The Governor

Theories as to why George W. Bush ran for the governorship of Texas in 1994 differ. It may have been to avenge the comment of the incumbent Governor, Ann Richards, who had referred to Bush's father as 'born with a silver foot in his mouth'. It may have been the ploy of Karl Rove in his quest to take over Texas and then national politics for the Republican Party. It may have been to promote the crony capitalism that his family's political dynasty was built on. It may have been to honour what George W. calls his 'charge to keep', the imposition of oppressive conservative Christian values on a broader sphere. It may have been that he loved being the centre of attention and that his offhand, back-slapping political style made him a natural at politics. Or it may have been that he knew that the corporate right was out of power and had lots of money to help a candidate of their liking get into office. They all probably have some relevance.

To promote his candidacy he brought together a political team that stayed with him on his journey to the White House. Don Evans, his old drinking and Bible buddy from the Midland rough-neck days, who had married one of Bush's childhood friends, became his finance chief. Karl Rove, who worked for George Senior at the Republican National Committee in the seventies and had since staged a takeover of Texas politics for the Republican Party, became his chief political adviser. Joe Allbaugh, a newcomer to Bush's life from Oklahoma, became his campaign manager.

Running for Governor was a great political education, and one of the first lessons that Rove and Bush learned was that politics go better with God. At the 1994 Texas Republican convention they tried to oppose the Christian right in selecting the head of the Texas Republican Party. They lost, and as Lou Dubose and Jan Reid point out, if Bush and Rove were going 'to govern on behalf of the corporate right, they would have to appease the Christian right' (Dubose et al. 2003: 91).

Once Governor, Bush promoted the domineering and special interests of conservative Christians. He supported the Religious Freedom Restoration Act, which created special rights for religious conduct and shifted the balance of power between state and religion in favour of religious institutions. He initiated a welfare reform programme that would turn state welfare functions over to Churches. Most significantly, however, he paid respect to the discipline and obedience that are basic to fundamental Christianity by enhancing the criminal justice system. Under his auspices the criminal detention system in Texas incarcerated 545,000 people, more than any other country in the world on a per capita basis. Texas executed a third of the people sent to the gallows in all fifty states and Bush signed over a hundred death sentence warrants, more than any other Governor had in the past.

Cronyism (Lind 2003: 104–5) with his corporate-right financial supporters was rampant throughout his administration. He appointed his friends to the University of Texas Regents. They privatized the school's endowment and gave $9 million of it to a company headed by Tom Hicks, one of the Regents and the man who paid Bush an overly generous price for the Texas Rangers. He lobbied Pennsylvania Governor Tom Ridge on behalf of his major campaign contributor, Enron. He promoted deregulation of the energy industry, which would result in consumers being charged for construction of nuclear plants. The director of the Texas Funeral Commission was mysteriously fired when she tried to fine a big Bush donor $450,000. He promoted a regressive tax plan that reduced the property tax, while increasing the sales tax. He eliminated the corporate franchise tax while imposing a new tax on small businesses and partnerships.

His environmental programme was a bonanza for his corporate friends, whom he allowed to comply with environmental standards voluntarily. Under his regime Texas became the most polluted region in the United States and Canada. Texas spent less

on protecting the environment than forty-eight other states. Bush
packed the Texas Resources Conservation Commission with his
political buddies, including a man from Monsanto and lobbyists
for the energy industry. The commission then proceeded to reduce
public input into environmental enforcement, lessened state over-
sight of environmental problems and terminated the practice of
making surprise inspections to violation sites.

As Governor of Texas, George W. acted as a great friend to the
oil industry, which contributed $5.6 million to his gubernatorial
campaigns. In return he allowed lax environmental laws that left
the state the most polluted region north of the Rio Grande. Houston, the capital of the petrochemical industry, 'is an ecological disaster, its coastal waters fouled by chemical spills and its air quality
the worst in the nation outside of Los Angeles' (Silverstein 1999).

Bush appointed oil and chemical industry employees to the
state environmental board. He also used industry advisers to
design an environmental regulation programme that depended
on market mechanisms and voluntary cooperation. An executive of Dupont involved in the consultation process wrote, 'The
"insiders" from oil and gas believe that the governor's office will
[push through] whatever program is developed between the industry group and the governor's office' (ibid.).

Headed Towards the White House

More than anything, however, Bush used the Texas governorship to launch himself towards the White House. Karl Rove says
he started thinking about running George W. for the presidency
in 1995. By March 1998, two years before the primaries, the campaign was going so well that Bush won a straw vote at the Southern Republican Leadership Conference, prompting the head of
the Mississippi Republican Party to say, 'the nomination is now
George W.'s to lose' (Berke 1998).

In 1998, while George W. pretended to be concentrating on his re-election as Texas Governor – during which he promised not to run for the presidency – Rove approached past Republican chair Haley Barbour about supporting Bush for the presidency. That year Rove set up campaign offices in every state and began the fund-raising effort that had become the hallmark of George W. Bush's campaigns.

From the very start of his political life George W. had excelled at collecting campaign contributions. When he lost his first political campaign in 1978, he outcollected his rival $400,000 to $175,000 (Dubose et al. 2003: 15). As Governor he set a record by amassing $41 million for his campaign chests.

By the spring of 1999, when Bush finally set up a presidential exploratory committee, he had been raising money for a year and the results were sensational. In the first six months of the official campaign he raised a record-breaking $37 million. His friend Ron Kaufman commented, 'this man is drawing numbers and money like no one has ever seen before'. Late in June 1999 he rolled into Washington, DC, for what CNN described as 'possibly the biggest presidential fund-raising day for a candidate that the nation's capital has ever seen'. After Bush raised $2.7 million at a $1,000-a-plate dinner attended by over 2,100 lobbyists and politicians, Steve Forbes's campaign manager observed, 'he has sold his soul to the Washington lobbyists'. Larry Mackinson of the Center for Responsive Politics chimed, 'It really shows the power of the purse. The funders have decided who the next nominee is going to be six months before anyone casts a vote.'

By the time he arrived at the Republican National Convention in Philadelphia, he had raised $125 million, most of it collected through his 'Pioneers', a network of corporate executives and lobbyists plumbing the corporate right for cash. Of the 214 Pioneers for Bush, six raised over $400,000. These included Richard Kinder and Ken Lay, both CEOs of Enron. When Bush was asked about his fund-raising prowess, he could only say, 'I've got a lot of friends.'

Frank Bruni, covering the campaign for the *New York Times*, agreed, saying that, 'Bush's velocity boiled down to the four letters in his last name and to his war chest of campaign contributions' (Bruni 2002: 31). But he also remarked on what a sensational back-slapping, storytelling, affectionate politician George W. proved to be. In his book on the campaign, Bruni relates that 'he pinched our cheeks or gently slapped them in an almost grandmotherly, aren't you adorable way. At least twice, on the campaign plane I felt someone's hand closing tight on my throat and turned around to see the outstretched arms of the future president of the United States, a devilish and delighted gleam in his eyes' (ibid.: 26).

The *Washington Post* describes his style as 'a visceral and energetic charm, sound political instincts, an easy and convincing sense of humor, a common touch'. It was a style that he had been born with, though his friends evoked surprise when he turned into a convincing speaker. A family member recalled Georgie 'performing and his parents laughing' (Lardner and Romano 1999). He led his gang on adventures and naturally gravitated to the heart of any activity.

Karl Rove saw the potential when he first met George W. in the 1970s. 'Huge amounts of charisma', Rove recalled of the young Bush, 'swagger, cowboy boots, flight jacket, wonderful smile, just charisma – you know, wow' (Dubose et al. 2003: 14). But by 1999, Rove knew that it would take more than that to be President. So the man George W. nicknamed Boy Genius and the press calls Bush's Brain started bringing tutors to the Texas Governor's mansion to educate George on the ways of the world. George Shultz, past Republican Secretary of State, showed up, as did a host of Washington politicians and an entourage of foreign dignitaries, including the Canadian Prime Minister, Qatar's foreign minister and the head of the British Conservative Party.

It was about this time that George and Laura Bush made a symbolic move. They bought a 1,600-acre ranch in Crawford, Texas, a few miles down the road from Waco, the notorious capital of 'wacko' Christian fundamentalism. The story of Waco did not begin with the Branch Davidians who brought the wrath of the federal government down on them when they killed a couple of federal agents trying to deliver warrants. Waco has had a history of Christian fundamentalism and racist brutality for a hundred years. Local lore says there are more churches per capita in Waco than anywhere else in Texas. It was a centre of the Ku Klux Klan where thousands of Klansmen paraded in the 1920s and became infamous for lynchings and a 1916 mob slaying when a black man was dipped in oil and cooked live on a bonfire in front of City Hall (Lind 2003: 9).

The next famous Waco fire, the burning of the Branch Davidian compound in 1993, gave Christian fundamentalists a symbol of their feared persecution by secular society. The Christian Republican right celebrates 19 April as a day of infamy. For the Christian fundamentalists Bush's move to Waco during his presidential campaign symbolized the fact that he was on their side.

But Bush would need a lot more than the help of God to get into the White House. Election day 2000 created such a débâcle that Bush forces had to reach new heights in their use of cronyism, bluster, corporate-right money, violence and pure, hardball political power to get their man out of the Governor's mansion in Austin and into the White House. In the end it was the US Supreme Court which made his move possible.

Since the late 1700s, when a closed convention of landowning, white males wrote the US constitution, people have complained that the US Supreme Court was given the power of a monarch. In the end, the American Revolution was not about democracy, but about installing a tribunal of judges appointed for life by the President and confirmed by the aristocratic upper house of the legislature. In December 2000, the presidential election came down to this tribunal. Five out of six Republican-appointed judges delivered the presidency to George W. Bush and the corporate right.

Who is This Man?

George W. Bush's life has created a complex and often troubled man. He covers over the dark shadows with an ebullient patina. More than anything else, as NATO spokesman Yves Brodeur says, 'he's a great salesman' (Hilton 2002). All his adult life George W. Bush has been a salesman. To his childhood chums, his multiple business associates and his political supporters he has been able to sell questionable schemes that often failed. Often what he sold was not what he portrayed.

While denying he was eyeing the presidency, Bush sold the voters of Texas on his re-election as their Governor even though he was the presidential front runner at the time and Karl Rove was setting up campaign offices in every state. Then he sold the religious right on the idea that he was the man to be President while dodging charges of drug use and drunken driving. Since becoming President he has been able to sell an excessive military policy even though he dodged the draft and purportedly deserted the military.

Such salesmanship requires a certain arrogance, which *New York Times* reporter Frank Bruni regards as a Bush family trait (Bruni 2002: 142). As the commander-in-chief of the most powerful military force ever assembled, as a man who feels God is on his side together with the US Supreme Court, the US Senate and House of Representatives, as well as the corporate right and the power of its money, it is not surprising that George W. Bush displays arrogance as President.

One political personality profile of George W. Bush concluded that his personality type is

Outgoing/gregarious and Dauntless/adventurous ... confident in

114

social abilities, skilled in social influence, charming, engaging [with] strong independence strivings, an ambition to excel, competitive, sensation-seeking, risk-taking ... overconfident, glib and superficial ... His personality-based limitations include a propensity for superficial command of complex issues, a tendency to be easily bored by routine, a predisposition to act impulsively, and a predilection to favor personal connections, friendship, and loyalty over competence in staffing decisions and political appointments. (Immelman 1999)

Rianne Eisler, who has written extensively on dominant personalities, identifies Bush as a strong dominator. Renana Brooks, a clinical psychologist writing in *The Nation* magazine, agrees with the dominator analysis and points out that 'Bush projects himself as the only person capable of producing results ... [he] describes the nation as being in a perpetual state of crisis and then attempts to convince the electorate that it is powerless and that he is the only one with the strength to deal with it' (Brooks 2003).

Psychologist Oliver James, writing in the *Guardian*, quotes Bush speechwriter David Frum as saying, 'Id-control is the basis of Bush's presidency but Bush is a man of fierce anger ... sometime in Bush's middle years, his id was captured, shackled and manacled, and locked away.' Then James goes on to point out that

the outcome of [his] childhood was what psychologists call an authoritarian personality ... [which] imposes the strictest possible discipline on themselves and others ... [and] is organized around rabid hostility to 'legitimate' targets, often ones nominated by their parents' prejudices. Intensely moralistic, they direct it towards despised social groups. As people, they avoid introspection or loving displays, preferring toughness and cynicism. They regard others with suspicion, attributing ulterior motives to the most innocent behaviour. They are liable to be superstitious ... [P]erhaps the group [Bush] reserves his strongest contempt for are those who have adopted the values of the 60s. He says he loathes 'people who felt guilty about their lot in life because others were suffering'. (James 2003)

University professor Katherine van Wormer, author of *Addiction Treatment: A Strengths Perspective*, worries that,

George W. Bush manifests all the classic patterns of what alcoholics in recovery call 'the dry drunk' ... Traits consist of: exaggerated self-importance and pomposity; grandiose behavior; a rigid, judgmental outlook; impatience; childish behavior; irresponsible behavior; irrational rationalization; projection [and] overreaction ... It was when I started noticing the extreme language that colored President Bush's speeches that I began to wonder ... Having worked with recovering alcoholics for years, I flinched at the single-mindedness and ego- and ethnocentricity in the President's speeches. In short, George W. Bush seems to possess the traits characteristic of addictive persons who still have the thought patterns that accompany substance abuse ... The fact that some residual effects from his earlier substance abuse, however slight, might cloud the US President's thinking and judgment is frightening.

Van Wormer then adds, 'One final consideration that might come into play in the foreign policy realm relates to Bush's history relevant to his father.' After citing George W.'s failure to match his father's successes, she points out that 'it would be only natural that Bush would want to prove himself today ... One motive is to avenge his father. Another seems to be to prove himself to his father' (van Wormer 2002).

Certainly George W.'s relationship with his father is a powerful and complex factor in his life. Frank Bruni, who covered George W. for years, talked about this relationship with George Senior in Kennepunkport. In that interview George H. W. Bush mused, 'I'm amazed – still amazed – at what he has done.' In these comments, and the way he admired George's brother Jeb, Bruni found 'a limit to the faith ... that George W. Bush's parents and sibling had in him'. George W. must have sensed this – must have spent a life-time sensing this. Then he went on to wonder whether George W. 'Bush, still at some level, might have felt that he had something to prove to his parents. Something to prove to himself.' It can be argued that George W. may even deeply resent his father. Once he moved into the White House, George W. chose to work at John Fitzgerald Kennedy's desk. His father's desk remained in storage (Bruni 2002: 149).

The Iron Triangle

If Bush's 'id was captured, shackled and manacled, and locked away', it was the 'iron triangle' of Karl Rove, Karen Hughes and Joe Allbaugh which performed this task. They were Bush's hand-lers whom he brought from Texas to Washington. Joe Allbaugh became head of the Federal Emergency Management Service at 500 C Street SW, but Rove and Hughes moved right into 1600 Pennsylvania Avenue. Hughes took on the title of Counselor to the President, overseeing his communications and PR operation. Karl Rove officially took on the management of the Office of Politi-cal Affairs, the Office of Public Liaison and the Office of Strategic Initiatives at the White House.

Rove and Hughes essentially carried on the jobs they had been performing for Bush since he ran for Governor in 1994. Rove has always been the consummate political operative and has, he claims, been so since he was born. In the early seventies, at a time when American youth was raging against the political establishment, Karl Rove worked for the corporate right, think-ing up dirty tricks to help get Republicans elected to office. His drive and notoriety boosted him to the head of the College Republicans, and from there he went to work for the Republican National Committee under George H. W. Bush. Big George sent

Rove to Texas, where he started a campaign consulting firm and transformed Texas from a strong Democratic state to a thoroughly Republican one.

Chuck McDonald, a Texas political consultant, says Rove 'plays for keeps. I always knew where I stood with Carl. I knew he was trying to kill me ... He approaches everything as life or death. He does not give off the vibe that you can go and have a beer with him when the game is over.' Ed Wendler, another Democratic political consultant, adds, 'the man's got no soul', and a third consultant intones that 'You have to understand that Karl Rove believes that you govern to be reelected. They were the most politically driven government we have ever had in Texas. And they are more politically driven now that they're in Washington' (Dubose et al. 2003: 242).

When Bush first ran for Texas Governor in 1994, Bill Cryer, the opposing press secretary, observed: 'All we'd heard about was Bush the playboy. Undisciplined in his personal life. We thought he'd get out there and start popping off, and the press would just cream him. But Karl had him ... on this mantra – Governor Richards called him a windup doll. And Karl very effectively kept him insulated from the press' (ibid.: 68). Besides keeping the Bush id under wraps and his boy on-message, Rove also reverted to one of his favourite political tools – dirty tricks. Rumours spread that Ann Richards, the incumbent Governor, was a lesbian.

At the Republican convention in Philadelphia, Rove and Bush were in charge and Rove created such a tightly controlled convention that Pat Robertson complained that 'it's prepackaged. It's slick. It's homogenized. It's pabulum.' In order to increase Bush's political acceptability, Rove included minorities and workers among Bush's supporters. He gave Bush general mantras such as 'no child left behind', 'restore civility to the process', compassionate conservativism and, of course, 'cut taxes'. But Bush also told people that he would not have 'an administration that gets involved in nation building', along with the admonition that if US troops did get involved overseas, 'I won't let it happen without an exit strategy.'

More than anything, though, Rove was the political strategist, tailoring Bush's message for the various regional markets around the country. Early on he realized that Bush could win the presidency by taking advantage of the weighted favouritism in the electoral college enjoyed by the American heartland, a concept that proved prescient given the outcome of the election.

In Rove's White House, everything became political. He orchestrated the appointment of John Ashcroft as Attorney General to keep the Christian right happy. Policy became political as all major legislative initiatives went through him as well as all judicial and cabinet appointments. In the aftermath of 9/11, once the neo-cons had captured the foreign policy initiative, both Rove and Karen Hughes undertook a major effort to project Bush's words and images as a competent and sure imperial leader.

Hughes has often been referred to as the 'Nurse Ratchet' and the 'enforcer' within the Bush hierarchy. Ever since the days of Bush's first campaign, when she berated a reporter for asking questions about Bush's avoidance of military service in Vietnam, she has ruled over the press's coverage of Bush. She favoured reporters loyal to the cause and ostracizes those who question what the Bush administration is doing.

At the White House she oversaw the offices of press secretary, media affairs, speechwriting and communications. She hired and fired press secretaries and quickly became known as the most powerful woman ever to work in the White House. Controlling Bush's vocabulary, which has included 'uninalienable' and 'misunderestimated', has been a major effort and she often mouths the words of his speeches. She was known to be closer to Bush than any other adviser, but her attempts to bring a 'mom's' perspective to policy was not well received by the corporate right and the oil interests in the White House. After a year she was moved out and sent back to Texas.

Oil Power

Along with his political cohorts, George W. Bush brought his corporate oil buddies with him to Washington. The Bushes had been involved in the oil industry since 1928 when Prescott Bush, working for the W. A. Harriman investment house on Wall Street, helped convert Dresser Industries into a publicly traded company. Dresser's CEO, Neil Mallon, became known as Uncle Neil to the Bush family and gave young George H. W. Bush his first job in the Texas oil business in 1948.

George W. kept up the cronyism. His good friend Don Evans worked with him in the oil industry in Midland, served as his political finance guru and became Secretary of Commerce after George W. became President.

George W.'s early years in the oil business were boom times when the industry was awash with cash. Middle Eastern oil money was looking for investment opportunities and some of that money, including some bin Laden money, may have financed part of George W.'s first company, Arbusto Oil. James Bath, a Bush family friend who helped usher Middle East money into the Texas oil industry, invested $50,000 in Arbusto at a time when he was investing money for Salem bin Laden, the brother of Osama bin Laden. Like George W., bin Laden's father had made money from the oil industry, operating one of the largest construction firms in the Middle East. Over the years Middle East oil, money often flowing out of the ill-fated Bank of Credit and Commerce International (BCCI), continued to filter through George W.'s oil businesses.

Most of George W.'s early money came from Wall Street, arranged by his uncle, Herbert Walker – including some from the publisher of the *Washington Post*. When George W. decided to take his business public as a move to avoid bankruptcy, a college friend of James Baker III stepped in to provide enough cash to make the books look good. Baker came from a long line of Houston oil industry lawyers and became a central player in the burgeoning Bush political dynasty. He worked in George H. W.'s cabinet in Washington as one of his closest confidants and headed up George W.'s effort to claim victory in Florida.

Not surprisingly, the Texas petrochemical industry became great supporters of George W.'s presidential bid. In May 2000, the CEO of Hunt Oil became chairman of the Republican National Committee's Victory 2000 Committee. Many of Bush's Pioneers, each of whom raised over $100,000 for Bush, came out of the Texas energy industry, including CEOs of Enron and Reliant. Both companies sought help from the Bush White House after they got into trouble for manipulating the California energy market.

Oil-industry-related executives and lobbyists filled many of the top posts in the Bush administration. Vice-President Dick Cheney came directly from the top post at Halliburton, the world's second-largest oil drilling services company. Bush's chief of staff, Andrew Card, was the chief lobbyist for General Motors. His National Security Advisor, Condoleezza Rice, served as a board member of Chevron.

With key players in positions of power, the oil industry wasted no time in making its stamp on national policy. Bush appointed Cheney to head the National Energy Policy Development Group with a remit to come up with a new national energy policy. The group's report favoured industry over regulation. Allegations that industry lobbyists and executives helped write the report kept its findings under a cloud.

An oil-industry-backed move by the Bush administration to withdraw from the Kyoto accord on global warming gave the first indication of the unilateralist and America-first policies that would become an increasing trademark of the Bush administration. Within days of Bush's inauguration the State Department sought to delay further negotiations on attempts to reduce green-house gases. Two months later, Bush rejected the treaty, saying, 'we will not do anything that harms our economy'.

The economy is what counts for Bush, and the corporate right is depending on him to maintain that posture. So is the Carlyle Group, an investment company that re-establishes the pattern of cartels that developed in Germany during the 1930s when government policy, government administrators, private government contractors and their employees became so intertwined that it was hard to distinguish who was helping whom.

Carlyle's offices are located between the White House and the US Capitol and many of its members have been involved in running the federal government. Besides George H. W. Bush, the Carlyle Group has also included James Baker and Colin Powell. As Peter Eisner, managing director of the Center for Public Integrity, says,

> It should be a deep cause for concern that a closely held company like Carlyle can simultaneously have directors and advisers that are doing business and making money and also advising the president of the United States ... The problem comes when private business and public policy blend together. What hat is former president Bush wearing when he tells Crown Prince Abdullah not to worry about US policy in the Middle East? ... Or when James Baker helps argue the presidential election in the younger Bush's favour? It's a kitchen-cabinet situation, and the informality involved is precisely a mark of Carlyle's success. (Burkeman and Borger 2001)

Carlyle got into the business of combining government and business when it recruited Reagan's Secretary of Defense, Frank Carlucci, first as managing director and then as its chairman. Carlucci, who was Rumsfeld's room-mate at Princeton, brought along a host of former government employees to cement the Carlyle–government connection.

Since then Carlyle has invested heavily in the arms industry and profited from arms sales to Saudi Arabia and other countries. Famed Washington personality Prince Bandar, the Saudi ambassador to the US, is also one of the investors. In one final twist, Carlyle was holding its annual investors' conference at the Ritz Carleton Hotel in Washington when American Airlines Flight 77 slammed into the Pentagon on 11 September 2001. Osama bin Laden's brother, Shafiq bin Laden, was there representing the bin Laden family interests in the Carlyle Group.

A Political Circus

On a cold winter night in January 2001, it was as if the American public and international observers were approaching a political tent supported by the pillars of the corporate right and the religious right. In the centre ring, George W. Bush performed as the master of ceremonies, a role he always loved. His nose no longer red from too much booze, his arrogance boosted by overwhelming support from an admiring peanut gallery, George W. made the most outlandish proclamations and issued the most frightening warnings. Strings running back to his political people controlled his most ardent outbursts. At times his unpredictable personality squirmed under the leash.

All his friends were given the best seats – oil people here, political buddies there; even his religious supporters occupied some prime spots. His parents and siblings sat to the side and shook their heads in amazement. Catching their eye, he upped the ante to make them smile. Whenever he needed support from the audience he chose a shill to provide needed assistance.

Unfortunately, there were no seats for the American public, who could only stand at the back and catch glimpses of the actions through a filtered view provided by the media, who seemed to be part of the show. The rest of the world, prohibited from entering, shivered in the freezing cold. Inside, soldiers marched in circles;

anyone in their way scurried for cover. Lasers illuminated the parapets. Rockets swung through the air. Burly CIA agents stuffed men into cages. Lines were drawn in the sand. Costs seemed not to matter. The people in the seats got in for free. The people at the back were paying the bill.

Suddenly the band struck up a tune. Satan had been detected. The crowd strained forward in their seats. The public cocked their ear to hear what came next. The people on the outside stopped and strained to catch the slightest clue.

George W. Bush raised his arms with a flourish and with a smile unrolled the Axis of Evil. What happened next is the rest of the story ...

The politics of fear: Bush hijacks 11 September

To those who scare peace-loving people with phantoms of lost liberty, my message is this: Your tactics only aid terrorists, for they erode our national unity and diminish our resolve. *Attorney General John Ashcroft*

For the first time in our history, American citizens have been seized by the executive branch of government and put in prison without being charged with a crime, without having the right to a trial, without being able to see a lawyer, and without even being able to contact their families. *Former Vice-President Al Gore*

It is an ironic twist of history that 11 September 2001 found George W. Bush in Florida, the very state he had seized from Al Gore in the disputed November elections the year before to become President of the United States. After being told of the attacks on the World Trade Center in an elementary school classroom, Bush boarded Air Force One and hopscotched around the country, winding up in Nebraska at the Strategic Command base for nuclear warfare. He finally returned to the White House at 6.30 in the evening.

Prior to 11 September many believed that Bush was under the control of a small group of cohorts, particularly Vice-President Dick Cheney. Indeed, on 9/11 Cheney, acting as virtual commander-in-chief in the White House, kept Bush flying around the country, allegedly to evade a terrorist attack. But once Bush arrived back in Washington he took charge. The overconfident and aggressive edge of his personality came to the fore as Bush determined he would use the events of the 11th to put his stamp on history. Without consulting Cheney, Secretary of State Powell or Secretary of Defense Rumsfeld, Bush told the nation on TV that night that the United States was at war and that in this war 'we will make no distinction between those who planned these acts and those who harbor them'. His National Security Advisor, Condoleezza Rice, cautioned him to tone down his remarks but he refused (Woodward 2002: 32). Never before in US history has a President with so little input from his cabinet taken the awesome decision to declare what amounted to an open-ended war.

In a meeting later that night in the White House bunker with his most senior national security advisers, Bush gushed, 'this is a great opportunity' (ibid.: 32). For Bush it was indeed an opportunity to rescue a presidency that had floundered during his first nine months in office. His job approval ratings just prior to 11 September stood at 51 per cent, according to the Gallup poll, noticeably low for new presidents, who usually enjoy a 'honeymoon' during their first year in office (Benedetto and Page 2003). The disengaged side of Bush predominated during the early months of his administration, and his lack of interest in detail undoubtedly contributed to the horrific events of 11 September. He had ignored repeated warnings in CIA briefings that al-Qaeda was about to pull off a stunning act. Bob Woodward, in his largely sympathetic portrayal *Bush at War*, notes that early on the morning of 11 September the Director of the CIA, George Tenet, had breakfast with former Democratic Senator David Boren, who had chaired the Senate Intelligence Committee. 'What are you worried about these days?' asked Boren. 'Bin Laden,' replied Tenet. Boren then said, 'Oh, George,' in disbelief. To which Tenet responded, 'You don't understand the capabilities and the reach of what they're putting together' (Woodward 2002: 3).

The truth of the matter was that Bush had fumbled badly during his early months in power. The withdrawal from the Kyoto Protocol on global warming, the abandonment of the Anti-Ballistic Missile Treaty, the refusal to go along with the establishment of the International Criminal Court in Rome, and the suspension of missile talks with North Korea – these unilateral actions and others convinced the world community, as well as many at home, that the Bush administration was incompetent and taking the United States down a dangerous path.

The administration itself was seemingly split between the 'hawks' or neo-conservatives congregating in the Defense Department around Donald Rumsfeld, and Colin Powell in the State Department, who argued for a more consultative, multilateralist approach to foreign policy. In the most notable foreign policy incident prior to 11 September – the forcing down of an American spy plane over China in early April 2001 – the Powell approach appeared to win out as the United States expressed 'sorrow' for having caused the death of a Chinese pilot when the US plane struck his jet (Bennis 2003b: 3–7). But this did little to change adverse world opinion of the United States. By August, Bush's ratings in Europe were dismal. In France 75 per cent had little or no confidence in Bush, while the Italians and the British had less confidence in Bush than in President Vladimir Putin of Russia to do the right thing in international affairs (ibid.: 14).

However, the fortunes of the Bush administration changed dramatically with the events of 9/11. Bush, as well as the neo-conservatives and militarists in his administration, quickly realized that this was the moment to stamp their ideological imprimatur on the world. As Rumsfeld told the *New York Times* in an interview, 11 September created 'the kind of opportunities that World War II offered, to refashion the world'. Bush himself recognized the importance of the attacks when he dictated into his tape recorder on the night of 9/11: 'The Pearl Harbor of the 21st century took place today' (Woodward 2002: 37).

The Open Door to War

In the aftermath of 11 September the plans to advance US global domination as advocated by the neo-conservative Project for the New American Century (PNAC) were quickly implemented. Europe and the rest of the world, out of solidarity with US suffering following the devastation and death of so many innocents in the World Trade towers, seemingly fell into line behind the United States. As *Le Monde*, France's leading newspaper, declared: '*Nous sommes tous les Americains*' (We are all Americans). Bush wasted no time in taking advantage of the shift in world opinion. In an address to a joint session of Congress on 20 September he stated: 'Every nation in every region now has a decision to make. Either you are with us or you are with the terrorists' (Bennis 2003b: 95). Bush went on to proclaim: 'Our war on terror begins with al-Qaeda but it does not end there. It will not end until every terrorist group of global reach has been found, stopped and defeated.'

Even before the congressional address, splits had emerged within the administration over how to proceed in this global war. On 12 September 2001, Rumsfeld, with the firm backing of his deputy secretary, Paul Wolfowitz, argued that Iraq should be attacked in the first round in the War on Terror (Woodward 2002: 49). Bush adopted a similar stance. Richard A. Clarke who was in charge of counter-terrorism efforts in the administration reports that on 12 September Bush in a White House meeting ordered Clarke to 'see if Saddam did it'. 'But Mr President, al Qaeda did this,' Clarke replied. The president insisted: 'I know, I know, but ... see if Saddam was involved.' The lack of any links to Hussein made it impossible for Bush to launch military strikes against him. The administration would need time to fabricate the lies for an invasion of Iraq.

As surprising as it may seem, shortly after 11 September Bush harked back to the Open Door policy at the turn of the twentieth century to explain the global war against terror. He stated: 'The terrorists attacked the World Trade Center, and we will defeat them by expanding and encouraging world trade.' The *New York Times* demurred, asserting that Bush seemed to imply 'that trade somehow was among the concerns of the terrorists who brought down the towers'. The *Times* was technically correct, but it missed the broader point, that trade and economic expansion were at the heart of what drove the US empire, even as it embarked on an open-ended war against terrorism. Bush himself subsequently expanded on this logic, declaring: 'Open trade is not just an economic opportunity, it is a moral imperative. Trade creates jobs for the unemployed.' In deceptive rhetoric reminiscent of former presidents from Woodrow Wilson and Harry Truman to Ronald Reagan, Bush added: 'When we negotiate for open markets, we're providing new hope for the world's poor. And when we promote open free trade, we are promoting political freedom' (cited in Tabb 2003).

The determination to relate foreign markets to the War on Terror was bound up with the difficulties that Bush and his immediate predecessor had faced in their efforts to advance corporate-driven globalization. Prior to 11 September, a virtual insurrection against global multinational and corporate interests had taken place in the streets of some of the largest cities in the world. After the Battle of Seattle in late 1999, anti-globalization demonstrators converged on Washington, DC, Quebec City, Canada, Prague, Czechoslovakia, in 2000, and then in Genoa, Italy, in June 2001. The Italian port city was besieged by hundreds of thousands of demonstrators as the leaders of the G8 nations, including George Bush, were forced to lodge on ships in the city's harbour.

Ambassador Robert Zoellick, the US trade representative responsible for negotiating new treaties to advance globalization and endorser of the Project for the New American Century, tried to link the demonstrators to the events of 11 September when he declared that the protesters had 'intellectual connections' with the terrorists (ibid.). This attempt to tie the opponents of the administration's policies to the terrorists was part of the administration's broader effort to instil fear and hostility among ordinary Americans to all those who dared to oppose or question its policies at home and abroad.

'Why Do They Hate Us?'

In the aftermath of 11 September, Bush asked the rhetorical question as to why the attackers of the World Trade Center hated the United States. His answer was: 'They hate us for our freedoms.' This was the first big lie that Bush foisted on the American people to create a climate of fear. While this statement was accepted at face value by many ordinary citizens, it flagrantly ignored the impact of repeated US interventions abroad, as well as the destructive effect of globalization on the Arab and Islamic worlds. Benjamin Barber's *Jihad Versus McWorld*, published in 1995, pointed out that a basic conflict was brewing between traditionalist, tribal and nationalist movements on the one hand and the forces of international corporate capitalism on the other. He applied the term 'McWorld' to the materialist, secularizing corporations whose sole objective was to make profits by spreading their corporate interests and culture around the globe.

At around the same time Samuel P. Huntington released *Clash of Civilizations*. It asserted that fissures or conflicts were developing between Western civilization and seven or eight other civilizations, including Islam. This thesis received much attention in the media and in foreign policy circles, particularly in the aftermath of 11 September. Cast in pseudo-intellectual terms, Huntington's thesis feeds into xenophobic tendencies among Americans. It is also the backdrop for understanding George W. Bush's early portrayal of this conflict first as a 'crusade', and then as a struggle of 'good' (us, the civilized in the West) versus 'evil' (them, the terrorists in the Islamic world).

There is indeed a global clash occurring. However, it is not between the Islamic and Western worlds, but between international corporate capital and the innumerable cultures, societies and civilizations that are undermined, uprooted and shattered as corporate capital expands its hold on the globe's peoples and resources. The many variants and tendencies of Islam have been particularly hard hit by this global trauma and upheaval. Throughout the Islamic world – from Indonesia, the Philippines and Malaysia to Afghanistan, Saudi Arabia and Nigeria – the values and interests of 'McWorld' have penetrated many of the most remote regions. Crass materialism, selfish individualism and the gross and often offensive imagery of Hollywood, with all its violent and frequently racist themes, are the concepts and experiences that are thrust upon much of the Islamic world.

Along with this clash of social and economic mores, entrenched in many of the Islamic countries is the most ruthless sector of international corporate capital – the petroleum companies. They may represent 'classic imperialism' in that these corporations were pursuing oil or 'black gold' in the Middle East and the Persian Gulf long before the advent of globalization. But with globalization, the quest for the lifeblood of the global economy has intensified and accelerated, generating new conflicts and wars in the Islamic world. It was after all Bush the elder who simultaneously proclaimed the New World Order (read globalization) while he constructed a wartime coalition bent on ensuring that Iraq and Saddam Hussein would not dominate the flow of oil from the Persian Gulf by taking over Kuwait.

The younger Bush and his ideologues also refuse to acknowledge that 'they hate us' because of recurring US interventions around the globe, including the overthrow of democratic governments and US support of international terrorism well before the rise of al-Qaeda. The first CIA coup that toppled an elected government took place in Iran in 1953, an event etched in the political memory of the peoples of the Gulf and the Middle East. Moreover, it is a historical coincidence worth noting that on 11 September 1973, exactly twenty-eight years before the jets flew into the World Trade Center, the United States helped overthrow the democratic socialist government of Salvador Allende in Chile and backed the military junta led by General Augusto Pinochet. Two years later a team of clandestine operatives sent by the Pinochet regime to Washington, DC, carried out the most sensational foreign-led terrorist action in the capital prior to 11 September 2001. Pinochet's operatives detonated a car bomb just blocks from the White House, killing a leading opponent of the regime, Orlando Letelier, and his colleague, Ronni Moffitt (see Burbach 2003: 154).

These assassinations were linked to the first international terrorist network in the western hemisphere, known as Operation Condor. Begun in 1974 at the instigation of the Chilean secret police, Condor was a sinister cabal comprised of the intelligence services of at least six South American countries which collaborated in tracking, kidnapping and assassinating political opponents. The CIA knew about these international terrorist activities and may even have abetted them. This network of Southern Cone military and intelligence units operated throughout Latin America at least until the early 1980s, sometimes with the knowledge of the CIA. Chilean and Argentine military units assisted the dictator Anastasio Somoza in Nicaragua and helped set up death squads in El Salvador. Argentine units also aided and supervised Honduran military death squads which began operating in the early 1980s with the direct assistance and collaboration of the CIA (ibid.: 148).

Similarities abound between the emergence of terrorist networks in Latin America and events leading to the rise of al-Qaeda. Osama bin Laden first became involved in militant Islamic activities when he went to Afghanistan in the 1980s to fight with the mujahidin against the Soviet-backed regime that had taken power in the country. According to the CIA 2000 Fact Book, the mujahidin were 'supplied and trained by the United States, Saudi Arabia,

Pakistan, and others'. Even in the 1980s it was widely recognized that many of those fighting against the Soviets and the Afghan government were religious fanatics who had no loyalty to their US sponsors, let alone to 'Western values' such as democracy, religious tolerance and gender equality.

In the mid-1980s, when the CIA was backing the mujahidin warriors in Afghanistan, Ronald Reagan likened them to our 'founding fathers'. Then in Central America, Reagan called thousands of former soldiers of Somoza's National Guard 'freedom fighters' as they were sent to wage a brutal war against the Sandinista government in Nicaragua. And when the Sandinistas went to the World Court to press charges against the United States for sending special operatives to bomb its major port facility in Corinto, the Reagan administration withdrew from the court, refusing to accept the rule of international law (Burbach 2002: 57).

Instead of acknowledging that these and other sordid US activities precipitated anti-American hostility abroad and fed the attacks on the World Trade Center, former US government officials and conservative pundits attempted completely to rewrite history in the aftermath of 9/11. Some were even bold enough to argue that bin Laden's international terrorist network flourished because earlier US collaboration with terrorists had been constrained or curtailed by congressional legislation. Henry Kissinger, who was in Germany on 11 September 2001, told the TV networks that the controls imposed on US intelligence operations over the years facilitated the rise of international terrorism. He alluded to the hearings of the Senate Foreign Relations Committee in 1975, headed by Senator Frank Church, which strongly criticized the covert operations approved by Kissinger, including the overthrow of Salvador Allende when Kissinger headed up the National Security Council. The Church hearings lead to the first congressional restrictions on CIA activities, including the prohibition of US assassinations of foreign leaders.

Other Republicans, including George Bush Senior, who was Director of the CIA when the agency worked with many of these terrorist networks, stood historic reality on its head by pointing the finger of blame at the Clinton administration for allegedly undermining foreign intelligence operations. They argued vehemently against the 1995 presidential order prohibiting the CIA from paying and retaining foreign operatives involved in torture and death squads.

Bin Laden and al-Qaeda are in fact an integral part of the brave new world erected by globalization and the imperial adventures of the United States. As Mary Kaldor notes in the pages of *The Nation* magazine, warring groups like al-Qaeda 'flourish in those areas of the world where states have imploded as a consequence of the impact of globalization on formerly closed, authoritarian systems, and they involve private groups as well as remnants of the state apparatus' (Kaldor 2001).

The Unilateral 'Coalition'

In the build-up to the war against the Taliban and al-Qaeda in Afghanistan, the Bush administration went to great lengths to make sure that those who were 'with us' did not place any limits on US prerogatives. The unilateralist hawks in the administration even shunned the 1994 dictum of Clinton's Secretary of State, Madeleine Albright, who said: 'We will act multilaterally when we can, unilaterally as we must' (Mahajan 2003: 23). After the United Nations General Assembly and Security Council passed resolutions of sympathy and support for the United States, Secretary-General Kofi Annan stated, 'this organization is the natural forum in which to build such a universal coalition. It alone can give global legitimacy to the long-term struggle against terrorism.' In response to Annan, a State Department official told the *Washington Post*, 'The United States welcomes a more active UN role as long as it does not interfere with America's right to use military force ... we don't think we need any further authorization for what we may have to do to get at the people that murdered American citizens' (Bennis 2003b: 106–7).

Even NATO was kept at arm's length. The day after the attacks on the Pentagon and the World Trade Center, NATO passed a resolution invoking the mutual defence clause of its charter by proclaiming that the attack on the United States was an attack on all nineteen NATO member states. In response Secretary of State Powell made it clear that the alliance did not have a direct role to play in the approaching war, nor could it impose any constraints on the Bush administration's military decision-making. Instead of consulting with NATO and assuming a 'collective security' mantle, the United States sent NATO members a shopping list of what it wanted, such as unlimited access to ports and airfields and access to early-warning aircraft (ibid.: 113). Later some NATO allies such as Germany sent troops to help occupy Afghanistan, but they did not go as part of a NATO mission.

In the run-up to the war against Iraq in 2003, it was largely forgotten by commentators that US disagreements with its allies began to surface in the days right after 9/11. In a meeting with Bush on 18 September 2001, President Jacques Chirac of France announced that he stood in 'total solidarity' with the United States, but he pointedly disagreed with Bush's formulation of the conflict with al-Qaeda as a 'war'. Prime Minister Tony Blair cast in his lot with Bush's war policy, but in London early dissent concerning his uncritical support of the United States quickly appeared. A British policy analyst wrote in *The Times* of London: 'Our Prime Minister should spend less time with his shoulder glued to President Bush's and more time applying it to the wheel back home.' A *Daily Telegraph* cartoonist showed Blair boarding 'Royal Air Force One' (ibid.: 112).

Within the Bush administration, Powell wanted to go to great lengths to try to forge as large a coalition as possible, even if this would constrict US actions. However, in a critical planning meeting for the Afghan war at Camp David on 15 September 2001, Bush made it clear that he sided with those in his administration who did not mind if the United States had to go it alone. Bush told Powell: 'At some point we may be the only ones left. That's okay with me. We are America' (Woodward 2002: 81).

Other voices, domestically and internationally, denounced the impending war in Afghanistan as likely to be ineffective in dealing with the real causes of terrorism. Judge Baltasar Garzon of Spain, who had gained fame in 1998 when he filed charges against General Augusto Pinochet for crimes against humanity, published an article entitled 'The West Shares the Blame' in early October 2001 in *El País*, a leading newspaper in Madrid. Garzon wrote: 'Lasting peace and freedom can be achieved only with legality, justice, respect for diversity, defence of human rights and measured and fair responses. It is impossible to build peace on foundations of misery.' In a warning to the Bush administration as it prepared for war, he added, 'Above all, it should not be forgotten that there will come a time when justice is demanded of those responsible for these mistakes and the loss of a historic opportunity to make the world more just' (Garzon 2002: 147).

In the United States anti-globalization demonstrations that had been planned before 9/11 against the World Bank and the IMF in Washington, DC, and San Francisco for the final weekend in September were quickly turned into the first major protests against the approaching war in Afghanistan. Even some relations of those who had died on 9/11 called for justice without war. David Potorti, whose brother perished at the World Trade Center, worked with the relatives of other victims to oppose the war in Afghanistan, participating in the 'Family Members of 9/11 Victims DC–NYC Peace Walk'. In an article entitled 'Coming to a Mall Near You: Just War', Potorti argued against the unending conflict being imposed on the American people: 'President Bush's guarantee of "a long, long struggle," absent a measurable goal, and without a quantifiable conclusion suggests that America will be in a permanent militarized state until the end of our days, forever erasing the distinction between "war time" and "peace time"' (Potorti 2002: 99).

While a vibrant, if limited, opposition to the US war took root at home, the established media acted as a propaganda monolith in backing Bush's war. During the Vietnam conflict, the press justified its sobriquet the 'fourth estate', as its independent investigative stance during that war and in the Watergate crisis ranked it as a power akin to the executive, legislative and judicial branches of the government. By the time of the Afghan war, however, the established media had largely become an appendage of the US government. Dan Rather, who had been ostracized by the Nixon White House for his critical reporting during the Watergate scandal, epitomized the transformation of the press from questioning adversary to submissive stooge. On 17 September 2001, on the David Letterman show, Rather gushed: 'George Bush is the president, he makes the decisions ... wherever he wants me to line up, just tell me where. And he'll make the call' (cited in Solomon 2002: 90). Rupert Murdoch, the arch-conservative owner of the Fox Network, proclaimed: 'We'll do whatever is our patriotic duty.' Not to be outdone by its Fox competitor, AOL Time Warner, the owner of CNN, issued a statement declaring: 'In deciding what to air, CNN will consider guidance from appropriate authorities' (ibid.: 91).

'Bush's Brain' at the White House, Karl Rove, told the media explicitly what to do and how to package the news in some instances. When Osama bin Laden released a video, Rove said to the press: 'The request is to report the news to the American people, but if you report it in its entirety, that could raise concerns he's getting this prepackaged, pretaped message out ... putting it into the hands of people who can read it and see something in it.' Rove and the Bush administration in effect believed that the American people could not be trusted, that they would somehow be confused and deceived if the press replayed a statement by bin Laden (ibid.: 89–90).

Bush even took on selling this war to the Muslims. The Pentagon hired John W. Rendon as a $100,000-a-month consultant to sell the war in Afghanistan. He helped create the Office of Strategic Information, which placed news stories around the world – some true, some purportedly not true (Berkowitz 2003). From the beginning it appeared that the Bush administration would go to any lengths to foist their imperial project on the world.

Within two weeks the Bush White House had two ad campaigns in full gear selling their images. They even got the reclusive Laura Bush to try to calm America's jittery nerves. The next month, Charlotte Beers, known as the Queen of Madison Avenue, a woman who has headed two of the world's largest public relations firms, was named Under-Secretary of State for Public Diplomacy. Her job was to sell the War on Terror to the Muslim world. Colin Powell referred to her effort as a 'change from selling the US ... to really branding foreign policy' (Rampton and Stauber 2003: 25).

As the bombs began dropping on innocent civilians in Afghanistan, her celebrity-packaged messages fell on deaf ears abroad. Sheldon Rampton and John Stauber point out in their book *Weapons of Mass Deception*: 'As a general rule of history, victims have much longer memories of injustice than the people who perpetrate their suffering.' Six months after she started her project, while America's military effort in Afghanistan was still terrorizing people, Charlotte Beers testified in Congress that only in Kuwait did more than a quarter of the population view the United States favourably, and that amounted to only 28 per cent of the people. In Saudi Arabia, the vaunted US ally in the Middle East, only 18 per cent viewed the USA favourably.

The Empire Confronts the Republic at Home

The founding fathers of the United States were constantly concerned with the possibility that the new republic would become a monarchy. As Benjamin Franklin asked, 'What have we got? A Republic or a Monarchy?' He cautiously replied, 'A Republic, if you can keep it' (cited in Gore 2003). In the aftermath of 9/11 the Bush administration, led by Attorney General Ashcroft, was determined to undo many of the basic freedoms that dated back to the constitution and the Bill of Rights. The process began at the meeting of the National Security Council on 12 September when Ashcroft told the Director of the FBI that he needn't worry about tampering with evidence in efforts to apprehend terrorists (Woodward 2002: 43). At another NSC meeting late in September, Aschroft said, 'We're thinking about a national neighborhood watch system,' in which citizens would call in or report strange behaviour or suspected terrorists. Ashcroft added, 'We want to convey the message that you're likely to be detected if you're doing something wrong' (ibid.: 169). In the United States a climate of fear was to be instilled right down to community level.

The USA PATRIOT Act, passed in October 2001, became the cornerstone of the administration's assault on basic liberties at home. The elaborate and self-righteous acronym of the act stood for 'Uniting and Strengthening America by Providing Appropriate Tools Required to Intercept and Obstruct Terrorism'. During the previous century no single act usurped or violated so many basic guarantees and rights. In the ambience of fear after 9/11, Congress rolled over when the Justice Department sent the proposed legislation to its chambers. The committee process was bypassed in the Senate, and the resolution was approved 99–1 with no discussion of amendments. In the House, after initial debate on an alternative measure, the bill the administration wanted was introduced in the middle of the night and was passed with virtually no debate. As Representative John Conyers of the House Judiciary Committee notes: 'Nobody had read it [the bill], nobody knew about it, but we had to vote out the administration's bill. It was a usurpation of the congressional prerogative' (cited in Forestel 2003: 269).

The PATRIOT Act restrained and restricted citizens' rights in three main areas: 1) it allowed for unprecedented secrecy on the part of the executive branch, with the voiding of many of the constraints imposed in the wake of the Watergate scandal and the revelations of the Church Senate Committee; 2) checks and balances within the governing system were upended, particularly the ability of the judicial branch to oversee actions of the executive and law enforcement agencies – to search a house for any reason vaguely related to terrorism, the government can now get a search warrant in a secret court, and it does not even have to tell the occupant about the break-in until months after the event; 3) rights to personal privacy are seriously abridged by the act. The government can search Internet e-mail and every website a citizen visits while keeping a list of everyone he or she sends or receives e-mail from. The same applies to telephone calls. The government does not even have to show probable cause that a citizen has done anything wrong. Once any information is obtained the investigators do not have to tell the courts what they've done. Federal investigators can also go to libraries to find out who reads what, and the local librarian is forbidden from telling anyone of the investigation (ibid.: 269–72).

Immigrants, whether legal or undocumented, can now be picked up and deported with no hearings. It is estimated that more than 1,200 people have been detained in this manner. Not since the Palmer raids in 1919 (Wipkipedia 2004) have so many foreign-born residents been stripped of all basic rights and sent back to their countries of birth, many after residing in the United States for decades. Even foreigners merely passing through the United States are detained. Perhaps the most notorious case of abuse is that of Maher Arar, a Syrian-born Canadian citizen, who was apprehended as he changed planes at John F. Kennedy airport in New York. He was interrogated by the FBI with no lawyer present, questioned again in Washington, DC, and then classified for 'extraordinary rendition'. This is a process by which the CIA sends alleged terrorists to third countries for interrogation and torture. Arar was first flown to Jordan, where he was beaten, and then to Syria, where he was imprisoned and tortured for ten months. He was finally freed and sent home to Canada. Neither the Canadian nor the US government has produced any evidence demonstrating that he is involved in any terrorist activities or organizations (Brown and Priest 2003).

Other executive decrees are just as egregious. The President now claimed the right to arrest and hold indefinitely any US citizen he labelled an 'enemy combatant'. Once anyone is detained under this classification the government is not required to charge them with any specific crime and they have no right to a trial, to see a lawyer or to call members of their family. Equally horrendous is the imprisonment of over 650 people captured abroad, mainly in Afghanistan, and sent to the US naval base at Guantánamo, Cuba. There they are imprisoned indefinitely with no rights in solitary cells measuring six feet eight inches by eight feet. Ultimately they can be tried and even executed by a military court. The United States refuses to recognize them as prisoners of war, or allow their status to be determined by a tribunal, as required under the Geneva Conventions (Conover 2003). A few of these prisoners have been released, and after being sent home they have told stories of systematic abuse, including torture.

Aside from a relatively well-publicized 'no-fly' list covering about a thousand people who are suspected terrorists, the US government also maintains a more secretive list of those it believes to be involved in anti-governmental activities. Using this list, two activists working with the small pacifist magazine *War Times* were prevented from flying out of San Francisco airport. A seventy-one-year-old Milwaukee nun embarking on a flight to an anti-war demonstration in Washington, DC, was also prevented from flying. And a leftist attorney is consistently strip-searched whenever he flies (*Independent*, 3 August 2003).

The famous CBS news anchor of the 1960s and 1970s, Walter Cronkite, likens this period of repression in the United States to the 'New Inquisition'. He compares Attorney General John Ashcroft to Tomás de Torquemada, a fifteenth-century grand inquisitor of the Spanish Inquisition, who tortured and burnt heretics, Muslims in particular. As Cronkite notes, 'there was something almost medieval in the treatment of Muslim suspects in the aftermath of Sept. 11. Many were held incommunicado, without effective counsel and without ever being charged, not for days or weeks, but for months or longer, some under harsh conditions designed for the most dangerous criminals.' Cronkite goes on to note: 'Nothing so clearly evokes Torquemada's spirit as Ashcroft's penchant for overruling US attorneys who have sought lesser penalties in capital cases. The attorney general has done this at least 30 times since he took office, according to the Federal Death Penalty Resource Counsel. In several cases, Ashcroft actually has overturned plea bargains negotiated by those government prosecutors' (*Denver Post*, 21 September 2003).

The Dirty War in Afghanistan

The creation of the climate of fear in the United States went hand in hand with the launching of the war against the Taliban government in Afghanistan. A Gallup poll taken in thirty-seven countries in September asked whether the US government should seek to extradite the terrorists or go to war. Only in the United States, Israel and India did majorities favour the war option (Mann 2003: 125). Knowing that it could incite most of the US public into backing its bellicose policies, the Bush administration gave no thought to limiting the conflict to policing operations and the use of international law. The day after 9/11 Bush stated, 'handing over bin Laden is not enough' to avert a full-scale war against the Taliban in Afghanistan (Woodward 2002: 43).

This war would be utterly ruthless, in line with Bush's declaration that he wanted Osama bin Laden 'dead or alive'. On 19 September, the director of the CIA Counterterrorism Center, Cofer Black, called into his office the leader of the first team of CIA operatives to be dispatched to Afghanistan. Black told 'Gary', the code name of the agent: 'You have one mission, go find the al Qaeda and kill them. We're going to eliminate them. Get bin Laden, find him. I want his head in a box.' Somewhat taken aback, Gary queried, 'You're serious?' Black responded, 'Absolutely,' stating he wanted bin Laden's head 'to take it down and show the President' (ibid.: 141).

Bush was irritated at the early meetings of his 'war cabinet' when he found out that it might take the US military weeks, if not months, to get troops positioned halfway around the world and to develop the appropriate war plans for invading Afghanistan. Bush declared, 'I want to get moving,' and he instructed Rumsfeld to push the military. In response to his call for immediate action, George Tenet, the Director of the CIA, drew up a plan that became the blueprint for the war. In the first stage it called for massive covert operations combining the use of intelligence-gathering resources, advanced technology and Agency paramilitary teams with the mobilization of opposition forces in Afghanistan to advance against the Taliban and al-Qaeda strongholds. These operations would be coordinated with the bombing of key targets in Afghanistan, to be followed by the insertion of special forces followed by US ground troops (ibid.: 44, 50–51).

Small CIA units were dispatched almost immediately into the limited areas controlled by the Northern Alliance, a group of largely discredited warlords who had been waging a sporadic war against the Taliban governmental forces for years. They had received limited CIA support in the past, but now millions of dollars were carried in suitcases by CIA agents to the warlords, with the hope that the funds would be used to embark on stepped-up operations against the front lines of the Taliban. In the early stages of conflict, the Northern Alliance was hesitant but once the United States launched massive bombing operations against Taliban front lines and strongholds the warlords began to move. The cutting off of supplies coming to the Taliban from Afghanistan, including petroleum, also proved critical to the war effort. Only when victory was virtually assured did US ground troops appear on the scene, along with a number of token units from Western countries (Mann 2003: 127).

The mythology of this war is that victory was achieved with few civilian casualties by the 'revolution in military affairs', meaning the use of 'smart bombs' and 'pinpoint air power'. What happened on the ground contradicts this high-tech interpretation of the war. As Marc Herold points out in *Blown Away*, the 'collateral damage' in Afghanistan was extensive, in spite of all the smart weaponry. 'A fundamental fact about recent US bombing campaigns is that as the US bombs get smarter, civilian casualties increase,' writes Herold (2004: 31). He goes on to note: 'The levels of Afghan civilian casualties have been caused less from mechanical or human errors, malfunctions, or faulty intelligence and more because of the decision by US political and military planners to use powerful bombs in "civilian-rich" areas where perceived military targets were located.' Based on an exhaustive study of reports from journalists, non-governmental organizations, health workers and other independent observers in Afghanistan, Herold concludes that a minimum of 3,007 to 3,514 civilians died as a result of the US bombings (ibid.: 4), more than the number that died in the World Trade Center on 11 September. The proportional impact on the Afghani population is even greater when one takes into account the fact that its population is only 26 million compared to the 290 million who live in the United States. Moreover, this death toll from bombing does not include other fatalities that 'surely followed from the destruction of infrastructure (including shelter, transportation for food, an incapacitated hospital system, etc.), lack of clean water, and from ordnance that either explodes later or causes long-term medical problems' (ibid.: 15).

The US media largely ignored the reporting of Afghan civilian deaths, deferring to the Bush administration and the Pentagon. When a reporter queried the Defense Secretary in October 2001 about 'collateral damage', he responded in Rumsfeldesque language: 'Are civilians going to be killed in a war? You bet ... No nation has done more to avoid civilian casualties than the United States in this conflict ... every single casualty in this war, be they innocent Afghans or innocent Americans, rest at the feet of [the] Taliban and al Qaeda.' This is an Orwellian explanation of what happened. All loss of innocent life caused by the US military is blamed on the enemy, as if the United States had no choice but to bomb heavily populated areas in a country that already lived in a virtual Stone Age (cited in ibid.: 5).

Bush and the Axis of Evil

A country often tries to refight its last successful war, regardless of its costs and brutality. Basking in the victory in Afghanistan, Bush, in his State of the Union address in January 2002, firmly aligned himself with the belligerent neo-conservatives in his administration. It was then that he coined his infamous phrase the 'axis of evil' to refer to Iraq, Iran and North Korea. Many commentators in the United States and abroad were initially shocked by this crude US policy statement, believing it to be one of Bush's rhetorical 'cowboy' flourishes that would probably not be followed up.

But less than five months later it became clear that Bush had embarked on a reckless and expansionist course in foreign affairs.

On a bright sunny day on 1 June 2002, on the shores of the Hudson river in New York, he gave the commencement address to the military cadets at the West Point Academy. With helicopters hovering overhead, snipers on rooftops and an entourage of bodyguards and security forces surrounding him, Bush proclaimed: 'For much of the last century America's defense relied on the cold war doctrine of deterrence and containment.' Noting that in the wake of 11 September 2001 the administration had determined that there were 'terror cells in sixty or more countries', Bush went on to assert: 'Deterrence, the promise of massive retaliation against nations, means nothing against shadowy terrorist networks ... the war on terror will not be won on the defensive. We must take the battle to the enemy, disrupt his plans and confront the worst threats before they emerge.' This would require 'preemptive action', he declared (Bush 2002a).

This marked the advent of what became known as the Bush Doctrine of Preemptive War. Just over three months later, in September 2002, it was set as official government policy with the release of 'The National Security Doctrine of the United States'. Staking out a unilateralist position in US foreign policy, it declared that the world's only superpower would not 'hesitate to act alone, if necessary, to exercise our right of self defense by acting preemptively'. In keeping with the historic commitment of the United States to the Open Door policy, the doctrine also declared: 'We will actively work to bring the hope of democracy, development, free markets, and free trade to every corner of the world' (cited in Tabb 2003: 81).

As described in Chapters 2 and 3, the US military aggressively imposed this capitalist model from the Caribbean to Vietnam throughout the first three-quarters of the twentieth century. But with the failure of the military approach in Vietnam strategists in the Reagan administration moved away from coercion and seized upon controlled democracies to impose 'consensual domination'.

The address at West Point and the Bush Doctrine brought coercion and consensual domination together as a joint strategy for expanding the American empire. Many critics assailed pre-emptive war as an outrageous moral depravity beyond the ideals of American society. While pre-emptive war appeared to be a break with the multilateral approach that had been ascendant since the days of Franklin Delano Roosevelt, the United States has practised pre-emptive war both overtly and covertly for at least a century and a half. From inventing excuses to take the northern half of Mexico in the 1840s to covertly removing democratic governments in Iran, Guatemala and Chile while overtly attacking Grenada and Panama, the United States has followed a doctrine of pre-emptive war almost since its founding. The only change is the openness with which the policy is pursued.

'The insistence that the United States must prevent potential adversaries from "surpassing, or equaling, the power of the United States"' (Kaplan and Kristol 2003: 112), however, advocates a change in the dynamics of global coexistence. For almost two centuries the world has depended upon a balance of power between potential adversaries to guarantee the peoples of the planet periods of peace. Now the US government is saying that it will be the pre-eminent power. This concept entails several problems.

First, it is disingenuous at best to promote democracy and self-government while insisting that the United States maintain a military that can impose its will anywhere at any time, even from outer space if necessary. Second, such a proposition is bound to elicit a continual succession of revolts from societies intent on pursuing self-determination. Third, the maintenance of such an imperial policy is bound to cost the United States dearly in outright expenditures and in lost opportunities to invest in the domestic needs that made the United States great. The American empire, as in the time of Caesar's Rome, could easily turn against the republic, creating a twisted, conflict-ridden society at war with itself.

Ostensibly a response to the terrorist attacks of 11 September, the Bush Doctrine has in fact become the post facto rationale for a rash of US military actions abroad, ranging from the war in Afghanistan to renewed US involvement in insurgent conflicts from the Philippines to Colombia. Most importantly, the doctrine established the framework for invading Iraq in the name of 'regime change'.

In the late summer of 2002 reports first began to surface of the administration's impending war plans against Iraq. At about that time Bob Woodward went to Bush's ranch in Crawford, Texas, for his last interview for the book *Bush at War*. Bush was in an upbeat, swaggering mood as he talked with the reporter. Riding high in the opinion polls in the wake of the Afghan war, he declared: 'I will seize the opportunity to achieve big goals' (Woodward 2002: 339). Bush even disparaged his father, noting that George Senior had derided the notion of a 'vision' or 'the vision thing' as unhelpful. In the garbled English George Junior is prone to use when excited or agitated, he went on to say: 'The job is – the vision thing matters. That's another lesson I learned' (ibid.: 341). Unfortunately for Iraq and the world, the hubris and depravity of George W.'s 'vision thing' was about to plunge the United States into a second devastating war on the other side of the world.

SEVEN

The drums of pre-emptive war

Every ten years or so, the United States needs to pick up some small crappy little country and throw it against the wall, just to show the world we mean business. *Michael Ledeen, Resident Scholar in the Freedom Chair, the American Enterprise Institute*

The American people will not relish the idea of any American citizen growing rich and fat in an emergency of blood and slaughter and human suffering. *Franklin D. Roosevelt, radio chat, May 1940*

Impetus for pre-emptive unilateral war on Iraq came from the mouth of a corporate lobbyist soon after Bush declared the axis of evil in his 2002 State of the Union address. It came at an invitation-only meeting Karl Rove held to outline his election strategy for the 2002 congressional elections. Regaining control of the Senate and maintaining control of the House of Representatives were important for the Bush administration's long-term plans. James C. Moore and Wayne Slater recount what happened at that meeting after Rove presented a strategy of fighting the Democrats on their own turf – social issues.

> This one big time Republican lobbyist just got up and said, 'Screw this. We can't run on education and social security and prescription drugs and all that other shit. We've done that. Let's run on taxes and terrorism. Fuck, we don't want to engage on that other stuff. We'll get killed on that.'
>
> Almost instantly, Rove's ideas were in trouble. The larger plan of the president, Cheney, and Wolfowitz could go nowhere if Karl couldn't even get this part right. The lobbyist, who represented large corporations that had been generous to Republican causes,

got angry and confronted Rove as the gathering dissipated into pointless debate.

The exchange was described as heated.

'Are you outta your fuckin' mind?' he asked Rove. 'Fuck these issues. The Democrats will run us to death on those issues. It's taxes and terrorism and nothing else.' (Dubose et al. 2003)

Concentrating on terrorism for the election meant scaring people into voting for Republicans. It also provided an opportunity to highlight Bush's War on Terror and the need for patriotic Americans to rally behind the flag to support their President and elect his party to majority positions in both the House and the Senate. Unfortunately, Osama bin Laden, the terrorist who had rained fear down on America on 9/11, could not be found. They needed to find a new terrorist to portray as evil incarnate. Saddam Hussein fitted the bill.

Removing Saddam and taking over Iraq also suited 'the larger plan of the president, Cheney, and Wolfowitz'. All sectors of the Bush administration could buy into it. Cheney and the militarists liked it because it promised permanent military installations in the heart of oil-producing country. Wolfowitz and the neo-cons liked it because it promised to inject 'NED-style democracy' (see Chapter 3) and the 'exceptional' American economic model into the heart of the world that had strongly rejected these themes. The Christian right and the Republikud liked it because it got rid of one of Israel's worst enemies and would perhaps enable a scenario under which Israel would gain sole control over the Temple Mount in Jerusalem. Karl Rove and Bush's political people liked it because it would arouse fear and patriotism to get voters out for the autumn 2002 congressional elections. But most of all Bush's financial backers liked it.

The people who had poured millions of dollars into his presidential bid saw this as the initiation of a campaign to spread corporate-friendly regimes through the geopolitical swath from Morocco to China. The military merchants saw a boom in an industry that was stagnating. The satellite industry suddenly sold all their excess capacity. Investors such as the Carlyle Group looked ahead to a boom in their defence industry holdings. Oil- and war-related construction firms such as Halliburton and Bechtel looked ahead to huge government contracts for the war reconstruction effort. Companies involved in oil production contemplated years of work restoring Iraq's oil production system.

It also fitted into the President's familial heritage. Bush wanted to seize 9/11 as 'the opportunity to achieve big goals'. As a man whose great-grandfather managed the money of a robber baron, whose grandfather helped finance the Nazis and whose father (as well as he himself) had promoted international oil, 'opportunity' had to do with increasing the opportunities for international investment. This plan to open up the region most resistant to global corporatization would do that. It was an audacious move that could bring the mighty United States either to universal domination or ruin. George W. Bush set out to sell universal domination. The costs of the project, which he failed to account for, promised to bring ruin.

Fear highlighted the sales pitch, and throughout the summer of 2002 Saddam Hussein was publicized as the super-terrorist, the butcher of Baghdad, the man who would gas his own people. They waited until late summer to roll out the idea of regime change because, as Andrew Card, Bush's chief of staff and a former lobbyist for General Motors, is famously quoted as saying, 'from a marketing point of view, you don't introduce new products in August' (Schneider 2002).

Cheney began the primal drumroll with a speech in front of the Veterans of Foreign Wars in Nashville right after Labor Day. He told the assembled war veterans that

Simply stated, there is no doubt that Saddam Hussein now has weapons of mass destruction. There is no doubt he is amassing them to use against our friends, against our allies, and against us. And there is no doubt that his aggressive regional ambitions will lead him into future confrontations with his neighbors – confrontations that will involve both the weapons he has today, and the ones he will continue to develop with his oil wealth ... This nation will not live at the mercy of terrorists or terror regimes ... Regime change in Iraq would bring about a number of benefits to the region ... With our help, a liberated Iraq can be a great nation once again. (Cheney 2002)

The Bush administration was blatantly advocating pre-emptive unilateral war in Iraq. It was such a brazen plan that even George Senior's former advisers, James Baker III, Brent Scowcroft and Lawrence Eagleburger, had their doubts. Baker urged instead that 'The United States should advocate the adoption by the United Nations Security Council of a simple and straightforward resolution requiring that Iraq submit to intrusive inspections anytime, anywhere, with no exceptions, and authorizing all necessary means to enforce it' (NewsMax Wires 2002).

Bowing to pressure for a multilateral consensus on his war plans, George W. Bush went to the UN. He declared that with weapons of mass destruction 'Saddam Hussein's regime is a grave and gathering danger'. Conveniently he forgot to tell his audience that the same man who told US intelligence agencies about Saddam's nuclear plans also told them that Saddam had destroyed all his nuclear and chemical weapons soon after the first Gulf war (Rampton and Stauber 2003: 81–2). Still Bush played on this theme. Then his belligerence came out as he proclaimed 'a regime that has lost its legitimacy will also lose its power'. In the end he taunted the members of the UN, asking 'Will the United Nations serve the purpose of its founding or will it be irrelevant?' (Bush 2002b).

He certainly failed to heed the words of his father. But maybe he was out to prove something to himself and the world. In both his book with Brent Scowcroft and in a *Time* magazine piece George Senior had advised against regime change in Baghdad when he wrote:

> Trying to eliminate Saddam, extending the ground war into an occupation of Iraq, would have ... incurred incalculable human and political costs. Apprehending him was probably impossible ... We would have been forced to occupy Baghdad and, in effect, rule Iraq. The coalition would instantly have collapsed, the Arabs deserting it in anger and other allies pulling out as well ... Going in and occupying Iraq, thus unilaterally exceeding the UN's mandate, would have destroyed the precedent of international response to aggression we hoped to establish. Had we gone the invasion route, the US could conceivably still be an occupying power in a bitterly hostile land. It would have been a dramatically different – and perhaps barren – outcome. (Bush and Scowcroft 1998)

History of US Intervention in Iraq

Interestingly, the official effort to remove Saddam Hussein from office emerged soon after the first Gulf war. In 1991, within months of the war's end, Bush Senior signed a CIA directive to get Hussein out of power. The CIA in turn hired a public relations man, John W. Rendon, to promote their efforts.

Rendon had been receiving $100,000 a month for his work supporting the Kuwaiti royal family in the run-up to Gulf war I (Rampton and Stauber 2003: 42). Over the next year he spent $23 million of CIA money to defame Hussein in movies, on radio and in comics. In 1992 he helped create what he called the Iraqi National Congress with, given its penchant for creating plans to pass Iraqi oil to the major American oil corporations, the appropriate acronym INC.

In the autumn of 1992, one of Rendon's associates and a neo-con favourite, Ahmed Chalabi, was appointed to head the INC. Chalabi was an Iraqi exile who had been convicted in Jordan of embezzling $70 million from his own bank. In the mid-1990s he helped channel $100 million (Suellentrop 2003) of CIA money into the effort to create at least a democratic shell government in Iraq. Accounting questions follow Chalabi's practices to this day. Former US ambassador to Saudi Arabia James Akins says, 'He's a criminal banker. He's a swindler. He's interested in getting money, and I suspect it's all gone into his bank accounts and those of his friends' (cited in Dreyfuss 2002b).

The National Endowment for Democracy (see Chapter 3) immediately jumped on to the Iraqi democracy bandwagon. Between 1991 and 1992 its funding in Iraq increased by over 400 per cent. Its efforts went to establish support for a 'liberal democracy' in Iraq among disaffected groups within Iraq and Iraqi exiles in Europe and North America. Within Iraq it concentrated its efforts in the Kurdish north, where Chalabi and his cohorts organized a military campaign to oust Saddam in 1995. Unfortunately, the Americans refused to support their efforts, various Kurdish groups turned against each other, and Saddam easily crushed their revolt.

The Clinton administration, which had refused to support the revolt at the last moment, hoped for a palace coup. General Anthony Zinni, Clinton's military 'proconsul' in the Middle East, referred to the INC as 'silk-suited, Rolex-wearing guys in London' (ibid.). The Clinton team turned their hopes to a group of ex-Iraqi army officers known as the Iraqi National Accord, which the British Secret Service had established after the Gulf war. The CIA recruited ex-Iraqi general Adnan Nuri, who was part of the INC, to head the Accord. It was Nuri who convinced the White House to abort its support of the 1995 coup attempt. Nuri was sure that the Accord could create a palace coup, remove Saddam, maintain stability and create an American-friendly regime in Baghdad. Of course, they never did.

Meanwhile the militarists and neo-cons of the Project for the New American Century (PNAC) sent President Clinton the January 1998 letter urging him to use military efforts to remove Hussein from power. In October of that year, PNAC helped the Republican Congress make covert US policy overt US policy with the passage of the Iraqi Liberation Act (1988). That bill declared that 'It should be the policy of the United States to support efforts to remove the regime headed by Saddam Hussein from power in Iraq and to promote the emergence of a democratic government to re-place that regime.' Suddenly the militarists and neo-cons started calling Ahmed Chalabi the 'George Washington of Iraq' (Rampton and Stauber 2003: 45).

Until they could get the President of the United States to do their bidding, however, their plans languished. As we have pointed out, their prospects improved when George W. Bush formally oc-cupied the White House in early 2001. On 20 September 2001 PNAC sent George W. a letter signed by Vin Weber, the head of the National Endowment for Democracy, among others. Besides supporting 'necessary military action in Afghanistan', the letter proposed: 'American forces must be prepared to back up our commitment to the Iraqi opposition by all necessary means ... the administration should consider appropriate measures of retalia-tion against [Iran and Syria], known state sponsors of terrorism.' They also suggested action against Palestinian groups resisting Israel's occupation of Palestine (Kristol et al. 2001). Like Bush, the militarists and neo-cons of PNAC saw 9/11 as their opportunity to implement world domination.

The Oil Connection

Big oil coyly watched from the sidelines. Chalabi had meetings with oil company representatives in mid-October 2002 during the selling of Gulf war II, but they refused to discuss the results. A pretender to the throne in Iraq was talking, however. Al Hussein, a cousin of the Iraqi king deposed in 1958, said, 'the Iraqi oil sector will be opened for all companies to participate, including the US majors. He added that all existing contracts will be reviewed to determine if they are in the interest of Iraq, in particular those oilfield development contracts with Russian and French companies, and if found lacking, they will be revoked and put up for tender' (Alexander's Gas and Oil Connection 2002). Former American ambassador to Saudi Arabia James Akins predicted that 'The American oil companies are going to be the main beneficiaries of this war. We take over Iraq, install our regime, produce oil at the maximum rate and tell Saudi Arabia to go to hell' (Dreyfuss 2002b).

This resonated with Dick Cheney's controversial 2001 energy plan developed during secret negotiations in the first months of the Bush administration, purportedly with energy industry representatives. Their report outlined a dour future for the United States where domestic demand for oil would skyrocket over the next twenty years and domestic production would decrease. It warned that 'This imbalance, if allowed to continue, will inevitably undermine our economy, our standard of living, and our national security' (National Energy Policy Development Group 2001: vii). It went on to point out that 'Our projected growing dependence on oil imports is a serious long-term challenge. US economic security and that of our trading partners will remain closely tied to global oil market developments' (ibid.: 1–13). One of its top recommendations was that 'the President make energy security a priority of our trade and foreign policy' (ibid.: 8–14). Certainly, securing the Iraqi oilfields would help fulfil that recommendation.

Even though they have kept quiet about their sentiments on the Iraqi war, big oil representatives would probably welcome regaining control of oil production in the Middle East. Iraq nationalized its oil in the early 1970s, creating a stir in Iraq and across the Middle East as well as in the boardrooms in New York City. Within years, all Middle Eastern oil had been nationalized and was providing most of the funding for the governments in that region. Any discussion about reclaiming control of production for the multinational oil companies is a touchy topic for the oil-producing governments of the region and the companies that refine and market the oil around the world.

So generally the oil companies kept quiet. But Robert Dreyfuss, writing in *American Prospect*, suggests that 'cautiously, the oil industry sees a war in Iraq as a way to win back what's been lost'. He did get one oil executive to admit that 'especially the US oil companies ... look forward to the idea that Iraq will be open for business'. Further on he confirms this with another quote from an oil company official, who pointed out that the oil majors 'want to return to greater direct control, perhaps through so-called production-sharing agreements that would give them both a direct stake in the oil fields and a greater share of the profits' (Dreyfuss 2002b).

The neo-conservative think tanks dealt with oil early in the campaign for war. In September 2002 the Heritage Foundation published *The Future of a Post-Saddam Iraq: A Blueprint for American Involvement*, which advocated the complete privatization of the oil industry. Earlier in 2002, Max Singer of the Hudson Institute wrote a piece called 'Free the Eastern Province of Saudi Arabia'. Commenting on that story, he said, 'I meant it seriously. Saudi Arabia is vulnerable not only to a US seizure of their land but to US unofficial participation in a rebellion by minority Shi'a in the Eastern Province' (ibid.). Eastern Arabia, of course, is where all the oil is.

Selling the War

The problem was that the majority of the American people and most of the international community opposed the United States pre-emptively going to war in Iraq. A *Washington Post* story published the week that the Bush administration rolled out its war plans pointed out that 'Substantial majorities in both the United

States and Europe say they believe the United States should invade Iraq only with UN approval and the support of US allies ... 71 percent in Europe and 62 percent in the United States gave the White House low marks for its handling of Iraq' (Franke 2002). Over the next month public support for the war continued to decline.

In response to this opposition the Bush administration made public relations a big part of the selling of the war. The White House formed the Office of Global Communications 'to communicate American policies and values' around the world. They produced 'Apparatus of Lies' about Saddam's propaganda operations as well as disseminating stories of 'torture and brutality in Saddam's Iraq'. John Rendon had his contract with the Pentagon renewed (Rampton and Stauber 2003: 5). In October 2002 Congress passed the Freedom Promotion Act of 2002, which instructed the US Secretary of State to 'Make public diplomacy an integral component in the planning and execution of United States Foreign Policy' (ibid.: 10). Torie Clarke, who had headed the DC office of the PR firm Hill and Knowlton, served as the chief Pentagon spokesperson. It was her idea to embed reporters with US army troops during the war.

By October 2002, the American Enterprise Institute, the Bush administration and their DC allies set about constructing organizations including the Committee for the Liberation of Iraq and the Iraq Public Diplomacy Group to promote the administration's pre-emptive war plans. George Shultz, former head of Bechtel and past Secretary of State, headed the advisory board of the Committee for the Liberation of Iraq (CLI), which he admitted 'gets a lot of impetus from the White House' (ibid.: 54). According to John Stauber and Sheldon Rampton, 'The group used humanitarian language on its website and strove for a bipartisan experience ... Overall however, its leadership and affiliations were decidedly conservative, militaristic and very much in step with the Bush Administration' (ibid.: 53). Randy Scheunemann, who directed CLI, had also signed the Project for the New American Century letter to Bush in September 2001 and served as treasurer of the Project on Transitional Democracies. This group is an NGO concerned with the integration of post-Soviet eastern Europe into the Western market economies. They feature stories such as the one about a neo-conservative investment banker who they claim was instrumental in securing the admission of eastern European countries into NATO in return for their support in the Iraq war (see Internet J). Laurence A. Toenjes identified CLI as one of the five primary groups in creating the rush to war (Toenjes 2003).

The Intelligence War

To find the rationales for unilateral pre-emptive war in Iraq, the neo-con and militarist advocates of the war turned to the intelligence community. They did not find what they wanted there, however, so they unfolded a three-pronged strategy. They created their own intelligence bureaus to give them the intelligence they wanted, culling existing intelligence and emphasizing only what helped their cause and putting pressure on the intelligence community to skew the information towards the results they were looking for.

A few weeks after 9/11 Paul Wolfowitz had neo-con Douglas Feith set up a Pentagon intelligence-gathering department focused on connecting Iraq to the attacks on the World Trade Center and the Pentagon. The official name for this unit was the Office of Special Plans (OSP.) Richard Perle referred to it as the 'Iraq war-planning group' (PBS Frontline 2003). Much of the fresh intelligence that came into the Pentagon originated from the Iraqi National Congress (INC) and likely came through the OSP. According to ex-CIA Director James Woolsey, 'A lot of what is useful with respect to what's going on in Iraq is coming from defectors, and furthermore they are defectors who have often come through ... the INC, that neither State nor the CIA likes very much' (Dreyfuss 2002a).

Both the State Department and the CIA had good reason not to like the INC. The State Department had cut off their funding when they could not account for $2 million they received for collecting intelligence. According to investigative journalist Robert Dreyfuss, 'most Iraq hands with long experience in dealing with that country's tumultuous politics consider the INC's intelligence-gathering abilities to be nearly nil' (ibid.). In their quest to get the information they wanted, however, the Pentagon started to pay the INC again for intelligence. According to former high-level CIA official Vincent Cannistraro,

> The [INC's] intelligence isn't reliable at all. Much of it is propaganda. Much of it is telling the Defense Department what they want to hear. And much of it is used to support Chalabi's own presidential ambitions. They make no distinction between intelligence and propaganda, using alleged informants and defectors who say what Chalabi wants them to say, [creating] cooked information that goes right into presidential and vice-presidential speeches. (ibid.)

Greg Thielmann, former director of the Strategic, Proliferation and Military Affairs Office at the State Department's Bureau of Intelligence and Research, adds, 'What seems to have happened is that the conclusions of the work that [OSP and INC] did somehow entered from the side into the policy community at a very high level, in a way that was invisible to those of us in the intelligence community producing intelligence' (PBS Frontline 2003).

Thielmann goes on to note that the twisted use of intelligence started as soon as the push for war began in August 2002. He calls it 'faith-based intelligence. Instead of our leadership forming conclusions based on a careful reading of the intelligence we provided them, they already had their conclusion to start out with, and they were cherry-picking the information that we provided to use whatever pieces of it that fit their overall interpretation' (ibid.).

Besides selectively using just the intelligence data they liked, the administration also created pressures for the intelligence agencies to produce intelligence that would support the rush to war. Robert Dreyfuss calls it 'part of a broader offensive by the party of war within the Bush administration against virtually the entire expert Middle East establishment in the United States – including State Department, Pentagon and CIA area specialists and leading military officers'. Cannistraro agrees, saying, 'There is tremendous pressure on [the CIA] to come up with information to support policies that have already been adopted' (Dreyfuss 2002a).

Over the six-month roll-out to the war, the Bush administration used this questionable intelligence to: connect Iraq to al-Queda; to guarantee the American people that Iraqis would welcome American democracy with open arms as soon as they were liberated from Saddam's heinous regime; and to scare the American public by suggesting that Iraq had nuclear and chemical arms which it was sure to use against the USA or its allies. The third contention, particularly a reference to Iraq's nuclear programme, was included in the President's State of the Union address in January 2003, even though the US government knew it was not true.

Congressman Mike Thompson (Democrat, California) wondered why the United States was going to war with a country it thought had nuclear weapons. When he suggested to the Bush administration that, once attacked, the Iraqis might use their nuclear weapons on their nearest enemy and the USA's nearest ally, Israel, he was dumbfounded to hear the reply that 'Israel will retaliate in a disproportionate manner' (interview, 18 November 2003, Washington, DC).

'It sounded like they were setting up a nuclear conflagration,' the congressman said in amazement (ibid.). It was only one of many concerns he had about the Bush administration's rush to war. Thompson, a fiscally conservative, Blue Dog Democrat (a group of conservative, mainly Southern Democrats who form a voting bloc in Congress) from noSthern California, is a decorated Vietnam war veteran who sat on the House Armed Services Committee as the Bush administration ramped up their drive to war.

'Every day the Bush administration gave us the same need – that we had to go to war with Iraq,' he says.

> But every day they also gave a different reason to justify the war. First it was that they had nuclear weapons, then it was that they had unmanned drones that would spray us with chemicals, and on and on. And they could never substantiate what they told us, and then they would give us another reason the next day. The Department of Defense, the Pentagon, the Defense Intelligence Agency, the CIA, they were all telling us these things. Whenever you asked them a question, they said, 'We're not going to talk about that.' (ibid.)

So Mike Thompson decided to go and see for himself. In September 2002 he obtained a licence from the Treasury and State Departments to join two colleagues on a trip to Iraq. What he saw there gave him the chills. 'The Iraqis held the American people in high esteem, but not the government. They were concerned about two things,' he said. 'One, that we were coming for their oil and two, that we were going to occupy their country. I could see that Baghdad was disastrous for urban combat. Our soldiers would be sitting ducks.'

The Republican need to control the information about Iraq became apparent when the congressmen returned. At that point Thompson says, 'the Republican National Committee went nuclear. They faxed and e-mailed everyone calling us "traitors" and various other things and that we were on a "rogue trip". It wasn't a rogue trip. We got licences from the Treasury and State Departments. I was on the Armed Services Committee. It was my responsibility to go see the situation for myself' (ibid.).

The House Joint Resolution Authorizing Use of Force against Iraq came to a vote in the US House of Representatives on 10 October 2002. Wording in the bill used the fear of attack to rationalize its passage. Selling the public on this disingenuous strategy was one thing but selling the legislators, who would, it was hoped, not be duped by campaign contributions and fear, was another. Still the wording of the bill pointed to 'Iraq's demonstrated capability and willingness to use weapons of mass destruction ... to launch a surprise attack against the United States or its Armed Forces or provide them to international terrorists who would do so', and stated that 'members of al Qaida ... are known to be in Iraq'. Most tellingly, however, it ended a list of twenty-four provisions using the word 'whereas' with 'Whereas it is in the national security interests of the United States to restore international peace and security to the Persian Gulf region ... The President is authorized to use the Armed Forces of the United States ... to defend the national security of the United States against the continuing threat posed by Iraq.'

According to the Center for International Policy, 'throughout the week or so before the vote, Congressional offices in the House and Senate, both Republican and Democrat, reported that a large majority of their calls were in opposition to war with Iraq' (Center for International Policy 2002). The Republicans had Karl Rove, however. Congressional insiders reported that House Minority leader Richard 'Gephardt fell into a White House [Rove] trap meant to divide Democrats and embarrass [Senate Majority leader Tom] Daschle' (*Washington Post* 2002). Gephardt made a deal with the White House, congressional opposition faded and Congress voted to give the President the war authority he wanted.

Multilateral Consensus?

Gephardt's compromise, which came to be known as the Rose Garden Deal, restricted US military action to Iraq and specified that the President would authorize military action only after he had determined that 'reliance by the United States on further diplomatic or other peaceful means alone either (A) will not adequately protect the national security of the United States against the continuing threat posed by Iraq or (B) is not likely to lead to enforcement of all relevant United Nations Security Council resolutions regarding Iraq' (HJ Res. 114 2002).

This meant that Bush had to go back to the United Nations and exhaust the mechanisms of that body before he entered the USA in a unilateral, pre-emptive war. In a historic confrontation within the United Nations, however, France, Russia and China used the threat of their veto power on the Security Council to rewrite the belligerent resolution originally put forward by the United States and the United Kingdom. Instead of allowing the Bush administration to decide whether Iraq was in material breach of UN resolutions and thus authorizing the use of military force, they insisted that the UN have that authority. Their new wording also limited the amount of military support that the weapons inspectors could count on, which nullified the possibility of a 'creeping invasion under the guise of weapon inspections' (Associated Press 2002).

On 8 November the Council adopted Resolution 1441, which 'set up an enhanced inspection regime with the aim of bringing to full and verified completion the disarmament process established by resolution 687 (1991) and subsequent resolutions of the Council'. Five days later Saddam's government accepted the conditions of the resolution. The first inspectors were due in Iraq early the following week and their first report by mid-February.

About the time the weapons inspectors arrived in Baghdad, George W. Bush was in Prague announcing the creation of a 'coalition of the willing to disarm' Saddam Hussein. Scholars at the Institute for Policy Studies assessed this new development and concluded that 'If Bush fails to get approval from the United

Nations for war, he will claim the right to move ahead with a military attack with this informal and unauthorized coalition' (Anderson et al. 2003).

Bush was in Europe on a dual mission – to collect members for the coalition of the willing and for NATO deliberations on accepting seven eastern European countries into the organization. According to news reports, 'Bush is a firm proponent of expanding [NATO] in part because many of the new members have been strong allies in the war on terrorism and voiced a willingness to offer bases and overflight rights if there is a US-led military confrontation with Iraq.' Did Bush make a quid pro quo offer to Bulgaria, Estonia, Latvia, Lithuania, Romania, Slovakia and Slovenia, by which they got NATO membership if they joined his coalition of the willing? In Prague he said that all nations would be free to choose whether they wanted to join. But certainly there could have been some threats or incentives to help them make up their minds. With an economy that controls 25 per cent of global economic activity and a military stronger than any of several of the next-largest militaries combined, the Bush administration had plenty of muscle to create the coalition of the willing.

Memories of the first Gulf war helped drive the creation of the coalition. A decade earlier George Senior assembled an impressive group of partners to give an international imprimatur of acceptability to the Persian Gulf war. That acceptability led to support from the United Nations. Now, however, with France, Russia and China influencing the final terms of Security Council resolutions, it appeared that the UN might not give George W. the moral authority for pre-emptive unilateral war.

So in Prague George Junior began his efforts to create his own cabal of war cronies. This effort elicited memories of the hardball politics that the first Bush administration had employed to create its list of allies. In that situation, 'when Yemen voted against the first Gulf war a US diplomat told the Yemeni ambassador, "That will be the most expensive 'no' vote you ever cast." Three days later the US cut its entire aid budget to Yemen' (ibid.).

In the intervening years the United States inserted provisos to legalize such actions into its dealings with other nations. In writing the Africa Growth and Opportunity Act, the USA inserted a requirement that countries 'not engage in activities that undermine United States national security or foreign policy interests' (ibid.). Then in August 2002, as the Republicans were orchestrating their war plans, the Republican-dominated Congress passed a similar amendment to the Generalized System of Preferences (GSP). The GSP allows qualifying countries to export various products to the USA duty free. The amendment permits the US government to revoke a country's GSP status if it 'has not taken steps to support the efforts of the United States to combat terrorism'.

Besides its economic power, the USA also exerts its overwhelming military influence to convince other countries to back its initiatives. Of the forty-nine countries that finally joined the coalition of the willing, a substantial number had governments that owed their existence to US military action. In fact five of the six coalition countries from the western hemisphere had governments that inherited their authority from US-financed military interventions in the past several decades. Of the other governments certainly Afghanistan, Kuwait, South Korea and the Philippines all owe a debt to the US military. Even Albania acknowledged that its support was due to US military intervention in the Balkans (Murati 2003).

Besides the stick, the USA also used the carrot to encourage countries to support its war efforts. Almost all coalition members had something to gain from their siding with the United States. Eritrea and Ethiopia, which have been warring over their common border for years, were both looking for US support in the resolution of their dispute. Other nations hoped to benefit in the war's aftermath or as locations of lucrative military bases.

Many of the members had anti-democratic traditions and

repressive policies. Over half the countries were either dictatorships or controlled democracies. The State Department's annual human rights survey describes the overall human rights situation in eighteen of the coalition countries as 'poor or extremely poor' (Anderson et al. 2003). It was not a group likely to create an enlightened, popular regime in Baghdad.

An oft-cited reason for regime change in Iraq was to give non-compliant countries a lesson as to what was in store if they defied the dictates of the United States. The USA now has bases in so many parts of the world, and has engaged or supported military solutions to its problems so frequently, that the threat of unprovoked and wanton violence raining down on a recalcitrant population is widely viewed as a distinct possibility. All these factors together provided a powerful incentive to join the coalition of the willing.

It must have been additionally attractive that their support was mainly in name only. The USA promised to supply the bulk of troops. Great Britain and Australia were the only other members to provide military personnel in any substantial quantity. The war was so unpopular across the globe that politicians in some coalition nations had to promise constituents that they would not send any troops. Territories such as Micronesia, the Marshall Islands and Mongolia are so small and distant from Iraq it is hard to know what benefits they could offer the war effort beyond their name. In all, the coalition represented only 20 per cent of the world's population, and in many countries, including Great Britain and Spain, a vast majority of the population opposed the war.

The Unwilling

In fact a vast majority of both the American and the world population opposed pre-emptive unilateral war on Iraq. Despite the inducements of fear and greed that the Bush administration depended upon to create its coalition of the willing, an overwhelming number of governments chose not to support what they saw as an expansion of the American empire. This included forty-nine of the fifty-three countries in Africa, each of which faced the direct threat of being cut out of the Africa Growth and Opportunity Act. Most of the countries of the western hemisphere declined to join the coalition, although almost all of them have at some point been the victims of US-instigated military attack in the past. Eleven of the fifteen Security Council members chose not to be among the willing, and the heart of Europe opposed the war.

German Chancellor Gerhardt Schroeder, the leader of a country that twice launched pre-emptive unilateral war on the world in the twentieth century, took a strong stance against the US position. In early August both he and the German foreign minister came out against foreign adventuring in Iraq during their re-election campaign. The German government repeated their concern after Cheney's speech before the Veterans of Foreign Wars, with the Chancellor stating that it was wrong for the US government to move towards a policy of unilateral war. There was such a strong anti-war sentiment in Germany that the next day the opposition candidate had to join the chorus and insist on war only with UN approval (see Internet E).

Perhaps even more critical than dissent within Europe was the dissent on the part of Iraq's neighbours. In the 1991 war almost all the neighbouring countries supported US policy. But a dozen years later only Kuwait, the beneficiary of the earlier war, chose to join the coalition of the willing. Jordan, a steadfast American ally, refused either to cooperate with the Iraqi opposition or let the United States use its military bases. Eighty-three per cent of Turks opposed allowing the USA to use military bases, although American diplomats were trying to gain favour in official circles by promising to help Turkey join the European Union. The Saudi foreign minister, Prince Saud al-Faisal, opposed war plans as soon as they were made public in August, and instead promoted the idea of Arab states overseeing the solution to the problem (*Observer* 2003). Iran and Syria, the two remaining neighbours, were understandably opposed to the unilateral American project since they saw themselves as the next target of America's war to remake the map of the Middle East.

By the middle of January resistance to pre-emptive unilateral American military adventurism in Iraq had spread around the world. In the middle of the month there were demonstrations in all parts of the planet, including Tokyo, Islamabad, Damascus, Moscow, Washington and San Francisco. Commenting on this phenomenon in the *Guardian*, Simon Tisdall (2003) noted that 'for every person who took to the streets, there are thousands, maybe tens of thousands, who share their concerns'.

In contrast to George Bush's original characterization of his War on Terror as a crusade, almost all the world's major religions opposed his pre-emptive war. The Pope, who occupied the position of the man who called for the first crusades a millennium earlier, derided the American plan. Beginning in the early winter he began to chastise the United States and Britain for promoting a 'preventative war' which he said was not a 'just war' (Tincq 2003). The US National Council of Churches joined the chorus of voices opposing the war. Fundamentalist Christian Churches in the United States proved to be about the only holy sanctuaries to preach war.

Domestic American opposition to the war had continued to grow since the first anti-war demonstrations erupted in October 2002. Both police and organizers in Washington called these the largest anti-war demonstrations in that city since the Vietnam war. '"Nebraskans for Peace" and "Hoosiers for Non-Violence" chanted alongside silver-coiffed retirees from Chicago and a Muslim student association from Michigan' (Reel and Fernandez 2002). On the same day there were also massive demonstrations in Rome, Berlin, Copenhagen, Denmark and Mexico City. By the end of the year many trade unions, the National Organization of Women and the National Association for the Advancement of Colored People had come out against the war. One hundred and sixty-seven local governments passed resolutions against the war, as well as a couple of state legislative bodies. In January, street protests doubled in size in both Washington and San Francisco. They were joined by demonstrations in cities across the nation and in thirty-two countries around the world.

Facing such opposition, the Bush administration felt compelled to go back to the United Nations to get a Security Council resolution supporting their pre-emptive war. Unfortunately, Russia, China, France and Germany were all staunchly opposed to an immediate war. The US government hoped to get a majority of the Security Council to support their effort and thus stave off a veto by either France or Russia. The United States pressurized what became known as the 'Middle Six' to join their cause. Tactics included bugging phones and threatening economic consequences.

On 15 February, however, there were even larger demonstrations. (See Chapter 1.) With millions of people around the world demanding a change in the American pre-emptive war policy, and faced with overwhelming opposition in the Security Council, the USA and the UK delayed their plans for a second resolution. The Associated Press quoted one diplomat as saying, 'In light of the circumstances, Washington is trying to be more creative' (Linzer 2003).

With strong public opposition in the United Kingdom, British diplomats were determined to get a second resolution. But Washington wanted to go it alone. On 20 February, George W. Bush, using his dry-drunk twisted view of the world, announced that 'for the oppressed people of Iraq, people whose lives we care about, the day of freedom is drawing near' (Bush 2003b). The next day the Bush administration announced that, with 200,000 troops around

Iraq, the US military was ready to go to war. The effigy of George W. Bush bobbing above the heads of the protesters in New York City came to life and dumped buckets of blood and oil all over the citizens of the planet.

EIGHT

Iraq and the imperial dead-enders

Few things are more dangerous than empires pursuing their own interest in the belief that they are doing humanity a favour. *Eric Hobsbawm*

Great empires do not die by murder, but suicide. *Arnold Toynbee*

The United States and Britain had been spilling blood throughout Iraq for over a decade. Following the first Gulf war the United States unilaterally instituted the no-fly zones in northern and southern Iraq which it used to traumatize the Iraqis for the next ten years. Former United Nations Secretary-General Boutros Boutros-Ghali confirms that the UN never authorized the no-fly zones. 'The issue of no-fly zones was not raised and therefore not debated: not a word,' he says. 'They offer no legitimacy to countries sending their aircraft to attack Iraq' (cited in Pilger 2002). According to a Reuters November 2002 story, 'The United States is alone among the 15-member Security Council member states in insisting that the no-fly zones are included in the resolution' (Reuters 2002). San Francisco University professor Stephen Zunes reports that the United States and Britain have used the no-fly zones to facilitate 'mission creep' whereby US and British forces have initiated increasingly aggressive tactics towards Iraq. Whereas initially they fired only on encroachments into the no-fly zone, they soon began firing on anti-aircraft batteries when they were fired on. After a time this advanced to firing on anti-aircraft batteries when they simply aimed at American and British war planes. Eventually the US and UK planes began attacking whichever military targets they chose within the no-fly zone, whether they were a threat or not, and finally, under Bush, they were attacking military targets anywhere in the country (Zunes 2002).

Following the autumn of 2002, Bush's aggressive authoritarian personality guaranteed that unilateral pre-emptive war would become a reality. 'There was a feeling that the White House was being mocked,' reported one source close to the deliberations. In December, Saddam Hussein's tactics pushed Bush over the edge. 'A tinpot dictator was mocking the president. It provoked a sense of anger inside the White House. After that point, there was no prospect of a diplomatic solution' (Peel et al. 2003). In fact, ever since late August, when Dick Cheney first announced unilateral pre-emptive war against Iraq, there had been over a hundred US and British special forces and CIA agents operating in Iraq, executing acts of war (Donnelly 2003). Military missions in the no-fly zone increased by 300 per cent after that point.

As the Bush administration rushed to war before the summer heat fried American troops in the sand, two divergent occurrences with future significance occurred. The Defense Department began granting almost a billion dollars in contracts to favoured corporations to help with the reconstruction of post-war Iraq. Simultaneously a last-ditch effort by the burgeoning global democracy movement pushed for a 'Uniting for Peace resolution' in the United Nations.

Halliburton and Bechtel, two companies with intimate connections to Cheney and Bush, signed non-competitive contracts to clean up the oilfields and other infrastructure damage that might be caused by the war. Cheney, of course, had spent the five years before he became Vice-President as CEO of Halliburton. George P. Shultz, who worked for Bush Senior as well as advising George W., had also headed Bechtel in the past. The early favouritism for these companies and the lack of competitive bidding indicated that unilateral, crony capitalism was going to fare well as the Bush administration spread the American empire into new lands.

Meanwhile, the global peace movement, the Arab League and a collection of non-governmental organizations pushed the United Nations General Assembly to pass the Uniting for Peace resolution. The use of this type of resolution goes back to the Korean war. According to the United Nations charter, 'if the Security Council, because of the lack of unanimity of the permanent members, fails to exercise its primary responsibility for the maintenance of international peace and security ... the General Assembly shall consider the matter immediately with a view to making appropriate recommendations to Members for collective measures ... to maintain or restore international peace and security' (IPO 2003). Uniting for Peace resolutions have been invoked ten times over the intervening years. When such a resolution was implemented during the 1956 Suez Canal crisis, France and Britain withdrew their troops from combat.

The American war against Iraq presented the model situation for utilizing this mechanism for maintaining peace. The Russian Duma and other political entities around the world passed motions supporting a special session of the General Assembly to promote peace. This convergence of civil society and dissident governments signalled the first fledgling attempts of a new global power to challenge pre-emptive unilateral US war.

The Bush administration reacted in fury and discarded any pretensions of supporting democracy. Using what one advocate of the resolution process called thinly veiled threats, the State Department sent special letters to all members of the United Nations, declaiming, 'Given the highly charged atmosphere, the United States would regard a General Assembly session on Iraq as unhelpful and as directed against the United States ... the staging of such a divisive session could do additional harm to the UN.' It called such steps 'provocative' and guaranteed that they 'will not change the path that we are on' (Brecher 2003).

Preventive War

When the bombs started dropping on Baghdad, the United States invoked the new Rumsfeldian strategy of war – psychology and flexibility. Secretary of Defense Rumsfeld sees it as the model for the future of the American military. It involves high-tech weapons and well-paid specialized soldiers with a lot of the grunt work jobbed out to private contractors; it involves space weapons and a 'new nuclear posture'. It is designed simultaneously to perform a regime change in Location A while stabilizing the situation in Location B until regime change can also be imposed there. At the same time enough troops will be left free to perform what Rumsfeld calls 'lesser contingencies or non-combat evacuations' (Lehrer 2003).

Speaking as the war was raging, Noam Chomsky pointed out that Iraq

> is a trial run to establish ... a new norm in international relations ... preventive war ... The doctrine of preventive war ... holds that the United States alone – since nobody else has this right – [can] attack any country that it claims to be a potential challenge to it. So if the United States claims, on whatever grounds, that someone may sometime threaten it, then it can attack them ... the US will rule the world by force ... it will do so for the indefinite future, because if any potential challenge arises to US domination, the US will destroy it before it becomes a challenge. (Chomsky and Ramachandran 2003)

Iraq seemed like a good place to perform this experiment. Their military had been deweaponized and aerially bombed for over a decade. Their culture and economy had been sapped of any vitality by onerous sanctions. The country had essentially been split into three parts and the enemies of the regime had been nurtured and coddled in both the north and the south for the past thirteen years. The arrogance of the Bush administration convinced it that after all these depredations, the people of Iraq would rise in wondrous applause at the coming of American troops.

That is not the way it turned out. Denied access from the north by Turkey, American troops had to fight their way through the heart of Mesopotamia, where civilization first dawned. Troops entering Baghdad depended on one long supply line that suffered from continual attacks out of the desert. Criticism of Rumsfeld started to rumble through the military with claims that his fast and flexible strategy did not put enough troops on the ground.

Initially these critiques seemed off base. The soldiers made it to Baghdad and occupied Saddam's palaces. Full of hubris, they marched their designated democratic government out of Kuwait behind the advancing troops. Once in Baghdad they used their Iraqi shills to create a great media event to show the world that America-the-good had been received as a hero. While American tanks protected the main square, the paid minions from the Iraq National Congress pulled down a towering statue of Saddam Hussein in the blazing lights of the international media.

But then the true shortcomings of the American strategy began to emerge. Baghdad went wild, but not in the manner the Bushites expected. As American troops approached Baghdad, Saddam declared that a unique resistance strategy had been devised – like nothing ever before, he said.

What happened next was more than American troops could or cared to handle. Instead of erupting in euphoria at their liberation by American troops, the whole city became a looters' paradise. From ministerial air conditioners to the priceless heirlooms of human antiquity, everything was up for the taking. And the Americans didn't stop it, except for orders from Washington to protect the oil and interior ministries. Beyond that, Baghdad was out of control.

The truth is, despite George W. Bush's promise, the Americans didn't really care about the Iraqis. As long as they had control of the oil and the intelligence data from the interior ministry they would let the Iraqis wallow in chaos. And civilian deaths from the war? They weren't worth counting.

The Non-existent Road Map for the Empire

History will record that the month of May 2003 marked the high point of Bush's imperial hubris. Right after he declared the 'end of major hostilities' in the Iraqi war on the USS *Abraham Lincoln*, Bush formally announced a 'road map' for the 'settlement of the Israeli–Palestine conflict'. Secretary of State Colin Powell started scurrying around the Middle East, meeting politicians and diplomats as part of the US effort to impose its pro-Israeli recipe for peace on the region. In Iraq a glitch did appear in early May as the Pentagon's anointed pro-Israeli satrap, former general Jay Garner, failed to quell the rising violence in the cities. But the situation was seemingly stabilized when J. Paul Bremer III became the new civilian administrator of Iraq on 13 May. At the end of the month Bremer confidently declared: 'Iraq is open for business.' Arguing for the imposition of the free market formula on Iraq, Bremer asserted: 'history tells us that substantial and broadly held resources, protected by private property, private rights, are the best protection of political freedom. Building such prosperity in Iraq will be a key measure of our success here' (*Washington Post*, 27 May 2003).

But the Bush administration's economic and imperial visions soon turned out to be mirages, like those that often afflict the lost in the hot desert sands of the Persian Gulf. By mid-June US postwar military casualties stood at almost half the number of total deaths caused by the war. The emergent Iraqi resistance, led by 'dead-enders', according to Secretary of Defense Rumsfeld, grew increasingly bold in staging attacks on the occupation forces. In response to the growing resistance, the United States launched its first counter-insurgency mission, dubbed 'Operation Peninsula

Strike', followed immediately by 'Operation Desert Scorpion'. According to a Pentagon statement, these operations were 'designed to identify and defeat selected Ba'ath party loyalists, terrorist organizations and criminal elements while delivering humanitarian aid simultaneously' (Operation Desert Scorpion 2003).

It was unclear what, if any, humanitarian aid was actually delivered, but the raids incensed the local populace in the area known as the Sunni Triangle. Rawah, a mid-sized farming city, was hard hit as US jets bombed the community, followed by army assaults, leaving seventy-eight people dead, most of whom had nothing to do with the armed insurgency. One resident, Hassan Ibrahim, stated: 'This town was safe before the Americans came here and made a lot of blood. Is this the democracy they were talking about?' A member of a family that owned farmland throughout the area added: 'If I get a chance, I would shoot an American, because they are now my enemies. Before this, 1 of 10,000 Rawah citizens would fight the Americans. Now, more than half would' (Lasseter and Brown 2003).

Even ardent sympathizers of the United States were alienated by the first US counter-insurgency offensive. As part of Operation Peninsula Strike, the army's Iron Horse unit raided the home of thirty-four-year-old Njim Rais in a provincial city 60 miles north of Baghdad. Rais loved America, and as he grew up he dreamed of visiting Niagara Falls. He was so captivated by a television programme set in Florida that he insisted his youngest sister be named Miami when she was born. At 2 a.m. on 10 June, Bradley fighting vehicles appeared in the street in front of the Rais family's house as four Apache helicopters hovered above. American soldiers burst through the door, training their weapons on everyone. Njim's mother screamed as they grabbed two of Njim's brothers and hauled them off as prisoners of war. They were released several days later, but Njim no longer has pleasant thoughts of America. Now, when his friends taunt him about his pro-American senti-

178

ments, he says: 'if I do not attack them with words, then I will keep silent'. His mother adds: 'We will never forget the night they came with their machine guns. I will never forget it until I die' (Barry and Bender 2003).

The Oblivious Empire

The die was cast. The United States had become bogged down in a lengthy war of occupation and attrition. How did this happen? How could the greatest power in the history of the world, bestowed with a seemingly unlimited number of well-trained policy analysts from universities and international study institutes, become mired in what amounted to a colonial war that harked back to the nineteenth and twentieth centuries?

A renowned British historian, Eric Hobsbawm, writing just after the end of the formal war in Iraq, captured the exceptionality of the US position compared to previous empires:

> The present world situation is quite unprecedented. The great global empires that have been seen before, such as the Spanish in the 16th and 17th centuries, and notably the British in the 19th and 20th centuries, bear little comparison with what we see today in the United States empire ... A key novelty of the US imperial project is that all other great powers and empires knew that they were not the only ones, and none aimed at global domination. None believed themselves invulnerable, even if they believed themselves to be central to the world – as China did, or the Roman Empire at its peak. (Hobsbawm 2003)

The truth of the matter is that the Bush administration is oblivious to the restraints and lessons of history. Few imperial rulers have ever demonstrated such incomprehension of how the real world functions as George W. Bush. The Bush neo-conservatives and militarists are convinced that the United States is somehow unique, that it is not bound by any of the constraints of prior empires, or even by the experiences and lessons that derive from the prior half-century of Pax Americana. One Pentagon adviser captured the cockiness of the administration's thinking when he stated: 'Knocking off two regimes [Afghanistan and Iraq] enables us to do extraordinary things' (Hersh 2003b).

The starting fallacy of the Bush administration is the belief that it can simply toss out the doctrine of containment that guided the United States for decades and replace it with the doctrine of pre-emptive war. The containment doctrine was aimed principally at the former Soviet Union, but its basic strategy is still relevant for curtailing the ambitions and intents of lesser powers in the post-cold-war era. Arthur J. Schlesinger Junior, a prominent liberal historian and adviser to presidents (who sharply disagreed with William Appleman Williams's view of the United States as an empire), wrote in mid-2003:

> President George W. Bush has made a fatal change in the foreign policy of the United States. He has repudiated the strategy that won the cold war – the combination of containment and deterrence carried out through such multilateral agencies as the UN, NATO, and the Organization of American States. The Bush Doctrine reverses all that ... Mr Bush has replaced a policy aimed at peace through the prevention of war by a policy aimed at peace through preventive war.

Schlesinger went on to quote Harry S Truman, who wrote in his memoirs: 'There is nothing more foolish than to think that war can be stopped by war. You don't "prevent" anything by war except peace' (Schlesinger 2003).

In line with their obsession with pre-emptive war, the people around Bush refused to accept the age-old adage that wars, even when they are won, lead to unpredictable consequences. With no second thoughts, the Bush administration began plotting the invasion of Iraq in the early autumn of 2002. The only outside 'advisers' it listened to were the meteorologists who reported that the extraordinarily hot climate of Iraq would make it impossible for a heavily clad army to fight a war after March, when temperatures would soar well over 100 degrees Fahrenheit.

Because the Bush administration was set upon waging a war in Iraq it had no real interest in the mission of the UN weapons inspectors, who re-entered Iraq in November 2002. The thinking of the administration was that it would simply be frosting on their war cake if the inspectors came back with any reports of chemical or biological weapons. Here, however, the administration got caught up in its own propaganda trap. When no weapons were found most of the international community, with the notable exception of Tony Blair and Great Britain, refused to endorse the invasion of Iraq. The determination of the administration to proceed with war in the face of international opposition led Bush to fabricate repeated lies in an effort to mislead the world. In his State of the Union address in 2003, Bush uttered the sixteen infamous words that even US intelligence agencies knew to be untrue: 'The British government has learned that Saddam Hussein recently sought significant quantities of uranium from Africa.' Moreover, another twenty-five words from the same speech were just as damning: 'Evidence from intelligence sources, secret communications and statements by people now in custody reveal that Saddam Hussein aids and protects terrorists, including members of al-Qaeda.'

The international community correctly perceived these and other statements as outright warmongering. However, the lack of support from other nations and international institutions was of little importance to Bush and his advisers. Here they flagrantly ignored another lesson of the post-cold-war period, the importance of working with others in a world that is increasingly interdependent. Their visceral hatred of William Jefferson Clinton and all that he stood for led them to reject the globalist orientation of his foreign policy. The Clinton administration did lead the USA into a series of interventions and conflicts, but it understood that the United States should not go it alone, even in Kosovo, where it secured NATO support when the Russians blocked UN participation. The Bush administration, on the other hand, opted for what amounted to a unilateral war that alienated most of Europe and the nations of the South, particularly the Arab world, as well as the Muslim nations that represented one-fifth of humanity. In its history the United States has never aroused such international antagonism and antipathy as it did in the second Gulf war. Here Arthur Schlesinger correctly compares the United States to Japan and the 'infamy' it aroused by attacking the United States at Pearl Harbor in 1941.

Anatol Lievin, a senior associate at the Carnegie Endowment for International Peace, draws a stark contrast between the foreign polices of Clinton and Bush:

> Clinton may well be justifiably seen by future generations as a particularly intelligent and valuable servant of American imperial capitalism, in a way that went beyond diplomatic cleverness. He seems to have understood three things that the Bush Administration has wholly or partly forgotten: that the American economy is utterly intertwined with the world capitalist order, depends on the health of that order and draws immense benefits from that order. This is indeed likely to be seen by future historians as the central tragic irony of the Bush Administration's world policy: that the United States, which of all states today should feel like a satisfied power, is instead behaving like a revolutionary one, kicking to pieces the hill of which it is king. (Lievin 2003)

A prior period of the US imperium invites comparison with Bush's adventurism – Teddy Roosevelt's 'gunboat diplomacy'. In a message to the US Congress in 1904, Roosevelt sought to justify repeated US interventions in Central America and the Caribbean basin by proclaiming the Roosevelt corollary to the Monroe Doctrine. He declared that 'chronic wrongdoing, or an impotence which results in the general loosening of the ties of civilized society ... may force the United States ... to the exercise of an international police power' (Roosevelt 1904). The logic of the Roosevelt corollary was virtually the same as that of the Bush doctrine; they both asserted that the United States had the right to intervention if it detected wrongdoing in uncivilized or 'rogue' states. The main difference is that the Roosevelt corollary was applied only to the western hemisphere, whereas the supposed right to pre-emptive war encompasses the entire world. Also, Teddy Roosevelt's adage, 'speak softly but carry a big stick', stands in sharp contrast to the rhetoric and hubris of the Bush administration.

Of course, the Bush administration has no interest in understanding the adverse historical consequences of gunboat diplomacy. While the Roosevelt corollary remained in effect for almost twenty-five years, historians generally recognize that the interventions carried out under its aegis did not bring stability or democracy to the countries of the Caribbean and Central America. Interventions to 'civilize' other countries aroused the wrath and resistance of Latin Americans in general, and the corollary was formally repealed under Republican President Calvin Coolidge in 1928.

The Incompetent Emperor

Aside from its fundamental policy flaws, the Bush administration also demonstrates a shocking ineptness in carrying out its policies. As Robert Kuttner notes, 'The hallmark of the Bush foreign policy has been a naive radicalism married to an operational incompetence' (Kuttner 2003). To a certain extent the Bush administration and the Pentagon had it right in their belief that they could win a quick ground war against Saddam Hussein. He had, after all, lost the first Gulf war to Bush's parent, and Saddam's regime was ravaged by international sanctions for the next dozen years. But the seizure of Baghdad on 9 April 2003 marked the beginning of the end of Bush's efforts to be the master of a new empire as he totally bungled the post-war effort.

As David Rieff points out in 'Blueprint for a Mess': 'The mess that is postwar Iraq is a failure of planning and implementation' (Rieff 2003). The key agency in the Pentagon responsible for 'cherry-picking' intelligence information in the run-up to the Iraqi war, the Office of Special Plans, was also directly involved in post-war planning. The office, headed by neo-conservative Douglas Feith, relied heavily on the exiled and US-funded Iraqi National Congress for pre- and post-war planning. It thus came as little surprise when the Pentagon, over the objections of the State Department, flew the leader of the congress, Ahmad Chalabi, along with 500 armed supporters, into Iraq in the hope that they would constitute the core of a new Iraqi army, and soon form a new government. But virtually no one in Iraq rallied to Chalabi, a convicted bank swindler who had spent the past twenty-three years living abroad.

To its credit the State Department established the 'Future of Iraq Project', which consulted with a wide number of Iraqis from monarchists to communists. They helped draw up a thirteen-volume report containing plans and options for post-war Iraq. Among its more insightful passages the report states: 'the period immediately after regime change might offer . . . criminals the opportunity to engage in acts of killing, plunder and looting'. But the Pentagon refused to use the report. Jay Garner, the first US administrator, says that Rumsfeld instructed him to ignore the Future of Iraq Project. Instead Garner fell back on the plans of the Office of Reconstruction and Humanitarian Assistance (ORHA), a unit he formed in the Pentagon eight weeks before the war started. Starting out with three or four people, the unit possessed virtually no one with expertise on the Arab world and was still understaffed when it accompanied Garner to Iraq in April (ibid.).

However, the Pentagon had been so focused on the invasion of Iraq that once it took Baghdad it relegated even ORHA to a secondary status. ORHA reconstruction teams became a de facto part of the military and they went out in military convoys to provide assistance, complete with flak jackets and military helmets. According to Judith Yaphe, a former CIA analyst and an expert on Iraqi history, 'In some ways, we're even more isolated than the British were when they took over Iraq' at the end of the First World War (ibid.).

While the Pentagon and Rumsfeld bear the major responsibility for the planning disaster in post-war Iraq, Garner became the first fall guy for the US failures. Bush replaced him with J. Paul Bremer on 6 May. Possessing no experience in the Middle East or the Gulf, Bremer had been a career diplomat for twenty-three years, serving as ambassador to the Netherlands before Ronald Reagan appointed him Ambassador-at-Large for Counter-Terrorism from 1986 to 1989. He then left government to become managing director of Henry Kissinger's consulting firm, and moved into the private sector, serving as a director of Air Products and Chemicals. Then, after joining the crisis consulting firm of Marsh & McLennan Companies (MCM) in 2000, Bremer caught the eye of George W. Bush, who appointed him to the President's Homeland Security Advisory Council in mid-2002 (MCM News 2002).

As might be expected, this neophyte in Iraqi affairs quickly created an even bigger mess in Iraq. Days after arriving in Baghdad he disbanded the 400,000-member Iraqi army and declared that some 50,000-odd members of the Ba'athist party could not hold public positions, measures that Garner had not taken because he feared creating even more antipathy towards the United States. As one US official noted, 'we made 450,000 enemies on the ground in Iraq' when Bremer took these steps against the old regime (Rieff 2003).

Bremer is a doctrinaire advocate of the free market, and his next major move was to begin planning the privatization of the Iraqi economy. By early July, in spite of the continuing turmoil in the country, his obsession with the free market led him to declare: 'Privatization is obviously something we have been giving a lot of thought to,' adding, 'everybody knows we cannot wait until there is an elected government here to start economic reform' (Reuters 2003). Two hundred of Iraq's largest state-owned enterprises, including electricity, telecommunications and pharmaceutical concerns, were put up for privatization as the US–UK Coalition Provisional Authority (CPA) abolished all restrictions on foreign investments outside the petroleum sector (Mate 2003). Of course, Bremer paid no heed to the fact that private foreign investment would not be interested in Iraq for months, if not years, because of the volatile political conditions in the country, and that the elimination of state sector enterprises would mean an even greater increase in the already massive ranks of the unemployed.

The Mirage of an Occupied 'Democracy'

Bremer and the Bush administration floundered about in an effort to devise a government for Iraq that would be properly subservient to US interests. After the collapse of Rumsfeld's scheme to instal Chalabi and the Iraqi National Congress as the new rulers, Bremer decided to exert direct rule over the country, much as General MacArthur did in post-war Japan. This approach appears to have been endorsed by Wolfowitz and other neo-conservatives, who thought they could transform Iraqi society in a few years into a Western-style democracy under US tutelage. But within a couple of months the growing violence and resistance made it apparent that the Iraqis would not tolerate direct imperial rule for a lengthy period. Garner than opted to create a façade for his rule by establishing the Iraqi Governing Council. Comprised of twenty-five members, hand-picked by the United States from collaborationist sectors of the anti-Saddam elite of Iraq, the council had formal control over the country's ministries and a rotating presidency. It was clear to all that the council was a puppet of Bremer and the United States.

The government situation in Iraq soon became eerily similar to that of Vietnam in the mid- and late 1960s. There one government had succeeded another in fairly rapid succession as the United States stepped up its counter-insurgency war. The significant difference was that in Iraq the United States could not even come up with a political formula for a nominally independent elected government as occurred in Vietnam. Bremer's neo-colonial approach only generated more hostility and resistance among the Iraqi populace. In early November the strife had reached new levels as the rate of US casualties climbed rapidly and four helicopters were downed in a two-week period. Most international reconstruction agencies were withdrawn as the coalition forces could not protect their personnel.

Bremer was recalled to Washington for emergency consultations. He returned to Iraq in mid-November with a new plan. It imitated the Afghani Loya Jirga model in that it called for local caucuses to select delegates that would in turn elect a national government. The local caucuses would be drawn from municipal and regional governing bodies that had been endorsed and/or selected by the US occupation authorities. This process was even more rigged than the Loya Jirga, which at least had a historic basis in Afghani society. The date for this Iraqi national government to take power was set for no later than 30 June 2004. It was not explicitly stated, but even after the installation of the government the US occupation army intended to remain in Iraq for an indeterminate period (for a good summary of early US efforts to establish a government in Iraq, see Internet G).

At about the same time the United States began mapping out this new governing scheme for Iraq, George W. Bush began trumpeting the merits of democracy in the Gulf and the Middle

East. No longer able to justify his invasion of Iraq on the ground that the country possessed weapons of mass destruction, in November 2003 Bush began to argue that his real mission was to bring democracy to the region. On the twentieth anniversary of the founding of the National Endowment for Democracy (NED) in Washington, DC, Bush proclaimed, 'The establishment of a free Iraq at the heart of the Middle East will be a watershed event in the global democratic revolution.' He hinted at his real US strategic interests in the region when he added: 'In many nations of the Middle East – countries of great strategic importance – democracy has not yet taken root' (Bush 2003d).

By a democratic Iraq, Bush meant an Iraq like the controlled democracies promoted by NED in other parts of the world. In the 1980s NED intervened repeatedly in the politics of Central America in an effort to establish US-backed regimes that opposed the democratic revolutionary movements that were sweeping the region. As US Republican Congressman Ron Paul has noted, 'The misnamed National Endowment for Democracy (NED) is nothing more than a costly program that takes US taxpayer funds to promote favored politicians and political parties abroad.' He goes on to quote a study of the NED which observes that ' ... the controversy surrounding NED questions the wisdom of giving a quasi-private organization the fiat to pursue what is effectively an independent foreign policy under the guise of "promoting democracy"' (Paul 2003). The interests that back the type of democracy Bush and his administration are promoting were illuminated by the fact that he gave his speech before the United States Chamber of Commerce, a major participant in NED programmes, and that the event was sponsored by the AT&T and AIG Insurance corporations.

In his statement, however, Bush tried to paint a rosy picture of NED's actions in Iraq: 'The National Endowment for Democracy is promoting women's rights, and training Iraqi journalists, and teaching the skills of political participation. Iraqis, themselves – police and border guards and local officials – are joining in the work and they are sharing in the sacrifice.' He made no mention of the fact that Bremer had closed down a number of newspapers in Baghdad for publishing views considered hostile to US interests. Nor did he note that while the United States issued decrees privatizing the Iraqi economy, a memo was sent out declaring that the old repressive labour laws of the Saddam regime remained in effect. Some trade unions are banned while strikes in general are prohibited. Just over a month after Bush's speech on democracy, US troops stormed the headquarters of a new trade union formed in June 2003, the Iraqi Workers Federation of Trade Unions. Eight of the members of the federation's executive board were arrested and hauled off along with office files. Ironically, the US soldiers tore down posters written in Arabic on the office walls which denounced terrorism (Bacon 2003).

The undemocratic nature of the government the United States sought to impose on Iraq was denounced by leading representatives of the Shiite Muslims, who represent 60 per cent of the Iraqi population. The main leader of the Shiites, Grand Ayatollah Ali Sistani, an opponent of Saddam Hussein's regime, rejected Bremer's plan to hand-pick a new government via local caucuses. He wrote: 'The occupation officials do not enjoy the authority ... General elections must be held so that every eligible Iraqi can choose someone to represent him.' As Juan Cole, an expert on the history of the Shiites, notes: 'Sistani is a genuine democrat. He believes that sovereignty resides in the body public. So if you're going to have a government that's legitimate, it has to be elected by the people on a one-person/one-vote basis' (Cole 2003). But Bremer refused to budge from his governing plan, falling back on the lame excuse that viable voting lists could not be compiled over a six-month period, even though the United States had managed to invade and occupy the country in three weeks.

The Counter-insurgency War

The seizure of Iraq soon turned into a nightmare for US forces. Given the strategic and operational incompetence of the Bush operatives, the US occupation will by no means endure as long as it did in Vietnam. But the toll will nevertheless be all too high among civilians as the occupation forces go to any extremes to impose their will on the country. As Bremer proclaimed in July 2003: 'We are going to fight them and impose our will on them and we will capture or ... kill them, until we have imposed law and order on this country. We dominate the scene ... ' (Brightman 2003).

Iraq is predominantly an urban country, whereas Vietnam was a nation of peasants and jungles. But the terrain makes little difference when the United States becomes engulfed in a people's war. As its early counter-insurgency operations such as Desert Scorpion reveal, the United States is only alienating more and more people with its search-and-destroy missions. The strategists in the Pentagon even resurrected the notorious Plan Phoenix from Vietnam, which targeted rural hamlet leaders for capture and assassination. As an American who advised the coalition authority in Iraq said, 'The only way we can win is to go unconventional. We're going to have to play their game. Guerrilla versus guerrilla. Terrorism versus terrorism. We've got to scare the Iraqis into submission' (Hersh 2003a).

In line with this thinking, in the autumn of 2003 the Pentagon created a new Special Forces Group comprised of members of the army's Delta Force, Navy Seals and paramilitary operatives. As with Plan Phoenix, their mission is to carry out 'manhunts' to 'neutralize' the Ba'athists and other insurgents. In the initial stages they rely on teams drawn from the upper ranks of the old Iraqi intelligence services to penetrate the insurgency. Once they have secured information from the infiltrators, US special forces are sent in to take out targeted leaders. As a former CIA station chief states in simple terms: 'There are Iraqis in the intelligence business who have a better idea, and we're tapping into them. We have to resuscitate Iraqi intelligence, holding our nose, and have Delta and agency shooters break down doors and take them out' (ibid.).

This attempt to hit the insurgents' networks won't work in Iraq any more than it did in Vietnam. Indeed, in Iraq the guerrilla cells appear to be even more diverse and autonomous than in Vietnam. There appears to be no central command as the cells act virtually on their own. Ray McGovern, a former CIA analyst for almost thirty years who is a critic of the Iraqi war, states:

> What is increasingly clear is that neither the present-day Pentagon whiz kids nor their patron, Vice-President Dick Cheney, have learned much from history. They encourage President Bush to insist, 'We are not leaving,' and Defense Secretary Rumsfeld to protest that this war is 'winnable.' But most of those with a modicum of experience in guerrilla warfare and the Middle East are persuaded that the war is not winnable and that the only thing in doubt is the timing of the US departure. (McGovern 2003)

In 1917, in words reminiscent of George W. Bush's declaration that he is freeing Iraq, British general Stanley Maude, on capturing Baghdad from the Ottomans, proclaimed, 'Our armies do not come into your cities and lands as conquerors or enemies, but as liberators.' The British settled in for a long occupation, but the citizens of the newly formed state of Iraq were not pleased. In the summer of 1920 a violent revolt erupted against the British led by 100,000 armed tribesman. Gertrude Bell, deputy to British Commissioner Arnold Wilson, warned in a letter to a friend against trying to 'squeeze the Arabs into our mould', because, as she wrote, she feared that the British would only 'have our hands forced in a year – who knows – perhaps less' (cited in Schell 2003). The revolt was brutally repressed and it took more than a year or two to get the British out, as they remained as colonial masters until 1932.

But Meade's time line and admonishment to the British commissioner actually apply more to Bush and his gang of neo-conservatives than to the former imperial rulers of Iraq. An anonymous refrain making the rounds is: 'Iraq is Vietnam on speed'. There will be no quick fixes for the United States in Iraq.

As in Vietnam, the US rulers on occasion become euphoric, thinking they have turned the corner in the war, as when they captured Saddam Hussein in mid-December 2003. But here again the United States was deluded, believing the resistance had no popular roots, that all it had to do was get rid of a few 'dead-enders' like Saddam. In fact Saddam had little to do with the insurgency. As Tariq Ali, a leading analyst of the Middle East who lost friends to the regime of Saddam Hussein, wrote: 'Those who were, till now, reluctant to back the resistance will now come out openly against the Occupation. Those in the United States and elsewhere who argued that the resistance was led by Saddam and the remnants of the old regime will now get a big shock.' He added: 'The Iraqi underground is vibrant and hopeful' (Ali 2003). This is a war that will end miserably for the United States. The real dead-enders are the pretentious rulers of a faltering empire, George W. Bush, Dick Cheney, Donald Rumsfeld and the satrap of Baghdad, J. Paul Bremer III.

NINE

The interregnum: an empire in descent confronts a world in upheaval

Resistance against American power mounts with every step away from the emerging global consensus. If the 'universal nation' does not uphold universal values, its world order will eventually collapse.
Parag Khanna, 'The Counsel of Geopolitics', Current History, November 2003, p. 393

Perhaps it's asking a lot to expect America to act differently from all the other empires of history, but wasn't that the original idea?
Bono, U2

The Bush administration took office in 2001 determined to secure the USA's position as the sole superpower of the twenty-first century. To prevent any other nation, or alliance of nations, from challenging US domination, the Bush strategists launched a new Star Wars programme, augmented US naval prowess on the high seas, and maintained US troops and bases on every continent. Nazi Germany was the last great power to believe it could escape the undulating tides of empire when Hitler proclaimed the 'Thousand Year Reich'. The Reich lasted twelve years. George W. Bush's empire will have an even shorter lifespan. Today, in the aftermath of the Iraqi war, it is eminently clear that the United States is in a state of imperial decline.

A few short years ago, at the turn of the millennium, virtually no one argued that the United States was destined for such a rapid decline. But the neo-conservatives and the militarists under George W. Bush have launched the United States on a path of imperial overstretch that follows almost to the letter the pattern of imperial ruin of previous empires outlined by Paul Kennedy in

The Rise and Fall of the Great Powers. Today the United States is inexorably wasting its national treasury on military spending and foreign adventures that will not be compensated for by increased revenues deriving from the empire's commercial and economic activities abroad.

It is well known that Spain in the seventeenth and eighteenth centuries declined as an imperial power because, unlike England, it did not develop a manufacturing base. But it managed to postpone its decline for centuries by extracting silver and gold bullion from the Spanish American colonies to cover its trade deficit. It was not until the Napoleonic Wars that financial reality fully caught up with the Spanish empire, leading to Spain's takeover by France and the separation of its American colonies. While the United States does maintain access to cheap raw materials abroad, its manufacturing base is rapidly disintegrating and it has no bullion flowing from colonies to provide it with the wealth necessary to cover its enormous trade deficit. Petroleum may be today's 'black gold' but the diversity of supplies and the growing difficulties of the US empire in the Gulf and the Middle East indicate that the United States is not destined to secure a stranglehold on this critical commodity.

Economic Overstretch

By mid-2003 the United States, like Spain, had mortgaged its future to finance its imperial war machine. Ninety-three per cent of its budgetary allocations destined for international affairs went to the military while the State Department got only 7 per cent. Of the 189 member countries of the United Nations, the United States had a military presence in 153, with large-scale deployments in twenty-six. Military treaties or binding security agreements were in place in thirty-six countries. To help sustain this mammoth military apparatus, the United States ran an internal budgetary deficit of $375 billion in 2003, with red ink of a similar or greater magnitude projected for years to come. The US international trade deficit with the world approached a figure of $435 billion, equal to about 2.5 per cent of the US gross domestic product (Johnson 2004: 288, 307). To cover its total current account deficit, including trade, the United States borrowed about $500 billion abroad. By contrast the British empire ran international current account surpluses averaging 3 to 4 per cent from 1850 to 1913. The United States has not had a positive trade balance since 1975. To cover these deficits, foreigners have been investing heavily in US assets, and foreign-owned assets in the United States are now valued at $2.5 trillion more than US-owned assets abroad. By mid-2003 foreigners owned 41 per cent of US treasury debt, 24 per cent of US corporate bonds and 13 per cent of corporate stock (Du Boff 2003).

Economist Max Sawicky of the Economic Policy Institute in Washington, DC, predicts that disaster will strike the US economy in one to four years. 'Both discretionary spending and defense spending are going up,' he points out. 'Debt is growing faster than GDP.' Sawicky believes the growing debt will activate a disciplining by the financial markets. As the United States borrows to cover its deficit, interests rates will go through the ceiling. This creates problems for loans tied to variable interest rates from credit card debt to highly leveraged business deals. Home mortgages, farming, construction and consumer durables will all be affected (interview, 17 November 2003, Washington, DC). As interest rates rise, the money supply collapses, businesses start going broke and people get laid off. This begins a cycle wherein the government receives a smaller amount of taxes and has to borrow more money, driving the interest rates higher. At best it will be reminiscent of the years following the Vietnam war when interest rates reached 15 per cent and the American family farm faced extinction. At worst the American and world economy will dive into a deep depression.

Sawicky is not alone in his concern. Middle East journalist Waseem Shehzad notes that 'since September 2001 foreign investment, hitherto the mainstay of the US's economy, has dried up, and an estimated $100 billion leaves the country annually'. Shehzad goes on to point out:

> The true obligations of the government are 10 times larger than the Treasury debt held by the public ... the current value of these unfounded obligations is a mind-numbing $43 trillion. The US Federal Reserve recently put the net worth of all American households at $39 trillion ... How is the government going to meet such obligations? One way is to rob other countries, as it has done for generations and is trying to do in Iraq, but this policy has to confront the reality that those who are being occupied will resist ... Militarily the US is so strong that nobody can meet it head on. Economically, however, it is vulnerable. (Shehzad 2003)

Perhaps the most damning indictment of the Bush administration's policies on the economy comes from the business community. On 17 March 2003 Jeffery Garten, who held foreign and economic policy positions in the Nixon, Ford, Carter and Clinton administrations and is now Dean of the Yale School of Management, wrote a commentary entitled 'Bush's Guns-and-Butter Dilemma' in *Business Week*.

> If the Administration continues its economic policies, we won't be able to afford our expansive efforts overseas ... the tab is likely to run into hundreds of billions of dollars over many years. Such amounts cannot be accommodated without aggravating an already acute fiscal problem. The Congressional Budget Office is already projecting cumulative deficits of $1 trillion for the rest of this decade ... To fund our foreign policy, President Bush would need to cancel virtually all of his proposed tax breaks, which currently add up to a projected $1.5 trillion over 10 years. A foreign policy that involves continual military interventions abroad while securing the US itself is bound to erode economic vitality ... Any-

way you cut it, however, there is a disconnect between national security and economic policy. History shows such a mismatch can be disastrous ... [the United States risks] imperial overstretch ... as it faces crises all over the world. (Garton 2003)

To be sure, before Bush took power the United States already possessed a global military machine that consumed enormous economic resources. But as the administration of William Jefferson Clinton drew to a close, there was a significant budgetary surplus, no talk of tax cuts for the rich, and the international scene was one of general optimism and cooperation as the United States enjoyed amicable relations with its allies. Even two neo-Marxists, Michael Hardt and Antonio Negri, in their provocative book *Empire*, maintained that the United States would dominate the globe for years to come, much as Rome did two millennia before. Writing in the late 1990s, they argued that as the world's hegemonist the United States acted to ensure the broader interests of the global system it dominated. America 'is imperial and not imperialist', they asserted, adding: 'In all the regional conflicts of the late twentieth century, from Haiti to the Persian Gulf and Somalia to Bosnia, the United States is called to intervene militarily – and these calls are real and substantial ... The United States is the peace police, but only in the final instance, when the supranational organizations of peace call [upon it]' (Hardt and Negri 2000: 181). They discuss the enormous human and environmental toll exacted by the empire and foresee an eventual rebellion by 'the multitude'. But they believe that at that historic moment the United States, by collaborating with the other major powers, could postpone the empire's demise.

Put another way, the interventions of Bill Clinton, and his predecessor, George H. W. Bush, responded to the needs of the dominant economic and political interests for global order. Gone were the old days of classic imperialism when a hegemonic power sought to advance the narrow interests of its particular ruling class at the expense of others. In the age of globalization the interests of the dominant classes of the globe are intermeshed.

The Interregnum

Since 11 September 2001 the world has appeared very different from the one portrayed by Hardt and Negri. So what went wrong? Is their analysis of the role of the US imperium flawed? Our argument is that it is not, that Hardt and Negri captured the position of the United States in the 1990s. But their world view failed to take into account the instability and upheaval that are occurring in the early phase of globalization. We are in an interregnum. The last imperial interregnum lasted for about thirty years, between the First and Second World Wars, when the United Kingdom confronted challenges to its hegemony from Germany, Japan and the United States, with the latter finally emerging as the new hegemonist in 1945. Our contemporary interregnum differs in that we are on the cusp of a transition from the nation-state system of intense competition to a new global order that is by no means complete or even clearly defined.

Clinton and presidents prior to him were bent on creating and reinforcing an array of international institutions that would lead to cooperation rather than conflict as we moved into this new global epoch. They were trying to construct a new form of international hegemony in which the United States would lead while acting in concert with the interests of the other leading nation-states. This explains not only the formation of the array of trade and financial agreements epitomized by the World Trade Organization, but also the emergence of a series of transnational elite forums such as the Trilateral Commission, the Davos World Economic Forum and the G8 annual meetings of the world's most powerful nations. Perhaps this globalist empire trajectory could have continued if Al Gore had wrested the presidency from

George W. Bush. But even as the sun set on the Clinton years, the globalization project was in trouble as the economy began to enter a recession and the protests against corporate-driven globalization spread around the world, with major mobilizations in Seattle, Quebec City, Canada, and Prague, Czechoslovakia. They culminated in the gathering of the first World Social Forum in Porto Alegre, Brazil, just as George W. Bush was taking power in Washington.

The Bush team has a very different agenda for the interregnum. It is reverting to the practices of a classic nation-state, bent on advancing its narrow interests at the expense of others, even its historic allies. Ethnic, religious and popular resistances to the US imperium are to be dealt with unilaterally, or at best with token allies. The belief of the Bush clique is that absolute military power, and if necessary unending warfare, should be used to repress and contain all challenges to the world's reigning superpower. The reliance on US military might to confront all challengers dovetails with the interests of the petro-military complex that is particularly powerful under George W. Bush.

The Pentagon's Corrupt Spartans

Viewed from the perspective of the empires of antiquity, the Bush militarists are like the Spartans while the Clintonian globalists can be viewed as Athenians. The Spartans established military bases and oligarchic regimes in the areas they conquered whereas the Athenians, in their drive for imperial ascendancy in Greece in the fifth century BC, founded settlements, expanded trade and backed democratic movements that opposed the oligarchs in other city-states (Doyle 1986: 68–75). The Athenian empire ultimately lost to the Spartans in the Peloponnesian War because of over-extension and internal divisions. But Sparta as the hegemonist of Greece was unable to reclaim the wealth and glory of the Athenian empire.

There is one significant difference between the Spartans and Bush's conclave of neo-conservatives and militarists. According to history the Spartans were austere and generally honest whereas the representatives of Bush's petro-military complex are corrupt, racking in huge personal fortunes as they seek to expand the imperial order. When it suits their interests, they even violate the principles of laissez-faire and neo-liberalism they so loudly espouse. As the second Gulf war began, the United States asked five engineering firms to submit bids for post-war reconstruction work in Iraq. The two winners were Kellogg Brown & Root, a subsidiary of the Halliburton company commanded by Dick Cheney until he became Vice-President, and the Bechtel Group, which had connections with the CIA and high-ranking Republicans dating back half a century. These contracts effectively represented insider trading between the Pentagon and the private sector (Johnson 2004: 308).

The corruption of the current regime is also embodied in the large number of military firms that line up at the public trough under the guise of 'privatizing' Pentagon military functions. Secretary of State Donald Rumsfeld harangues the old military commanders and generals for not doing enough to 'outsource' military functions, including even the contracting of covert operations to what are called Private Military Forces. As Peter Singer points out in *Corporate Warriors*, 'at a time when downsizing and increased deployment have left US forces stretched thin, private firms have provided the United States with an array of services: security, military advice, training, logistics support, policing, technological expertise, and intelligence' (Singer 2000: 15). It is as if we are returning to the early modern period of European history when the monarchies relied on paid mercenaries to fight their wars for empire. The personal security detail for the US-anointed president of Afghanistan, Hamid Karzai, is provided by a unit of DynCorp made up of about forty ex-US special forces troops. In

Afghanistan as well as Iraq, the Pentagon and the CIA run special units that meld privately contracted soldiers with covert operatives on the public payroll. Farther downstream in the Pentagon's food chain, private military forces play an ever-expanding role in providing non-lethal aid and assistance. The more than 650 Taliban and al-Qaeda suspects captured by the United States are housed in the military prison in Guantánamo Bay built by Brown & Root for $45 million (ibid.: 17).

The Empire's New Frontier

Bush's quest for a permanent global empire is primarily centred on redrawing the map of the vast region extending from the Caucasus of Europe to central and south-western Asia, including the Persian Gulf, North Africa and the Middle East. The reason why even mainstream commentators debate the emergence of a new American imperium is because the United States has projected its massive military power into this region. The *Wall Street Journal* called the repositioning of US forces in the Gulf and south-central Eurasia 'the most radical redeployment of American forces since the end of the Cold War' (cited in Klare 2003b). Today, Afghanistan, Georgia, Kyrgyzstan, Pakistan and Uzbekistan host American troops and facilities, while the United States provides significant military aid to Azerbaijan and Kazakhstan (ibid.). In the Gulf proper, the United States has well over 100,000 troops in Iraq, and major military bases in Saudi Arabia, Qatar and Kuwait, with additional bases in Oman and the United Arab Emirates (Johnson 2004: 242). All these troops, bases and military outposts are under the control of the US Central Command. Created in 1983, its commander-in-chief, or CinC, is now the most powerful figure in the region. General Tommy Franks served as the head of the Central Command in the 2003 war against Saddam, and his successor, General John P. Abizaid, is in charge of the counter-insurgency wars being fought in Afghanistan and Iraq.

The rub for the Central Command is that it is seeking to implant US imperial power in the most volatile and unstable area of the world. The formation of an empire stems from a disparity of power as a large and powerful country seizes control of weaker nations. But the existence of an empire is also conditioned by its international relations with other great powers and by the characteristics of the peripheral societies that the imperial nation seeks to rule over (Doyle 1986: 130). The region the Central Command is seeking to dominate is extremely complex with very diverse cultures and social systems. Today many of the nations of central and south-west Asia are wealthier and markedly different to what they were in the early twentieth century when the European powers tried to maintain their hold on the region. Some nations of the region are tribal and rural with the trappings of modernity, some possess large immigrant populations, and others are highly urbanized. And some countries in the region are a mixture of all these elements.

While George W. Bush refuses to discuss the United States as an empire, he is nevertheless leading the charge to remake the societies and politics of the Islamic states in the US image. He bluntly states that his mission is to spread the neo-liberal model and its attendant political system along with an 'open door' for US investors. As history demonstrates, this is an impossible mission, particularly in the political and social spheres. In the Caribbean and Central America in the first quarter of the twentieth century the US empire failed in its efforts to 'civilize' the societies and politics of the countries it invaded in the age of gunboat diplomacy. As we saw in the second chapter, the United States withdrew its troops and military garrisons from the region by the end of the 1920s as virtually all of Latin America turned against 'Yanqui imperialism'. If the United States could not alter relatively simple societies in its back yard almost a century ago, how can it possibly transform the political structures of diverse Islamic societies halfway around the world? Of course the United States occupation forces will leave an imprint on the region, but the impact will not be positive, nor will it facilitate the spread of democracy.

Afghanistan is a test case which demonstrates the total inability of the United States to create a stable society with evolving democratic institutions. At the end of 2003, just over two years after the United States invaded and occupied Afghanistan, the economy was in ruins. The main source of international exchange (next to the revenue injected by the US occupation forces) was the country's poppy fields and the heroin trade. Under the previous Taliban government, poppy production had been banned and virtually eliminated.

In early January 2003, the country's Loya Jirga, a gathering of tribal and community representatives, drew up a new constitution for the country which on paper seemed to usher in a more open political system. But the country remained under the thumb of the old mujahidin warlords who had fought against the Soviet Union in Afghanistan in the 1980s with massive CIA assistance. After the defeat of the Soviets, the mujahidin occupied and pillaged the capital city of Kabul from 1992 to 1996 as they fought internecine wars, leaving rotting bodies strewn in the capital's streets. Small wonder that a fanatical Islamic group, the Taliban, took control of most of the country from 1996 to 2001. They at least stood for a few simple bedrock principles, such as no raping, banditry or pillaging of peaceful citizens.

The United States ousted the Taliban rapidly in late 2001 because it once again became the patron of the mujahidin warlords who were languishing in the northern Afghan provinces. The CIA brought in bags of money and a slew of CIA operatives to ensure that the warlords fought and that some of the money trickled down to the rank-and-file soldiers. Perhaps even more importantly, CIA operatives and special forces helped coordinate the massive bombing of the Taliban strongholds in Afghanistan, shattering their ability to resist.

Back in the saddle, the mujahidin military leaders once again carved out their territorial fiefdoms in Afghanistan, and in effect made President Hamid Karzai the mayoral puppet of Kabul. The United States poured hundreds of millions of dollars into the country, but none of it really improved the country's social infrastructure or changed the lives of the overwhelming majority of the populace, who live in absolute poverty. As John Sifton of Human Rights Watch noted after a field trip to Afghanistan in late 2003:

> Some projects to rebuild the country started in a few places, but for the most part the entire country has plodded along since then: very little progress on reconstruction; very little progress on good governance – you know, making the ministries work better, starting to have a real civil service; very little progress on building up democratic institutions, civic society groups, political parties, laws and groups like that ... There are a few places ... Herat, the city in the west, and Kabul, a city in the east, have seen reconstruction privately. But for the most part, if you scratch the surface, you'll see that those reconstruction projects are underwritten by factional leaders, by warlords and such. This isn't really a legitimate reconstruction. It's a sort of power elite that's paying for some of this reconstruction. And then outside of those cities, in the rural areas – nothing, absolutely nothing. (quoted in Gross 2003)

One major Afghan infrastructure project financed by the United States was completed – a 300-mile highway from Kabul to Kandahar. Lauding this as a major US achievement, Bush declared on 16 December 2003 that the road 'will promote political unity between Afghanistan's provinces, facilitate commerce by making it easier to bring products to market, and provide the Afghan people with greater access to health care and educational opportunities' (US Department of State 2003). What Bush failed to mention is that the road is actually a military priority for the Pentagon. Kandahar is the former stronghold of the Taliban and the province around it is the scene of stepped-up fighting as the Taliban regroup and begin to kill US soldiers on a regular basis in the region. Kandahar is also the centre of the Pasthun tribe that makes up almost 70 per cent of the Afghan population. While Hamid Karzai is from this tribe, the Pasthun people have been largely marginalized in the re-building of Afghanistan as the northern-based mujahidin warlords embezzle most of the money and dominate the country's politics (Internet C).

The failure of the reconstruction effort, not to mention the inability to create democratic institutions, helped precipitate the resurgence of the Taliban. By late 2003 the United States was run-ning frequent bombing missions in areas suspected of harbour-ing Taliban militants and soldiers. Just as in Iraq, the bombing, often with allegedly 'smart' weapons, alienates the local people from the US forces. In a three-day period in December, US aircraft killed fifteen children when they targeted two villages in eastern and southern Afghanistan. According to local sources, no Taliban militants were killed in the strikes.

Can one imagine what the reaction would be in the United States if the aircraft of a 'friendly' nation, let alone a terrorist cell, dropped or set off a bomb that killed fifteen children? Bush would moralize ad infinitum about the event and the Homeland and Defense departments would get tens of billions in new fund-ing. However, in the case of Afghanistan the children's deaths merited little more than a brief mention in US news coverage. The Afghan families who lost their children undoubtedly feel powerless to do anything about the terrible tragedy they suffered, but they will surely go to their graves hating American soldiers and the occupiers of their country.

The low-intensity war being fought in Afghanistan could easily tie down the ten thousand US troops stationed there for years to come. The Taliban receive support and supplies from the funda-mentalist Wahabi Muslims of Pakistan and Saudi Arabia. Sectors of Pakistan's powerful intelligence agency, the ISI, also provide some assistance. The Taliban will certainly outlast the Bush administration, even if it wins a second term. In sum, Afghanistan, by US and Western standards, will remain a 'failed state' as along as the United States remains there. Corruption is rampant in the government, the mujahidin maintain their own armies and have turf battles with each other, the country's link to the international economy is tied to the violence-prone drug sector, and US soldiers continue to die in Afghanistan. If democratic values do take root they will be in reaction to the US occupation rather than because of it.

Iraq Around the Clock

Nation building as espoused by George W. Bush cannot and will not work in central Asia and the Gulf. The tragedy of Afghanistan is being repeated in Iraq, albeit with more profound consequences given the extent of the US invasion and occupation of the country. Even some neo-cons and sectors of the Christian right are convinced that Bush, Cheney and Rumsfeld have dangerously overstretched the American empire in Iraq. They use the phrase 'Iraq Around the clock' to describe the full-time effort that the Bush administration is being forced to commit to the deteriorating situation. The Christian right's concern is that the military in general as well as individual soldiers are overstretched. The neo-cons complain that the Bush administration does not have the time or energy to handle any of the other critical situations around the globe, including a suspected nuclear programme in Iran and the well-known arsenal of nuclear weapons in North Korea.

At the end of 2003, the Christian right *World Magazine* published an article entitled 'Iraq Around the Clock'. In it Richard Miniter reported from Baghdad that the pressure on air transport is so bad that Defense Department officials are flying around with human remains. Meanwhile the grunts don't worry about becoming human remains as much as the fact that 'they can't explain to their families why their deployment orders and return dates keep changing'. As for the officers, they are concerned about a 'number of potential crises that could emerge in Iraq in the coming year ... from military to political, economic, and cultural. Some officials worry about a "winter offensive" of high-profile terror strikes ... that the Iraqi economy will collapse, and ... that constantly changing troop rotation schedules will sap morale.' While generals complain about the lack of high-tech tools, administrators complain that they do not have enough translators. The biggest problem, however, is that the troops are ready to go home. 'We are in a condition of descending consent,' the commander of an armoured unit in Baghdad told Miniter. 'We've got a year at most to do this job and go home' (Miniter 2003).

If the hyped fears and predictions of the neo-cons are realized, then the demise of the empire may be more dramatic than the neo-cons in the Defense Department could ever imagine. These fears were revealed on 17 November 2003 at an American Enterprise Institute forum entitled 'The IAEA[1] Reports: Does Iran Have a Nuclear Weapons Program?' The plush Wohlsetter conference suite where the conferees met sits on the twelfth floor of the same DC office building that houses not only the American Enterprise Institute but also the Project for the New American Century, the Weekly Standard and any number of other neo-conservative institutions. Among the people speaking that day were Patrick Clawson from the Washington Institute for Near East Policy (WINEP) and Reuel Marc Gerecht from the American Enterprise Institute (AEI). Both AEI and WINEP were instrumental in driving the rush to war in Iraq, and it appeared that they were pushing for the same solution in Iran.

During the course of the conference all the speakers confirmed their sense that the Bush administration is overwhelmed by the events in Iraq. Each analyst promoted the view that Iran was well on the path to acquiring nuclear weapons. They all advocated some sort of intense US intervention to stop this eventuality. They often mentioned a military solution, even though one analyst suggested that military action in Iran would make the situation in Iraq look mellow. In the end they all agreed that the Bush administration was too overstretched to do anything but try to delay the construction of nuclear weapons in Iran. They were convinced that if the administration remained overstretched then Iran would ultimately attain nuclear weapons. Clawson pointed out that nukes in Iran would have several ramifications: they would lead to a nuclear arms race in the area; the Iranians could give nukes to a terrorist group; or Iran could use nukes to bully its neighbours (American Enterprise Institute 2003). Of course, Israel already has nuclear weapons, and if threatened would have no hesitation in taking pre-emptive action. It would probably react, as predicted by a US government official, in a 'disproportionate manner'. Who knows where that would end? It would certainly be the end of the world as we know it.

Such conclusions are perhaps fear-mongering rhetoric on the part of quasi-political think tanks trying to promote their neo-conservative views. But their insights into the overloaded workings of the Bush administration do present a view of an executive branch too involved in the minutiae of Iraq to maintain an overview of the big picture.

Michael Lind, a former neo-conservative who has turned against the New Right and the Bush administration, brusquely states: 'The United States lacks the economic, military and political power to dominate the world ... ' He adds, 'the United States may have the world's most powerful military. But US military power should not be exaggerated' (Lind 2002). Today the United States accounts for about 20 per cent of the globe's economic output, whereas at the beginning of the 'American Century' after the Second World War it accounted for almost half of its industrial production. The European Union may at present have a lethargic growth rate, but that could change. Even now the high growth rates in China and other parts of Asia mean that the relative weight of the United States in the world economy will inevitably diminish.

The computer and technological revolutions did give the United States an economic edge in the 1990s, but with the international spread of technology, particularly in countries such as China and India, this technological lead will erode. We need to remember that in the nineteenth century Great Britain was the laboratory of the industrial revolution, but Germany, Japan and the United States soon caught up with the British by borrowing and adapting their technologies. Population trends may also contribute to the decline of the United States. At present it accommodates 4 per cent of the globe's inhabitants (owing in large part to its continued reliance on immigration), but as the world's population increases to a projected total of about nine billion people, the US share will in all probability drop to 2 per cent or less. It is hard to believe that 2 per cent of the world's people can impose its will on the other 98 per cent.

For Lind, even the current US superpower military status is no guarantee of imperial dominance. The United States may now spend more than the next fourteen countries combined on its military machine, but given the fact that it is an 'island' country, the costs of imposing US firepower in Asia or the Gulf are enormous. China, which probably represents the principal military challenge to the United States in the twenty-first century, can move its military forces anywhere in the Asian theatre at a fraction of what it costs the United States.

The World in Revolt

We are indeed in an interregnum of conflict and upheaval. 'Globalists' similar to Clinton may retake power in the United

States and try to secure a more benevolent form of the US imperium. Or George Bush and his unilateral conception of empire may hold sway for the immediate future. But neither project will be able to control and direct the emergent forces of opposition. Just as there are failed states, we are also witnessing the advent of a failing empire. Indeed, the very concept of empire in any form is proving antiquated and incompatible with the winds of popular change, resistance and upheaval that have been unleashed in the epoch of globalization.

In the interregnum, there are three main destabilizing forces for the US imperium. First is the increasing tension among the dominant powers of the North over whether to continue the process of globalization or to revert to intense competition with each other for control of the world's resources. When there is relative prosperity, as during the Clinton years, the tendency will be to collaborate. But when the global economy heads downwards, as seems increasingly likely in the coming years, competition and antagonism intensify among the great powers. It is no accident that the unilateralism of the Bush administration coincides with a downward spiral in the global economy. This interpretation is reinforced by the fact that even the Democratic Party appears to be adopting a more antagonistic approach towards free trade agreements and is favouring new forms of protectionism.

The second major breach in the interregnum is the fundamental split between the countries of the North and the South. The polarization of wealth and power between these two realms has never been as extreme as it is today. The revolt of the South manifests itself in a number of ways. Its most portentous form is the rise of radical movements such as al-Qaeda which claim to be fundamentalist. In reality they are not strictly following the original prophets. Rather they use texts such as the Koran to justify their reactionary attacks on the evils of modernity. These radical movements are also rebelling against the failure of the old Arab nationalists and the national liberation movements of the South, which once in power usually comprised new elites of privilege that dictated to, and often exploited, the masses of their own countries.

Just as importantly, many of the contemporary governments of the South are rebelling against US domination. From Latin America to the Middle East, most of these countries opposed Bush's invasion of Iraq. They are also exercising increasing autonomy in trade and commercial disputes with the United States. At the World Trade Organization meetings in Cancún, Mexico, in September 2003, Brazil emerged as the leader of a bloc of twenty-two countries from the South, including India and China, that refused to go along with US demands to enhance the ability of multinational corporations to penetrate their economies. Then, at the meetings of the Free Trade Area of the Americas in November, Brazil stood out as the leader of the countries of Merosur and of the Andean Community in compelling the United States to abandon its goal of imposing the free trade area on all of Latin America by 2005 (Du Boff 2003: 14).

The third major strand of opposition to the American empire is what can be called the anti-corporate globalization movement, or the 'Spirit of Porto Alegre'. It is a broad movement that marches under the banner of 'Another World is Possible'. While the 'Battle of Seattle' in late 1999 marked its eruption on the global scene, its roots go back to 1968, when an 'anti-systemic' rebellion erupted that extended from Paris and Mexico City to Vietnam and Czechoslovakia. This movement (perhaps with the exception of Vietnam) rejected the old left, whether it was embodied in the Kremlin or the Communist Party of the USA, as a failure. These anti-systemic movements also denounced Western political systems, whether represented by the Social Democrats in West Germany under Willy Brandt or the rightist government of Charles de Gaulle in France. In its early years the anti-systemic movement focused its wrath on the US empire and the holocaust it visited on south-east Asia (see Wallerstein 2003).

The neo-liberal icons of the 1980s, Margaret Thatcher and Ronald Reagan, mounted a counter-offensive against this broad anti-systemic and counter-cultural movement. But it was by no means defeated. Gains continued at grassroots level with the advances of gay rights, the growth of indigenous and anti-racist movements and the clamour for human rights. Finally the rise of a movement opposed to the trade agreements that promoted the interests of the dominant social classes and the intensified exploitation of the poor by the rich, of the South by the North, has exposed the extreme injustices of the global system of neo-liberal free trade policies.

The broad anti-systemic movement for global justice is at this stage very amorphous, including an incredible diversity of popular and social organizations, ranging from trade unionists, environmentalists and marginal urban dwellers to anarchists, leftist political formations and radical land reform movements. At this moment in history its strength is in its very diversity. In the United States the principal reason why Attorney General John Ashcroft has not been able to move decisively against the anti-war movement is because it is so broadly based. This was not the case in the early 1950s, when a climate of fear and oppression took hold in the United States as the cold war McCarthyists launched a modern-day inquisition against the Communist Party and its 'fellow travellers'. It was possible to hound, persecute and imprison these opponents of the US system because they had a relatively limited social base. This is not the case today with the anti-war and global justice movements. From the streets of San Francisco, Los Angeles and Denver to those of Milwaukee, New York and Washington, DC, militant demonstrators by the tens of thousands are willing to fill the jails to defend their basic rights and those of others. John Ashcroft may be trying to usurp the Bill of Rights, but given the broad base of opposition even conservative courts dominated by Republicans are revoking some of Bush's executive decrees that infringe civil liberties.

Another strength of the anti-corporate globalization movement is that it overlaps the schism between the governments of the North and the South. The movement influences even 'mainstream' governmental representatives of the southern elites. In Seattle in 1999 and in Cancún, Mexico, in 2003, many of the official delegates from the South who participated in the meetings of the World Trade Organizations openly acknowledged that the protesters in the streets played a decisive role in empowering them to stand up to the demands for one-sided trade concessions made by the countries of the North.

The environmental and peace contingents The environmental toll exacted by the American empire is becoming too much for the world as imperial America, its war machine and the corporations poison the planet. A coalition of civil society organizations and progressive governmental leaders has evolved over the years to oppose this systematic destruction of the globe. One of the most enduring features of this movement has been its drive to control the spread of toxic industrial chemicals.

Twelve chemical compounds are on a list of persistent organic pollutants (POPs) that 'can cause nervous system damage, diseases of the immune system, reproductive and developmental disorders, as well as cancers' (IPEN 2001). An additional problem with these materials is that scientists have found 'evidence of long-range transport of these substances to regions where they have never been used or produced' (UN Environmental Programme 2001). One of the most insidious aspects of them is that they migrate to the polar regions. Thus they 'pose a critical threat to northern indigenous people, whose survival, health and well being depend on their traditional relationship with the ecosystem and the food it provides ... the Inuit living on Baffin Island carry seven times as many PCBs in their bodies as people living in lower latitudes' (Cray 2002).

Cognizant that market mechanisms had failed to stop this poisoning of the planet, non-governmental organizations started lobbying for a solution in the 1970s. Finally the 1992 Rio Earth Summit adopted an agenda that led to the Stockholm Convention on Persistent Organic Pollutants. Organized through the United Nations Environmental Programme, this international POPs treaty utilizes the precautionary principle on the development of new chemicals and seeks to eliminate the production of the twelve compounds on the short list of POPs, as well as other chemicals wherever feasible. Ninety countries initially signed this Global POPs Treaty in May 2001. Since then that number has grown to 151.

Corporate interests driving the American empire have led the fight to derail this crucial initiative almost since its inception. The United States and a handful of industrialized allies worked to weaken the use of the precautionary principle and avoid termination of production of the chemicals. One expert on the treaty noted that this group has 'become a significant part of the problem, not the solution' (ibid.).

Nevertheless, concerned governments and dedicated civil society organizations managed to keep the essential sections of the agreement intact. Their efforts point to an example of limited but critical victories of the rising global community against the authority of the American empire on an issue crucial to the survival of the planet. Over forty of the minimum of fifty governments needed to make the convention operational had ratified the treaty by the end of 2003. Supporters are optimistic that the treaty will become a reality in the near future.

The New Internationalism

This is only one example of what Phyllis Bennis of the Institute for Policy Studies calls 'the new internationalism'. As the IPS Fellow in New Internationalism she has been working on this issue since 1990. She envisions 'global civil society and a rotation of governments challenging the empire and using the United Nations' as a forum for these struggles. She goes on to point out that 'It is particularly easy for these countries to challenge the empire when their people are rallying in the street' (interview, 18 November 2003).

The great coming together of the world's people on 15 February 2003 to say 'no to the war in Iraq' illustrated the rise of a new 'second superpower' to challenge the American empire. The subsequent ability of a coalition of countries to defeat the United States in the United Nations represented another pivotal advance for the new internationalism. In large part the strength of the anti-war movement among the German populace was responsible for the German government's falling out with the Bush administration. As the direct descendants of the main propagators of the last global war, the Germans are deeply aware of the horrific costs of war and the quest for empire.

The global push by both civil society and a large number of governments for a Uniting for Peace resolution at the United Nations General Assembly to stop Bush's war against Iraq was a further move in this direction. Initiated by the Arab League and orchestrated by civil society organizations such as the Center for Constitutional Rights and Greenpeace, this effort brought together both governments and civil society in a way that enabled them to play a proactive role in global events. It was supported by such diverse political bodies as the lower house of the Russian legislature and the Senate Standing Committee on Foreign Affairs of Thailand. Popular democracies that have arisen across Latin America in response to the American neo-liberal agenda also called for a special session of the General Assembly to discuss Iraq. The chief executive of Indonesia, as well as many other countries from the non-aligned movement and the South, supported the initiative. Jules Lobel, an international policy specialist from the University of Pittsburgh, insisted, 'the United States is ignoring international law. In this situation, the General Assembly must act' (Deen 2003).

Speaking to the Transnational Institute in Amsterdam in May 2003, Phyllis Bennis allowed that 'the threatening letters sent [by the United States] to most UN member states in February 2003 demanding that they refuse to consider a General Assembly debate on Iraq seem to have worked'. But she offers a strategy and hope for the future. 'Responding to the more-or-less spontaneous emergence of this global movement', she said, 'means helping provide a space for strategic planning among key actors in the key countries, and helping to shape a political/intellectual framework on which a world-wide peace and justice movement can transform itself into a politically conscious movement challenging empire while building a new internationalism' (Bennis 2003a). As Immanuel Wallerstein states in *The Decline of American Power*: 'A new kind of historical system will be constructed in the next half century. The worldwide battle has already begun over what it will look like ...' (Wallerstein 2003: 237, 257).

The Bush administration's reaction to the new internationalism's successes proves that they are aware that the worldwide battle has begun. In Miami, Florida, in November 2003, the Bush brothers colluded in an attempt to derail the support that street protesters provided to insurgent Latin American governments attending the eighth ministerial meeting of the Free Trade Area of the Americas (FTAA). President Bush diverted $8.7 million of the money he had deemed essential for the stability of Iraq in order to help his brother, Governor Bush, equip a police state intent on intimidating, harassing and frustrating the actions of thousands of citizens who came to Miami to participate in legal street protests against the FTAA.

Bedecked in factory-fresh protective gear, and carrying shiny red crowd-control rifles and tear-gas launchers, police uttered threats such as 'I smell human blood'. Arranged in a perimeter around Miami's luxury bay-front hotels, they created an enclave for Bush's buddy, Commerce Secretary Don Evans, whose task was to try to convince FTAA delegates that 'free trade offers hope, opportunity, and expanded freedom', and to assure them that the protesters offered only 'to perpetuate inequality and preserve economic hardship'. Delegates were told to stay away from the protesters, and that it was dangerous on the streets.

Meanwhile, the only danger came from the police. They not only harassed the protesters with tear gas and rubber bullets, but also chased them through Miami's streets. In a desperate effort to minimize the impact of the protests, police stopped up to 185 buses from entering the city and reaching the protest site outside the FTAA enclave.

But Latin American delegates stayed tough. Supported by the street protesters they could watch on television, they forced acceptance of what some called FTAA à la carte, some FTAA Lite and some FTAA zero. They defeated the attempted invasion of free-range American capital, which hoped to conquer their countries. They fought off the imposition of intellectual property rights that threatened to privatize their national heritage. Facing such opposition, the American empire was forced to retreat. They closed the conference a day early, no doubt fearing that the 'other America' touted by the protesters was suddenly possible.

Certain fundamental beliefs and values for 'another world' are emerging from the movement for global justice and against corporate globalization. Among them are demands for participatory democracy, an end to all forms of racism and a rejection of the 'commodification' of all aspects of life which global capital is

217

bent on imposing on us. This rejection is crucial to demystifying and replacing the capitalist system that dominates the world. Our struggle is not for the end of the market, nor even for an end to private property in non-corporate forms, but rather for decommodification, which means an end to the buying and selling of commodities for profit. It is not Pollyanna-ish to believe in this struggle. It is at an early stage, and largely defensive at present. We see it in the struggles of Bolivians to prevent the privatization of their water supplies, in the demand of Brazilian peasants for land and in the struggles to prevent the takeover of non-profit hospitals and public universities by greedy corporate capitalists. These decommodification struggles are also present in alternative currencies such as those used in the barter markets of Argentina or the shops of Ithaca, New York. Achieving the decommodification of 'everything' will be a long struggle, lasting perhaps centuries. But ultimately it is the only way to change the global system of capitalism that burst out of western Europe half a millennium ago, mediated by conquest and empire.

We are entering an interregnum between an international system bullied by a rogue empire and the dreams and demands of the multitude. Will that future be controlled by an economic plutocracy? Or will the vast majority of humanity come together and create a world that believes in a harmonious and liberated future for the planet? As Wallerstein says, 'History is on no one's side. It depends on what we do.'

Note

1 UN International Atomic Energy Agency.

Bibliography

Alexander's Gas and Oil Connection (2002) 'Iraqi National Congress Lays Out Plans for Iraq's Oil and Gas Resources', 18 October, <www.gasandoil.com/goc/company/cnm24616.htm>.

Ali, Tariq (2003) 'The New Model of Imperialism: Saddam on Parade', *Counter Punch*, Petrolia, CA, 16 December.

American Enterprise Institute (2003) 'The IAEA Reports Program Conference', Washington, DC, 17 November.

American Humanist Association (2003) 'Humanists Call for Fundamentalist General's Dismissal', Washington, DC, October 22. <http://www.americanhumanist.org/press/Gen.'sComments.html>.

Anderson, Sarah, Phyllis Bennis and John Cavanagh (2003) 'Coalition of the Willing or Coalition of the Coerced? How the Bush Administration Influences Allies in Its War on Iraq', Institute for Policy Studies, Washington, DC, 26 February.

Arrighi, Giovanni (1994) *The Long Twentieth Century: Money, Power and the Origins of Our Times*, Verso, New York and London.

Associated Press (2002) 'Security Council Approves Resolution on Iraq', 8 November, <www.globalpolicy.org>.

Bacon, David (2003) 'The United States Arrests Iraq's Trade Union Leaders', e-mail report, 10 December.

Barry, Ellen and Bryan Bender (2003) 'US Support in Iraq Fades after Raids', *Boston Globe*, 15 June.

Bartley, Russell H. (2001) 'The Piper Played to Us All: Orchestrating the Cultural Cold War in the USA, Europe and Latin America', *International Journal of Politics, Culture and Society* 14(3): 571–619.

Behan, Richard (2003) 'The Triumph of the Diligent Dozen', AlterNet, 6 June.

Beinin, Joel (2003) 'Pro-Israel Hawks and the Second Gulf War', MERIP, Washington, DC, 6 April, <www.merip.org/mero/mero040603.html>.

Beisner, Robert L. (1968) *Twelve against Empire: The Anti-Imperialists, 1898–1900*, McGraw-Hill, New York.

Bello, Walden (2003) 'The Crisis of the Globalist Project and the New Economics of George W. Bush', *Focus on the Global South*, 10 July.

Benedetto, Richard and Susan Page (2003) 'Bush's Approval Lowest since 9/11', *USA Today*, 13 January.

Bennis, Phyllis (2003a) 'Going Global: Building a Movement against Empire', *Foreign Policy in Focus,* May, <www.fpif.org>.

— (2003b) *Before and After: US Foreign Policy and September 11*, foreword by Noam Chomsky, Olive Branch Press, New York.

Berke, Richard L. (1998) 'Reporter's Notebook; Southern Republicans Pick Gov. Bush in Straw Poll', *New York Times*, 2 March, p. 13.

Berkowitz, Bill (2003) 'Marketing the Invasion of Iraq', Working for Change, 13 August, <www.workingforchange.com>.

Bernstein, Richard (2003) 'Foreign Views of US Darken since Sept. 11', *New York Times*, 11 September.

Bloom, Harold (1999) 'The Preacher, Billy Graham', 14 June, <www.time.com/time/time100/heroes/profile/graham03.html>.

Bookman, Jay (2003) *Atlanta Journal-Constitution*, 17 April.

Boot, Max (2003a) 'Does America Need an Empire?', Fleet Admiral Chester Nimitz Memorial Lecture at the University of California, Berkeley, 12 March.

— (2003b) 'American Imperialism? No Need to Run Away from Label', *USA Today*, 5 May.

Borosage, Robert (2002) 'The Mighty Wurlitzer', *The American Prospect*, 6 May.

Boutros-Ghali, Boutros (2003) 'The Future of the United Nations', *The Hindu*, online edn, 3 April, <www.thehindu.com/thehindu/2003/04/03/stories/2003040302021100.htm>.

Brecher, Jeremy (2003) 'UN General Assembly Provides Crucial Opportunity for Global Peace Movement', *Counter Punch*, Petrolia, CA, 2 April.

Brightman, Carol (2003) 'Repeating Mistakes of the Cold War', AlterNet, 11 August.

Brooks, Renana (2003) 'Bush Dominates a Nation of Victims', *The Nation*, 24 June.

Brown, DeNeen L. and Dana Priest (2003) 'Deported Terror Suspect Details Torture in Syria (Canadian's Case Called Typical of CIA)', *Washington Post*, 5 November.

Bruni, Frank (2002) *Ambling into History: The Unlikely Odyssey of George W. Bush*, HarperCollins, New York.

Burbach, Roger (2001) *Globalization and Postmodern Politics: From Zapatistas to High-Tech Robber Barons*, Pluto Press, London.

— (2002) 'September 11, Day of Infamy in the United States and Chile', in Burbach and Clarke (2002).

— (2003) *The Pinochet Affair: State Terrorism and Global Justice*, Zed Books, London.

Burbach, Roger and Ben Clarke (eds) (2002) *September 11 and the US War: Beyond the Curtain of Smoke*, City Lights Books, San Francisco, CA.

Burkeman, Oliver and Julian Borger (2001) 'The Ex-Presidents' Club', *TheGuardian*, 31 October.

Bush, George H. W. and Brent Scowcroft (1998) 'Why We Didn't Remove Saddam', *Time*, 2 March.

Bush, George W. (1999) *A Charge to Keep*, William Morrow, New York.

— (2002a) speech to the US Military Academy's graduating class at West Point, 1 June.

— (2002b) speech to the UN, 12 September, <www.cnn.com/2002/US/09/12/bush.transcript>.

— (2003a) weekly radio address, 15 February,<www.whitehouse.gov/news/releases/2003/02/20030215.html>.

— (2003b) 'President Meets with Small Business Owners in Georgia', speech at Harrison High School, Kennesaw, GA, 20 February, <www.whitehouse.gov/news/releases/2003/02/iraq/20030220-2.html>.

— (2003c) 'Freedom and the Future', speech at the American Enterprise Institute's annual dinner, Washington, DC, 26 February.

— (2003d) 'President Bush Discusses Freedom in Iraq and Middle East', remarks by the President at the 20th anniversary of the National Endowment for Democracy, 6 November.

Callahan, David (1999a) '$1 Billion for Ideas: Conservative Think Tanks in the 1990s', special report from the National Committee for Responsive Philanthropy, 12 March.

— (1999b) '$1 Billion for Conservative Ideas', *The Nation*, 8 April.

Center for International Policy (2002) 'Vote Analysis Shows Deep Distrust of Iraq Policy in Congress', 13 October.

Cheney, Dick (2002) 'Vice President Speaks at VFW 103rd National Convention', Nashville, TN, 26 August, <www.whitehouse.gov>.

Chomsky, Noam (1993) 'What Uncle Sam Really Wants', Znet, <www.zen.secureforum.com/Znet/chomsky/sam/sam-1-2.html>.

— (2003) 'On Imperialism', interviewed with David Barsamian, MIT, Cambridge, MA, 11 September.

Chomsky, Noam and V. K. Ramachandran (2003) 'Iraq is a Trial Run', *Frontline* (India), 2 April.

Christeler, Agnes (2003) 'Dick Cheney and Halliburton: A Chronology', Citizen Works, <www.citizenworks.org/corp/warcontracts/cheney-halliburton.pdf>.

Cole, Juan (2003) interviewed with Jim Lehrer on *The News Hour*, Arlington, VA, 2 December.

Collier, Ellen C. (1993) 'Instances of Use of United States Forces Abroad, 1708–1993', Congressional Research Service, Library of Congress, CRS Issue Brief, 7 October, <www.fas.org/man/crs/crs_931007>.

Combs, Roberta (2002) 'Christian Coalition Commends Rumsfeld for Defense of Israel', Christian Coalition of America, 7 August.

Commonweal Institute (2004) 'There is an Imbalance in the Marketplace of Ideas', <www.commonwealinstitute.org/thereis.html>.

Conover, Ted (2003) 'In the Land of Guantanamo', *New York Times Magazine*, 29 June.

Covington, Sally (1998) 'Right Thinking, Big Grants & Long Term Strategy. How Conservative Think Tanks Transform US Policy', *Covert Action Quarterly* 63.

Cray, Charles (2000) 'US Undermines POPs Treaty', *Rachel's Weekly*, Environmental Research Foundation, 13 July, <www.rachel.org/search/index.cfm?St=1#703>.

Cronkite, Walter (2003) 'The New Inquisition', *Denver Post*, 21 September.

Crouse, Charity (2001) 'Money Shouldn't Equal Power: Why an "Anti-AIPAC" isn't Enough', Jewish Unity for a Just Peace, <www.junity.org/proposals/notenough.pdf>.

Dear, John (2003) 'The Soldiers at My Front Door', CommonDreams.Org, 29 November.

Deen, Thalif (2003) 'NGOs Lead Move to Use UN General Assembly to Stop War', Inter Press Service, 31 January, <www.globalpolicy.org/security/issues/iraq/attack/2003/0131ga.htm>.

Diamond, Sara (1995) 'The Christian Right Seeks Dominion: On the Road to Political Power and Theocracy', <www.publiceye.org/eyes/sd_theo.html>.

Donnelly, John (2003) 'US Operatives Are Said to Be Active in Iraq', *Boston Globe*, 5 January.

Donnelly, Thomas et al. (2000) 'Rebuilding America's Defenses: Strategy, Forces and Resources for a New Century', Project for the New American Century, September.

Dowie, Mark (2001) *American Foundations: An Investigative History*, MIT Press, Cambridge, MA.

Doyle, Michael (1986) *Empires*, Cornell University Press, Ithaca, NY.

Dreyfuss, Robert (2002a) 'The Pentagon Muzzles the CIA. Devising Bad Intelligence to Promote Bad Policy', *The American Prospect*, 16 December.

— (2002b) 'Tinker, Banker, Neocon, Spy: Ahmed Chalabi's Long and Winding Road from (and to?) Baghdad', *The American Prospect*, 18 November.

Du Boff, Richard B. (2003) 'US Hegemony: Continuing Decline, Enduring Danger', *Monthly Review*, December, pp. 3–4.

Dubose, Lou, Jan Reid and Carl M. Cannon (2003) *Boy Genius*, Perseus Book Group, New York.

Easterbrook, Gregg (1986) 'Ideas Move Nations: How Conservative Think Tanks Have Helped to Transform the Terms of Political Debate', *The Atlantic*, January.

Edgin, Eric (2003) speech at the Mendocino Community School, Mendocino, CA, 5 December.

Farrel, John (2003), interviewed by Jim Tarbell, Caspar, CA, 6 December.

Feffer, John (2003) 'The Self-Limiting Superpower', TomPaine.com, 6 October.

Forestel, Herbert (2003) 'The USA Patriot Act: Uncensored', in Peter Phillips and Project Censored (eds), *Censored, 2004: The Top 25 Censored Stories*, Seven Stories Press, New York.

Francisco, Luzviminda Bartolome (1985) 'The First Viet Nam', in *Conspiracy for Empire*, Foundation for National Studies, Quezon City, Philippines.

Franke, Glenn (2002) 'In Public Opinion, US, Europe More United than Apart', *Washington Post*, 4 September, p. A01.

Freidman, Thomas (1999) *The Lexus and the Olive Tree*, Farrar, Straus, Giroux, New York.

Frontline PBS (2003) 'The War Behind Closed Doors', <www.pbs.org/wgbh/pages/frontline/shows/iraq/etc/wolf.html>.

Gardner, Lloyd (1964) *Economic Aspects of New Deal Diplomacy*, University of Wisconsin Press, Madison.

— (1976) *Imperial America: American Foreign Policy since 1898*, Harcourt, Brace, Jovanovich, New York.

Garten, Jeffrey E. (2003) 'Commentary: Bush's Guns-and-Butter Dilemma: Financing Foreign Wars and Boosting Homeland Security is Bound to Erode US Economic Vitality', *Business Week*, 17 March.

Garzon, Baltazar (2002) 'The West Shares the Blame', in Burbach and Clarke (2002).

Gore, Al (2003) 'Freedom and Security', speech delivered in the Daughters of the American Revolution Constitution Hall, Washington, DC, 9 November.

Graham, Bob (2003) 'I Just Pulled the Trigger', *Evening Standard*, 19 June.

Graham, Bradley (2003) 'Pentagon to Probe Remarks Made by General', *Washington Post*, 22 October.

Gross, Terry (2003), interview with John Sifton, Human Rights Watch, *Fresh Air*, 22 December.

Haass, Richard (2000) 'Imperial America', paper presented at the Atlanta Conference, *Foreign Affairs* 11 November.

Hardt, Michael and Antoni Negri (2000), *Empire*, Harvard University Press, Cambridge, MA.

Hatfield, J. H. (2000) *Fortunate Son*, Soft Skull Press, New York.

Herold, Marc (2004) 'Blown Away', Common Courage Press, Monroe, ME.

Hersh, Seymour (2003a) 'Will the Counter-Insurgency Plan in Iraq Repeat the Mistakes of Vietnam?', *New Yorker*, 8 December.

— (2003b) 'Moving Targets', *New Yorker*, 15 December.

Hilton, Dominic (2002) 'Postcards from the Edge', Opendemocracy.org, 29 November, <www.opendemocracy.net/other_content/article-794-worlddiary.jsp>.

History of the CIA (2003) <www.cia.gov/cia/ciakids/history/cia_history.shtml>.

HJ Res. 114 (2002) 'To Authorize the Use of United States Armed Forces against Iraq', House of Representatives, 107th Congress, 2nd Session, 2 October.

Hobsbawm, Eric (2003) 'After the Winning of the War', *Le Monde Diplomatique*, June.

Huntington, Samuel P. (1989) 'The Modest Meaning of Democracy', in Robert A. Pastor, *Democracy in the Americas. Stopping the Pendulum*, Homes and Meier, New York, pp. 12–13.

Ignatieff, Michael (2003) 'The Burden', *New York Times Magazine*, 5 January.

Immelman, Aubrey (1999) 'Political Personality of George W. Bush', St John's University, St Joseph, MN, August.

Internet A, <www.aei.org/events/eventID.329,filter./event_detail.asp>.

Internet B, <www.aei.org/events/eventID.428,filter.all/event_detail.asp>.

Internet C, <www.en.wikipedia.org/wiki/Pushtu>.

Internet D, <www.fas.org/man/smedley.htm>.

Internet E, <www.germnews.de/dn/2002/09/18-2002/08/03>.

Internet F, <www.iacenter.org/f15-world-2.htm>.

Internet G, <www.juancole.com>.

Internet H, <www.mtholyoke.edu/acad/intrel/nsc-68/nsc68-1.htm>.

Internet I, <www.people.cornellcollege.edu/a-free/feb15content.htm>.

Internet J, <www.projecttransitionaldemocracy.org/html/PTD_press.htm>.

Internet K, <www.smplanet.com/imperialism/joining.html>.

IPEN (International Pops Elimination Network) (2001) *The Pops Handbook for the Stockholm Convention on Persistent Organic Pollutants*, September, Version 4, <www.ipen.ecn.cz/index.php?z=&l= en&k=handbook>.

IPO (International Progress Organization) (2003) 'War on Iraq – United Nations, Call by International NGOs for Invoking Uniting for Peace Resolution', Vienna, 27 March, <www.i-p-o.org/nr-ipo-iraq-uniting-for-peace-27mar03.htm>.

Iraq Bodycount (2003) <www.iraqbodycount.net>.

Iraqi Liberation Act (1998), Public Law 105-338, 31 October.

Isaacson, Walter and Evan Thomas (1986) *The Wise Men*, Simon and Schuster, New York.

IWW (International Women's Working) (1997) Conference, 'Women and Children, Militarism and Human Rights', Naha City, Okinawa, Japan, 1–4 May.

James, Oliver (2003) 'So, George, How Do You Feel about Your Mom and Dad? Psychologist Oliver James Analyses the Behaviour of the American President', *Guardian*, 2 September.

JINSA (Jewish Institute for National Security Affairs) (2004) 'JINSA Military Academies Program in Israel', <www.jinsa.org/about/programs/programs.html>.

Johnson, Chalmers (2004) *The Sorrows of Empire: Militarism, Secrecy and the End of the Republic*, Metropolitan Books, New York.

Kaise, Robert G. (2003) 'Bush and Sharon Nearly Identical on Mideast Policy', *Washington Post*, 9 February, p. A01.

Kaldor, Mary (2001) 'Wanted: Global Politics', *The Nation*, 5 November.

Kamen, Al (2003) 'Road Map in the Back Seat?', *Washington Post*, 27 June.

Kaplan, Lawrence F., and William Kristol (2003) *War over Iraq*, Encounter Books, San Francisco, CA.

Kennedy, Paul (1987) *The Rise and Fall of the Great Powers: Economic Change and Military Conflict from 1500 to 2000*, Random House, New York.

Kirschbaum, Erik (2003) 'Boycott of American Goods over Iraq War Gains', Reuters, 11 September.

Klare, Michael (2003a) 'The New Geopolitics', *Monthly Review*, July/August.

— (2003b) 'The Empire's New Frontiers', *Current History*, November, p. 383.

Koerkamp, Geert (2002) Groot Radio Netherlands, 15 February, <www.rnw.nl/hotspots/html/kyrgyzstan020215.html>.

Krehely, Jeff, Meagan House and Emily Kernan (2003a) Interview, National Committee for Responsive Philanthropy, Washington, DC, 18 November.

— (2003b) *Draft Conservative Philanthropy Study*, National Committee for Responsive Philanthropy, Washington, DC, November.

Kristol, Irving (1997) 'The Emerging American Imperium', *Wall Street Journal*, 18 August.

— (2003) 'The Neoconservative Persuasion', *The Weekly Standard* 8(47), 25 August.

Kristol, William et al. (2001) 'Letter to President Bush on the War on Terrorism', Project for the New American Century, 20 September.

Kuttner, Robert (2003) 'A Foreign-Policy Emergency', *The American Prospect*, 1 November.

Lardner, George Jr and Lois Romano (1999), seven-part series on George W. Bush, *Washington Post*, July.

Lasseter, Tom and Drew Brown (2003) 'US Attack Threatens to Create Thousands of New Iraqi Enemies', Knight Ridder Newspapers, 15 June.

Lehrer, Jim (2003) PBS Online Newshour, 10 September.

Lievin, Anatol (2003) 'The Empire Strikes Back', *The Nation*, 7 July.

Lind, Michael (2002) 'Is America the New Roman Empire?', *The Globalist*, 19 June, <www.theglobalist.com/DBWeb/StoryId.aspx?StoryId=2526>.

— (2003) *Made in Texas: George W. Bush and the Southern Takeover of American Politics*, Basic Books, New York.

Linzer, Dafna (2003) 'US, UK Plans on Iraq Snarled at UN', Associated Press, 19 February.

Lobe, Jim (2003) 'Foreign Policy Experts Target US "Empire-Building"', OneWorld.net, 17 October.

McGovern, Ray (2003) 'Helicopter Down', TomPaine.com, 3 November.

Mahajan, Rahul (2003) *Full Spectrum Dominance: US Power in Iraq and Beyond*, Seven Stories Press, New York.

Mann, Michael (2003) *Incoherent Empire*, Verso, New York and London.

Mate, Aaron (2003) 'Pillage is Forbidden: Why the Privatization of Iraq is Illegal', *The Nation*, 6 November.

MCM News (2002) <www.mmc.com/news/newsOperatingCompanies_bremer_06_02.php>.

Miniter, Richard (2003) 'Iraq Around the Clock', *World Magazine* 18(47), 6 December, <www.worldmag.com/world/issue/12-06-03/international_1.asp>.

Murati, Shaban (2003) 'Why Albania Joined the Coalition of the Willing', *Southeast European Times*, 14 April.

National Energy Policy Development Group (2001), *National Energy Policy*, May.

National Priorities Project (2003), Factsheet, <www.nationalpriorities.-org>.

Nearing, Scott (1921) *The American Empire*, Rand School of Social Science, New York.

Nearing, Scott and Joseph Freeman (1925/1970), *Dollar Diplomacy: A Study in American Imperialism*, Arno Press, New York.

NewsMax Wires (2002) 'Baker Voices Caution on Iraq Regime Change', 26 August.

Nussbaum, Bruce (2003) 'The High Price of Bad Diplomacy: Mismanaging the Runup to War Will Do More than Squander Goodwill and Damage Alliances', *Business Week*, 24 March.

O'Brien, Thomas (1999) *The Century of US Capitalism in Latin America*, University of New Mexico Press, Albuquerque.

Observer (2003) 'Where the World Stands on an Invasion of Iraq', 12 January, <www.globalpolicy.org/security/issues/iraq/roadindex.htm>.

Ochieng, Philip (2003) 'Kenya: A US Base Would be Suicidal', *The Nation* (Kenya), 22 June, <www.afrika.no/Detailed/3728.html>.

Operation Desert Scorpion (2003). <www.globalsecurity.org/military/ops/desert_scorpion.htm>.

Page, Susan (2001) 'Norquist's power high, profile low', *USA Today*, 1 June.

Painter, David S. (1986) *Oil and the American Century: The Political Economy of US Foreign Policy, 1941–54*, Johns Hopkins University Press, Baltimore, MD.

Paul, Ron (2003) 'National Endowment for Democracy: Paying to Make Enemies of America', 12 October, <www.antiwar.com/paul/paul79.html>.

PBS Frontline (2003) 'Selective Intelligence', 9 October, <www.pbs.org/wgbh/pages/frontline/shows/truth/why/selective.html>.

Peel, Quentin, Robert Graham, James Harding and Judy Dempsey (2003) 'How the US Set a Course for War with Iraq', *Financial Times*, 26 May.

Pilger, John (2002) 'The Secret War: Iraq War Already Under Way', *Daily Mirror*, 20 December.

Pitt, William Rivers (2003) 'Of Gods and Mortals and Empire', Truthout.org, 21 February.

Priest, Dana (2003) *The Mission: Waging War and Keeping Peace with America's Military*, W. W. Norton, New York.

PNAC (Project for the New American Century) (1997) Statement of Principles, 3 June, <www.newamericancentury.org/statementofprinciple s.htm>.

— (1998) 'Letter to President Clinton on Iraq', 26 January, <www.newam ericancentury.org/iraqclintonletter.htm>.

Potorti, David (2002) 'Coming to a Mall Near You', in Burbach and Clarke (2002).

Powell, Lewis F. (1973) 'Confidential Memo Attack on the American Free Enterprise System', <www.mediatransparency.org/stories/ powellmanifesto.htm>.

Rabe, Stephen G. (1988) *Eisenhower and Latin America: The Foreign Policy of Anti-Communism,* University of North Carolina Press, Chapel Hill.

Rampton, Sheldon and John Stauber (2003) *Weapons of Mass Deception. The Uses of Propaganda in Bush's War on Iraq*, Tarcher/Penguin, New York.

Reel, Monte and Manny Fernandez (2002) 'Antiwar Protest Largest since '60s', *Washington Post*, 27 October.

Reuters (2002) 'Annan Says Iraqi No-fly Zone Firing No Violation', 19 November.

— (2003) 'Bremer Touts Privatization in Iraq', 8 July.

Rieff, David (2003) 'Blueprint for a Mess', *New York Times Magazine*, 2 November.

Robinson, William I. (1996) *Promoting Polyarchy: Globalization, US Inter-vention and Hegemon*, University of Cambridge Press, Cambridge, MA.

Roosevelt, Theodore (1904) 'The Roosevelt Corollary to the Monroe Doctrine', Annual Message to Congress, 6 December, <www.uiowa. edu/~c030162/Common/Handouts/POTUS/TRoos.html>.

Schell, Orville (2003) 'No Exit Strategy?', TomDispatch.com, 21 November.

Schlesinger, Arthur Jr (2003) 'Eyeless in Iraq', *New York Review of Books*, 23 October.

Schneider, William (2002) 'Marketing Iraq: Why Now?', CNN, 12 Sep-tember.

Shehzad, Waseem (2003) 'Bush Facing Growing Concerns about US Econ-omy', 18 July, <www.mediamonitors.net/waseemshehzad10.html>.

Siddiqui, Haroon (2003) 'Real American Agenda Now Becoming Clear', *Toronto Star*, 4 May.

Silverstein, Ken (1999) 'The Polluters' President', *Sierra Magazine*, November/December.

Singer, Peter W. (2000) *Corporate Warriors. The Rise of the Privatized Mili-tary Industry*, Cornell University Press, Ithaca, NY.

Solnit, Rebecca (2003) 'Fragments of the Future: The FTAA in Miami', tomdispatch.com, 25 November.

Solomon, Norman (2002) 'Media War without End', in Burbach and Clarke (2002).

Steele, Jonathan (2003) 'Body Counts', *Guardian*, 28 May.

Suellentrop, Chris (2003) 'Ahmad Chalabi: Why Shouldn't a Politician be President of Iraq?', Slate, 9 April, <www.slate.msn.com>.

Tabb, William K. (2003) 'The Two Wings of the Eagle', *Monthly Review*, summer, p. 81.

Tarpley, Webster G. and Anton Chaitkin (1992) *George Bush: The Unauthorized Biography*, <www.tarpley.net/bush1.htm>.

Tincq, Henri (2003) 'Pope Confronts US, UK, Directly on "Preventive War"', *Le Monde Diplomatique*, 3 December.

Tisdall, Simon (2003) 'World Opinion Moves against Bush', *Guardian*, 23 January.

Toenjes, Laurence A. (2003) 'US Policy towards Iraq: Unraveling the Web', June 2003, <www.opednews.com/toenjessummary.htm>.

Truman, Harry (1947) Address to Congress, Washington, DC, 12 March, <www.cnn.com/SPECIALS/cold.war/episodes/03/documents/truman/>.

UN (1944) Opening remarks by Henry Morgenthau Jr, US Treasury Secretary, United Nations Monetary and Financial Conference, Bretton Woods, NH, July.

UN Environmental Programme (2001) 'Persistent Organic Pollutants', <www.ipen.ecn.cz/handbook/html/index.html>.

US Department of State (2003) 'Bush Hails Completion of Afghan Highway', International Information Programs, 16 December.

Van Wormer, Katherine (2002) 'Addiction, Brain Damage and the President', *Counter Punch*, 11 October.

Wallerstein, Immanuel (2003) *The Decline of American Power: The US in a Chaotic World*, The New Press, New York and London.

Washington Post (2002) 'For Gephardt, Risks and a Crucial Role', 3 October.

Williams, William Appleman (1973) *The Contours of American History*, New Viewpoints/Franklin Watts, New York.

— (1980) *Empire as a Way of Life. An Essay on the Causes and Character of America's Predicament, along with a Few Thoughts*, Oxford University Press, New York.

— *The Tragedy of American Diplomacy* (1992) 2nd edn, revised and enlarged, Dell, New York.

Bibliography

Wipkipedia (2004) 'The First "Red Scare"', <www.en2.wikipedia.org/wiki/Red_Scare>.

Woodward, Bob (2002) *Bush at War*, Simon and Schuster, New York.

Yergin, Daniel (1992) *The Prize: The Epic Quest for Oil, Power and Money*, Simon and Schuster, New York.

Zunes, Stephen (2002) 'The Abuse of the No-fly Zones as an Excuse for War', *Foreign Policy in Focus*, 6 December.

— (2003) 'Bush Working to Ensure Sharon's Re-election', *Common Dreams*, 18 January.

Index

Some titles of related interest from Zed Books

Rogue State: A Guide to the World's Only Superpower UPDATED
   EDITION
   William Blum
   hb ISBN 1 84277 220 1   pb ISBN 1 84277 221 X

Killing Hope: US Military and CIA Interventions Since World War II
   William Blum
   hb ISBN 1 84277 368 2   pb ISBN 1 84277 369 0

On Imperialist Globalization
   Fidel Castro
   hb ISBN 1 84277 268 6   pb ISBN 1 84277 269 4

North Korea: The Paranoid Peninsula – A Modern History
   Paul French
   hb ISBN 1 84277 472 7   pb ISBN 1 84277 473 5

State Terrorism and the United States: From Counter-Insurgency to
   the War on Terrorism
   Frederick Gareau
   hb ISBN 1 84277 534 0   pb ISBN 1 84277 535 9

Another American Century: The United States and the World Since
   9/11
   UPDATED EDITION (Global Issues Series)
   Nicholas Guyatt
   hb ISBN 1 84277 428 X   pb ISBN 1 84277 429 8

Iran in Crisis? Nuclear Ambitions and the American Response
   Roger Howard
   hb ISBN 1 84277 474 3   pb ISBN 1 84277 475 1

Genocide, War Crimes and the West: History and Complicity
   Adam Jones
   hb ISBN 1 84277 190 6   pb ISBN 1 84277 191 4

Enemies of the Ayatollahs: The Iranian Opposition and its War on
   Islamic Fundamentalism
   Mohammad Mohaddessin
   hb ISBN 1 84277 530 8   pb ISBN 1 84277 531 6

A System in Crisis: The Dynamics of Free Market Capitalism
   James Petras
   hb ISBN 1 84277 364 X   pb ISBN 1 84277 365 8

Fat Cats and Running Dogs: The Enron Stage of Capitalism
Vijay Prashad
hb ISBN 1 84277 260 0   pb ISBN 1 84277 261 9

Global Intelligence: The World's Secret Services Today (Global Issues Series)
Paul Todd and Jonathan Bloch
hb ISBN 1 84277 112 4   pb ISBN 1 84277 113 2

Free Trade for the Americas? The United States' Push for the FTAA Agreement
Paulo Vizentini and Marianne Wiesebron (eds)
hb ISBN 1 84277 312 7   pb ISBN 1 84277 313 5

Tinderbox: US Middle East Policy and the Roots of Terrorism
Stephen Zunes
hb ISBN 1 84277 258 9   pb ISBN 1 84277 259 7

For full details of this list and Zed's other subject and general catalogues, please write to: The Marketing Department, Zed Books, 7 Cynthia Street, London N1 9JF, UK; or e-mail <sales@zedbooks. demon.co.uk>. Visit our website at <http://www.zedbooks.co.uk>.